DATE DUE

JUN 22 '11			
JUN 27 '11			

Library Store #47-0108 Peel Off Pressure Sensitive

PROBLEMS OF

OPERA PRODUCTION

Indiana University
Staged by Hans Busch

AIDA
By Verdi

PROBLEMS OF
OPERA PRODUCTION

By

Walther R. Volbach

Original Drawings by John R. Rothgeb

SECOND REVISED EDITION

ARCHON BOOKS, 1967

Library of Congress Catalog Card Number 67-24032
Printed in the United States of America

To Claire

CONTENTS

ILLUSTRATIONS

PREFACE TO THE REVISED EDITION

I am indeed very grateful to the editor of Archon Books for his decision to publish the revised version of my book on opera production. Its first edition was soon out of print, yet conditions did not make it feasible to prepare a second printing despite the favorable reaction to the appearance of my book. From many colleagues I received appreciative letters with sound recommendations regarding topics to be covered more elaborately or less thoroughly. Many of these suggestions have been incorporated in the present publication. I have been, and am, very grateful for all the advice. I am much obliged to those who have sent me their opinion, both favorable and critical, for when writing the first edition I was not always certain of the direction I should select, since this was the first treatise on an extremely complex subject matter.

The aim of the revised edition is the same as originally envisioned, namely to create a guidebook for people desirous of working in the lyric theatre, either on stage or backstage, in the pit or in the office, and to delineate for them the best means of how to achieve productions of the highest possible standard. The interval of more than a dozen years made it advisable to re-evaluate the first version on the basis of the recent proliferation of operatic activities, the growing interest in the performing arts demonstrated by councilmen, legislators and congressmen, in addition to my own observations and experiences.

My hope is that, even more than before, I succeed in clarifying my conception that music, which expresses emotion but not a definite action, is the dominating element. The feeling of music remains an individual matter. But an understanding of operatic art can be obtained only through study and experience combined with a deep knowledge of musical style and technical requirements.

The new shape of this book extends to the picture material. The old one had turned dated under the impact of changing styles. Therefore, new photographs were collected. Moreover, I have concentrated on pictures of American productions and I am indebted to the many professional, civic and educational groups who were kind enough to send me photographs. My only regret is that not all of them could be included. A further change is the broad emphasis on original sketches and floorplans for whose creations I am expressing my sincere thanks to John R. Rothgeb.

To name all those whose ideas helped form this new edition is not feasible, but I want to mention at least those who contributed a great deal to the original version and took the trouble to communicate with me again after its publication: Clifford E. Bair, Edward J. Dent, Senator Jacob K. Javits, Vern O. Knudsen, Thomas Ph. Martin, Gian-Carlo Menotti, Wilfred Pelletier, Joel Rubin, Bruno Walter, Terry Wells, and Werner Wolff.

I gratefully acknowledge the permission given by the editors of periodicals to use material from essays of mine: *Bulletin of the National Theatre Conference, Dramatics, Educational Theatre Journal,* and *Players Magazine.* I wish to express my sincere thanks to the publishers who authorized me to quote from their books: Brentano *(Inside the Moscow Art Theatre* by O. Sayler), Boosey and Hawkes (Preface to *Intermezzo* by Richard Strauss), E.J. Burrow and Co. *(The Sadler's Wells Book)*, F. Calmus *(On Conducting* by Felix Weingartner), Harvard University Press *(Harvard Dictionary of Music* by Willi Apel), A.A. Knopf *(Theme and Variation* by Bruno Walter, also *Man and Mask* by Feodor Chaliapin), Reinhold *(Theatres and Auditoriums* by H. Burris Meyer and E.E. Cole), Scribner's Son *(Memoirs of the Opera* by Giulio Gatti-Casazza), and Theatre Arts Books *(My Life in Art* by Constantin Stanislavsky).

Some essential data could not have been secured without the splendid cooperation of more than fifty groups which answered a brief questionnaire of mine. Valuable information was culled from official and private memoranda which were kindly made available to me. Above all, I want to express my gratitude to my wife to whom this book is dedicated, for she is my critic and my conscience; in short, without her this volume cannot be imagined.

W.R.V.

Amherst, Massachusetts
March 23, 1967

PROBLEMS OF
OPERA PRODUCTION

OPERA, A PART OF OUR CULTURAL LIFE

Historical Background

Unlike drama, opera was rather slow in setting foot on the shores of the new continent. With the exception of a ballad opera, *Flora or The Hob of the Well*, by Cibber, known to have been staged in Charleston, S.C., in 1735, and of others of this type produced in cities along the East Coast before the middle of the 18th century, opera was not presented in this country prior to the end of that century. At this time, French and Italian traveling companies visited North America, followed later by German troupes. Some of their standard works were performed in English as early as 1819. During the first decades of the 19th century, New York became the center of Italian opera, while in the South New Orleans gave emphasis to French opera. Both Italian and French works were mostly produced in the language of their origin, whereas German operas were presented in English as well as in German.

Shortly after 1850 New York acquired a theatre which proudly carried the title Astor Place Opera House. In other cities, too, new buildings arose, designed specifically for the presentation of opera. Toward the end of the 19th century it became the fashion of the day for small and distant places to possess an "opera house" in which the appearance of famous singers with their companies alternated with vaudeville. Culminating the operatic development, the opening of the Metropolitan Opera House in New York in 1883 became a landmark. Here French, German and Italian masterpieces performed by a galaxy of international stars found a home. British and American operas appeared in the repertoire years later.

Until World War I, opera was almost entirely in the hands of foreigners or foreign born artists. Native composers, singers, conductors and stage directors had only a slight chance for acceptance by managers and audiences. To circumvent this prejudice ambitious young artists studied in Europe and, in some cases, even altered their names to give them a foreign sound.

A turn came after 1915. Not suddenly, but gradually, almost unnoticed at the time, confidence in native talent began to grow. The depression of the thirties finally accelerated this trend. It was at the Met where a change became most conspicuous. Wealthy sponsors had suffered great losses and could no longer be counted on as its sole supporters. Other patrons had to be found. Thus this comparatively small group of rich sponsors was augmented by a larger organization whose members would provide the financial backbone of the productions. The "democratization" of opera set in.

The first most striking support came from an oil corporation which, since

3

1931, has been paying for the privilege of broadcasting the Met's Saturday matinees on a national circuit. Financial aid has also been provided by the Metropolitan Opera Guild, an independent organization, yet closely affiliated with the renowned company. Its beginning in 1937 was infinitesimal, but within ten years the group became a substantial factor in the Met's public relations. Its position as the mainstay in the Met's financial operations has been growing stronger every season.

The outward signal of the changed conditions was the disappearance of the "Diamond Horseshoe," the once famous row of boxes occupied by millionaires. They gave way to an increase in seating capacity. At the end of the thirties the reorganization of the Met Opera Association was completed, although its financial troubles remained unsolved. In any event, it was now clear to every opera lover that not only an evolution had taken place but a revolution as well.

After World War II, opera received a strong impetus. Perhaps the expansion of operatic activities would have come earlier if the restrictions, imposed by the War, had not interfered with the development. On the other hand, the returning soldiers were a driving force in this development. Thousands of veterans had attended performances in Europe and undoubtedly contributed to the generally growing interest in opera. This interest has been nourished chiefly by the weekly broadcasts from the Met whose millions of listeners can be considered potential patrons of live performances. Artistically of immense value were the operas in concert form of the National Broadcasting Company conducted by Arturo Toscanini with an outstanding ensemble. Operas, adapted for the film medium, were not impressive and created no stir. Other works such as *Der Rosenkavalier*, filmed in an opera house, or *The Tales of Hoffman*, shot in a studio, did not fare much better; in spite of their splendid artistic conception and laudable technical execution, they were ineffective in promoting this art form. Television, the new mass medium, added operatic productions to its program; seen in many thousands, one is induced to say millions, of homes, they contributed to the knowledge of and enhanced a liking for opera which cannot be measured.

To analyze the organization of the many American opera groups is not an easy task. In contrast to Europe where operatic productions are almost exclusively directed and performed by professionals (the few amateur groups do not count at all), conditions in the United States are quite complex. There are three categories, each of which represents an essential part of the overall picture: they are professional, semi-professional and amateur groups. Yet it is extremely difficult, sometimes impossible, to draw a dividing line between them. Few companies are fully professional, where all participants belong to a union and earn their living, or most of it, by working in opera houses.

In the first category, the Metropolitan Opera stands at the top. During a season of now thirty weeks in New York and six additional weeks on the road, this company offers approximately twenty different operas of the international standard repertoire, although rarely securing a new American or foreign work. The weekly broadcasts and its annual tour to cities in the north and south have

4

made the Met so widely known throughout the United States that it has become a national institution.

In 1944 a second opera company, the City Center Opera, was founded in New York. This ambitious group gives many opera aficionados an opportunity to hear the best of the standard works and, more important, a number of almost unknown older ones and a long list of contemporary operas. Limited by the inadequate technical facilities of its first theatre building and a small budget, the City Center Opera, nevertheless, has achieved a high standard in its productions. During its two brief annual seasons, one in the fall and the second in the spring, it offers close to one hundred performances. In the Middle West the Chicago Opera Company had an excellent reputation for many years; its season was a center for all opera lovers of the entire region. Financial difficulties forced its closing during the depression, but its successor, the Lyric Opera, initiated a few years ago, promises to revive the old spirit in a more modern conception. Another important professional organization has existed for a long time on the West Coast. The fall season of the San Francisco Opera Company has become a high point of the city's cultural life. The policy of this company is to include in its repertoire the production of one or more significant comtemporary works. After the close of its San Francisco fall season, the entire company appears in Los Angeles and other cities in California. In recent years the management has also scheduled a spring season in San Francisco for which instead of famous stars young singers are engaged and thus presented to a large audience.

The second category, hardly known prior to World War II, has expanded at a tremendous pace. This type has as its predominant feature a conductor-in-residence who sometimes has the title musical director or general manager. He rehearses the local orchestra and chorus but relies largely on name guests for the solo roles, though singers of the particular city are usually considered for minor roles. The musicians and the stage crew of these civic organizations are members of their respective trade group, as are the guest singers. Those who take on the small parts, the choristers and dancers, usually join a union for the duration of the season. To make the conductor the manager or to engage a specialist for this position became necessary when such a company expanded its artistic activities from one or two productions a year to four and more. As long as the ambition remains limited to a few productions, the management is, as a rule, in the hands of lay people who are willing to serve on the board of directors and thus to contribute their time and efforts to a community venture. About thirty of the civic companies have reached the highest possible standard and can be designated as professional. To classify most of them as semi-professional is done without derogatory connotation; this term merely refers to the type of organization, that is the membership of all participants in a union.

Among the first civic groups aiming at perfection were those in Boston, Pittsburgh and New Orleans. They flourished before the depression of the thirties. The financial strain of that time and then the war forced many of the civic groups to limit their activities or to suspend them. The postwar period brought about an immense expansion in this field, the end of which is not yet in sight.

If it is not easy to reach a decision about the professional or semi-professional status of the divers undertakings, it is impossible to draw the line between the semi-professional and the third category, since the latter, though basically consisting of amateurs, at times engages professionals in order to raise the standard, to fill roles for which no local talent is available, or to attract more patrons. Several civic groups have chosen this approach, in addition to some music schools, colleges and universities. Theoretically at least, educational institutions adhere to the amateur status; actually they do not, because their conductors, many of their musicians, and also some of their stage directors are union members or, at any rate, have had professional experience though they are now teachers.

Music schools such as the Peabody Conservatory of Music (since 1909), the Juilliard School of Music and the Eastman School of Music included operatic productions in their program almost from the start. Universities likewise at an early time added opera to their activities. Louisiana State University has probably the longest tradition, having performed operas since 1929. Among the newcomers, Indiana University, The Universities of California, of Southern California and of Illinois devote great effort to the preparation of their opera productions. In addition, Indiana and Southern California have set up separate opera departments and other institutions are contemplating this organizational change.

Companies, specifically initiated for summer offerings, deserve to be mentioned too. The majority of them specialize in musicals and operettas, yet several concentrate on light and grand opera. In the Rocky Mountain area, Central City gained much fame with performances of standard and original works in its historic opera house. Elsewhere the productions were staged in open-air theatres until about 1950 when tents and solid buildings with an arena stage became fashionable. To list even the best known of this kind would take up too much space. Among the open-air theatres, the Municipal Opera in St. Louis reaches a high standard; so does Cincinnati which continues to attract good crowds to its theatre in the Zoo. A few years ago a magnificent place was chosen for opera in the hills north of Sante Fe to stage not only the old favorite operas, but also unusual contemporary works. All these summer ventures operate with professionals. Lately a few educational institutions have added summer productions to their program. The famed National Music Camp at Interlochen decided several years ago to concentrate on contemporary American and foreign one-act works. More ambitious is the plan of Indiana University whose opera department has staged demanding operas like *Aida* and *Turandot* with guest singers in the title roles.

A comparison of current operatic activities with those of twenty-five years ago testifies to a tremendous increase. Before World War II, the number of professional companies, civic groups, music schools and colleges which regularly offered operas, was small indeed; it probably never surpassed one hundred. Surveys, made around 1950 by *Musical America* and *Opera News*, showed the total had climbed to about two hundred and fifty groups; included in these listings are one-hundred and fifty civic groups and fifty colleges. That this number did not cover the entire extent of the interest in musical productions has been proven. A thorough investigation by the American Educational Theatre Association, compiled in 1958, reveals that the current interest far exceeds that number. This survey mentions not only all opera companies, but also those producing musicals and operettas, not merely those which stage several works in a season, but also the many others which prepare an opera or operetta occasionally. The amazing result demonstrates the tremendous expansion in these activities during less than a generation. There were 678 groups (workshops) in colleges, universities and music schools; more than 320 are listed under civic, summer and winter stock companies; 205 high schools returned a positive answer to a questionnaire; and there were many more in the categories called industrial, folk, church, children, social center and armed services. In 1958 the grand total amounted to 1,363. As no all-embracing study has been made since, it is anybody's guess how much this number has grown during recent years.

Basic Aims

Theoretically opera can be presented like drama as a business venture or an artistic endeavor for the purpose of entertainment or enlightenment. Business and entertainment, however, need not necessarily exclude art and enlightenment. A scanning of history will teach that opera as a purely commercial enterprise has rarely been successful. Opera began as a hobby of princes and for a long time it remained the task of kings and men of abundant means to guarantee the anticipated deficit. With the development of an influential middle class in Europe, the financial responsibilities shifted ever more to groups of wealthy citizens, city and state governments. Since opera seldom paid for itself, yet was widely favored by admirers in all classes who insisted on its preservation, government agencies had to support the art form. In many countries the care of an opera house became an artistic and cultural affair of great importance. But state and city officials, legislators and city councils, have been unwilling and unable to grant a subsidy without limitations. The budget, once approved, has to be kept and therefore the business concern can never be ignored. Operatic presentations must not only be of high artistic value; they must, in addition, be attractive to a large segment of the public. Enlightenment is the foremost component of cultural offerings which must contain also some entertainment value in order to stimulate the interest of a large number of potential patrons.

If we interpret opera in this way, we shall want to know what, or how much, operatic productions contribute to the culture and entertainment of people; in other words, what is their value for the life of a community? There are in fact millions who listen to the broadcasting of operas from the Met and thus hear an ensemble of singers which another city in the United States can hardly afford to offer. Nevertheless, the work itself cannot possibly be appreciated and enjoyed through a loudspeaker as it will in a live performance. The greatest benefit naturally will come to those citizens who are able to participate in the orchestra, the chorus, or in small and leading roles. Civic associations should make it a point, therefore, to allot parts to young artists, thus giving them an opportunity to gain priceless experience before they try out for membership in leading companies. Of course the producers must strive to present good performances, which means performances based on modern artistic ideas and thorough rehearsals.

The social aspect of community life as a whole is enriched by operatic productions. The preparatory work alone keeps the minds of many people creatively busy for a long time; their gatherings are stimulated by their interest in a common cause. New congenial groups are formed to study a particular opera or to take part in committee work. When after weeks and months of hard work, these volunteers have assisted in bringing about a successful performance, their happiness and excitement are sometimes a better reward than any money can afford them. After all, citizens boast of their parks, libraries, orchestras and little theatres. Now they can be just as proud of their accomplishments in operatic production.

Business men will appreciate the value of publicity. Good opera is an attraction to out-of-town patrons, who are so highly welcomed by every chamber of commerce. Furthermore, if the management of a civic association is relying chiefly on resident talent for staff, and on local firms to make the settings and costumes, a large part of the money raised for the productions will be spent in the city itself. Mr. Clifford E. Bair, founder of the National Association for Opera, who developed the operatic festivals in North Carolina, writes: "Our Chamber of Commerce considers the cultural advantages which our vital program of community arts can give its citizens a deciding factor in bringing to the city new industrial, commercial and governmental agencies—in particular those of skilled labor—who demand cultural advantages, and these days most of them do." The author adds that singers and other artists collaborating in community productions secured good opportunities in other cities or received higher salaries in local employment.

At the initiation of her operatic venture, Miss Lilian Baylis, who for a generation managed the famous Old Vic Theatre and Sadler's Wells Opera in London, extolled the intrinsic merit of good opera productions for the cultural life of a city and a nation: "Great music and great drama at cheap prices are very real necessities in the life of people... I have said often before, and I repeat, that nowadays we cultivate physical fitness in every possible way; and everybody knows that the full enjoyment of one's bodily faculties is only possible after exercise and effort. But what about the mental fitness of our younger generation? This, too, can only be acquired by exercise and effort; and it is toward this full realization of the great kingdom in our minds, that we shall labor at Sadler's Wells." Another firm endorsement comes from Mr. Otto H. Kahn who, together with a group of friends, sponsored and supported the Metropolitan Opera Association in both good and dangerous days: "I have faith that the people as a whole know a good production and a good play or opera when they see and hear

8

it. They accept a poor one for lack of a better one but it is a rare case when they misjudge a good one. I wondered often at the people's capacity of digesting and enjoying art problems... Much is done for education, art is part of education, part recreation, and of the latter we need not more but better things."

In the United States the vision and perseverance of many opera lovers have born fruit. In a good number of cities opera has become an integral part of civic life. Several developments in recent years document this fact. A very remarkable sign was the plan and the creation of the Lincoln Center in New York for the Performing Arts, a venture in which Federal, State and City agencies collaborated in the most beneficial manner with private persons in order to solve the numerous problems, among them a total cost of some 165 million dollars. Spurred by this successful collaboration Washington is making great efforts to materialize its own blueprint for a Center for the Performing Arts. Close to one hundred cities and universities have already built or are making plans for an art center. Most significant is the interest in the arts demonstrated by legislators in Washington and several state capitals.

Training of Artists

There is no lack of native talent in the United States. Scores of American singers have proven that they equal those in other countries and some have gained international renown. Many have left these shores for Europe, since it is still difficult for them to make a career at home in their chosen field, one which offers so few opportunities. Every year more good singers graduate from music schools and colleges and come from private teachers, but the prospect they face is not promising. Where can they gain experience, where can they develop their talent until they are mature enough to approach the few leading companies? What is needed for so much talent is more opera companies extending their seasons and their repertoire.

A gap of available artists is noticeable in the field of leadership, which means there are not enough experienced American conductors and stage directors. To a high degree the older companies rely for these positions on foreigners who after a rigorous schooling have an excellent chance to acquire invaluable experience in the middling and leading opera houses of their native countries. To be sure, outstanding artists and singers as well as conductors and directors have always been welcome in the United States and it can be expected that this attitude will not change; yet the cultural life of the nation will certainly benefit from the participation of more American artistic leaders.

It should be an intriguing task for our institutions of higher learning to aim at offering ever greater opportunities to aspiring conductors and directors. A few music schools and universities have well-developed opera departments (not merely opera workshops); other institutions are making well-devised plans to offer courses and productions which will enable young artists to acquire the necessary theoretical and practical background. This is a hopeful sign. Soon an aspiring conductor, director, designer and singer will be in a position to gain this most urgently needed practical experience. The shortage is particularly

9

acute in the domain of coaching. Coaches are the indispensable assistants of the conductors, and a conductor, before tackling the demanding job of directing entire operas, should have a thorough knowledge of all scores, a task which can best be learned through coaching. If students can be trained in the diverse arts and techniques within the next ten years, we shall have gone a long way toward securing the services of well-trained and experienced artists.

The accent must be on "well-trained and experienced," for superficiality in the concept and execution of this program would do more harm than good. Those in charge and those in training must be aware that only long and hard work will let them arrive at the desired goal. All should realize that an undergraduate degree in music or theatre does not suffice but that graduate work specifically in opera is necessary to strengthen the program. Serving as a journeyman with civic and summer companies should complement the college work. Students, who have a professional career in mind, are advised to work, as is feasible, with all kinds of companies and even clubs. Young singers sometimes succeed in being engaged with very little experience provided their voices are outstanding, but all those anxious to become conductors and directors must go through a longer and more demanding training program before an opera group will entrust them with a production.

In due time opera will conquer a place of its own in our institutions of higher learning, if not in all, certainly in scores of our music schools, colleges and universities. The purpose of the training program will vary of course. It will be of general value to those who merely wish to become acquainted with operatic works and their productions. This aim in itself should not be underrated as an educational factor; not only does such knowledge raise the general level and improve the taste of the audience, it provides future theatre-goers with most essential and valuable experience. It prepares others for teaching in colleges or high schools, a most important feature, since good teachers are essential to instruct and fascinate the young students. For others, there are many ways to participate in amateur and semi-professional productions. Only in exceptional cases the goal can and will be a professional career. At any event the requirements must be high, as only thus the standard can be raised. Specific requirements must of course be applied to those who want to become professionals. This concerns singers, conductors, directors, designers, all who intend to devote their life and career to operatic productions.

The prospect for the development of operatic activities in the United States is excellent. We have the artistic talent and the managerial and technical skill to solve the basic questions and to push on into the highest sphere. What is necessary is the will to solve the manifold problems, to find the right leaders, to assemble the artists and technicians, and to create favorable conditions that make it possible to achieve the very best.

10

PROBLEMS OF OPERA PRODUCTION

The Elements

The first contact with the complex structure of opera might be bewildering and perplexing to the layman who wishes to enjoy this art form. Even without previous knowledge of theories he discovers that opera may easily please him indeed, but that, on the other hand, it is extremely difficult to understand its intricate style. Music has a direct appeal to our emotions, more so than the spoken word in a play. But this strange interplay of symphonic web, spoken words, singing, action, thought, and scenic effects challenges reasoning.

Before we examine the various components of an operatic work, we shall try to determine what opera as an art form means. Is it drama, or another musical form, like symphony? Since composers approached it with the idea of having it staged, opera ought to be a branch of theatre arts. All arguments about the pre-dominance of music notwithstanding, the original concept in the 16th century was related to the resurrection of the Greek tragedy, based on a misunder-standing, namely, that Greek drama was sung. Disregarding this peculiar fact we can still apply to opera Aristotle's definition of drama, which contains these elements: plot, character, thought, diction, melody and spectacle. Opera is in essence composed of the same elements, except that here, melody—music—takes a lead to which all other parts become subordinated.

The inceptors of opera made the composer alone all important. Repeated efforts of composers like Gluck, Weber and Wagner to reinstitute drama in its proper place show that music tends to superimpose its own weight whenever possible. Opponents of the reformers apparently consider opera a kind of ex-tension of oratorio, or a new form of music. Some historians of the theatre arts fail even to mention opera in their writings. Authors of books on music some-times take a similar attitude, barely dealing with it. Such views of students and scholars reflect the widespread uncertainty about the category to which opera esthetically belongs and what it actually means. A stepchild in many respects, it remains, for all its contradictions, nevertheless a favorite with many. The more successful works are performed again and again. They are standard pieces of our repertory and people wish to see them year after year.

People may delight in just listening to an opera, as radio and concert per-formances have amply demonstrated. Yet many listeners confess that something is missing—the scenic frame and the action. Lovers of pure music, on the other hand, maintain that they do not even look at the stage in an opera house, since action "distracts" them from enjoying the music. This can be the case whenever poor acting or unsatisfactory settings bring about incongruity of performance. In perfect productions even the "puritans" can be fascinated by the spectacle on stage.

Unlike drama in which it has a subordinate or supporting role, music predominates in opera. Surveying the other components, we find diction in a constant argument with music, as it were; thought definitely taking a secondary part in most works, despite all intentions and reforms by composers; character frequently of less importance, since many librettists and composers create stereotypes rather than individuals; and plot sometimes disorganized and superficial. Yet spectacle is next to music the most essential element in opera. It includes action, settings, costumes, lighting, and properties, in short everything we witness on stage. Opera represents a synthesis of all the arts, and this all-embracing property implies also imperfections and contradictions. A few great composers strove to achieve the ideal solution, among them Christoph Willibald von Gluck and Richard Wagner. The latter alone arrived at his goal and he only in the greatest of his music dramas. It seems almost as though creating the *Gesamtkunstwerk* is too far-reaching an attempt.

Opera means to most of its lovers music and music alone—excellent singing included. The difference in the popular approach becomes clear when we compare the dramas and operas of the repertoire. When we speak of *Hamlet, Faust, Tartuffe, The Doll's House,* or *The Sea Gull* we think of the authors as well as the characters. But of operas such as *The Magic Flute, Otello, Carmen, Faust, Tosca, Salomé,* theatre-goers remember the composer and the singers, while the librettist and his work are forgotten or neglected. Critics and advertisements support this prejudice by always giving the name of the composer, but rarely or in small print, the name of the librettist. The one exception to this custom are the works by Gilbert and Sullivan.

Scholars are conscious of the inconsistencies and contradictions inherent in opera. The layman, however, is lost in a labyrinth through which he has to fight his way with difficulty. It might therefore be advisable to point out these inconsistencies, since awareness of them can benefit a production. Less than in drama, it is possible to define the elements conclusively because they vary from opera to opera. Experts have so far set a norm for a style already known but no one as yet has succeeded in formulating a definition as comprehensive as Aristotle's statement about drama. In opera the disputed subjects are still being discussed as hotly as ever.

The Libretto

The fundamental question is the relationship of librettist and composer and the importance apportioned to each one of them. The ideal is, of course, the unification of author and composer in one personality, an ideal that has become reality in a few exceptional cases, such as Lortzing, Wagner, Moussorgsky and Menotti. The majority of composers rely on the collaboration of writers who specialize in this field. In general, the composer is in search of an author who is able to either write a book based on the composer's ideas, or to adapt his own script to the composer's wishes. On the whole, the librettist provides, as it were, the plot and its characters; the composer, the mood and the poetic atmosphere. Frequently the writer has been the composer's employee, seldom his close associate. Mozart, for one, ordered librettos from Da Ponte and was quite satisfied with the submitted material, but he suffered deeply when he "collaborated" with Schikaneder, the author of *The Magic Flute*, who was a theatre manager rather than a poet. Verdi, as a neophyte, adopted the custom of the day in having librettos tailored to his own ideas. He repeatedly altered verses at will, substituting words he considered more suitable for his melodies, inserting sounds like *ah* or *si*, regardless of their meaning. Later when he received excellent cooperation from Arrigo Boito, Verdi gave up his wilful alterations and *Otello* and *Falstaff* are the results of an intimate exchange of views. Of course the composer must have some latitude in adapting the text, but the question is how far he may go. Obviously the words in a coloratura passage need not necessarily make sense nor do they in an ensemble passage. Even Wagner, the great reformer, sinned against the meaning of words, as for instance, in the beautiful quintet in act three of *The Mastersingers*.

To a certain degree there is a conformity of procedure. Nevertheless national peculiarities can well be detected. The Italian composer often conceived music first and then added words, a method not unknown to many modern composers of "hits." The French musician began with the libretto as a basis for which he tried to find suitable melodies. This was adopted by the German in the beginning, but he soon gave music pre-eminence in his opera. There was also a time when melodies, even entire numbers were selected from one production and transferred to another. The text was all that was new. It is an axiom widely accepted that the mood as expressed in music supersedes the text. Music remains victorious even over excellent drama as libretto. Who remembers today that *The Barber of Seville* and *The Marriage of Figaro* were popular comedies written by Beaumarchais toward the end of the 18th century? Who thinks of Goethe or of Shakespeare at a performance of *Faust* or *Otello?* Even the authors of the two great modern plays *Salomé* and *Pelléas and Mélisande* are hardly mentioned. Whoever has seen these two works, both as drama and opera, is indeed inclined to concede that the mere spoken word can no longer be thoroughly enjoyed because music has so enriched the original form. This is true similarly of Alban Berg's music to George Buechner's drama *Wozzeck*. The strange position of the libretto is further accentuated by the fact that composers sometimes have selected a book in a foreign language, which they had not always mastered. Handel composed in Italian and English, Gluck in French and Italian, Mozart in Italian, Salieri in German, Meyerbeer and Offenbach in French. If, at this point, we add the problem of translations into other languages, the relationship of libretto and music becomes confused indeed.

The text of the average opera suggests a preference for certain situations and characters on the part of the writers. Hence one may conclude that the book must be typical and simple to be successful. A pattern of standardized events and characters can be recognized, much like those in the *commedia dell'arte*, the *blood and murder* drama and the *melodrama* which today makes us laugh so heartily. There are scores of drinking and hunting songs, serenades, duels, scenes of disguise, abduction, seduction, intrigue and heroic liberation, camp, church and cemetery scenes and, to be sure, love scenes of every sort. In addition, librettists and also composers seem to be fond of all the phenomena of nature from moon and stars to terrific thunderstorms. Animals too appear repeatedly. Certain situations have been copied so often that repetition seems to be epidemic. Lastly, it is evident that characters have become too stereo-typed. The lover-hero is a tenor, the villain a baritone or bass, the serious father a *basso profundo* and his funny counterpart, an uncle or padre turns out to be the *basso buffo*. The soprano, loved by the tenor, has our sympathy, as against the alto who is either funny or mean. There are exceptions to this formula, but despite many efforts at reforming, the standard characters have not entirely disappeared. They have been accepted and applauded for centuries and will, in all likelihood, remain with us as long as opera exists.

Dialogue and Recitative

Some cognoscenti ignore operas interspersed with dialogue scenes, because to them these works are not deserving of that term. A few outstanding examples, such as *Fidelio*, refute this concept. As a matter of fact, dialogue became an essential part of opera in its beginnings. It would be just as absurd to neglect operas with recitatives. For all its changes in style, modern opera contains not only recitatives in a modified form, but also lines of straight dialogue. The argument whether such passages should be sung or spoken has led to odd results. For a while it was customary to convert the recitative in Italian operas into dialogue. Thus *The Marriage of Figaro, Don Giovanni, The Barber of Seville* and others were staged with dialogue as though they had derived from the German *singspiel* or the French comic opera. Toward the end of the 19th and in the early 20th centuries the opposite trend came to the fore. Mozart's masterpieces were universally restored to their original beauty, but now the fundamental peculiarity of the German *singspiel* was sometimes vio-lated by the change from dialogue to recitative. The reason given for this change was that the musical atmosphere could be better preserved and that singers, often poor speakers, could remain in their own province, i.e. singing. *Singspiele*, like *The Abduction from the Seraglio*, with *secco* recitatives, or *Fidelio* and *Der Freischuetz* with *recitativo accompagnato* suffered from this offense against the style of these pieces. Indeed a few operas were so successful in the new version that their dialogue seems all but forgotten. They are above all *Carmen* and *The Tales of Hoffmann*. The orchestra recitatives composed by

Ernest Guiraud are heard in most of our performances, as are those of *Mignon*, arranged by Ambroise Thomas himself, for England and Italy. The original dialogue is now rarely heard in these operas. This is regrettable indeed because in the adapted musical form of the recitatives allusions essential to incidents and characters have been omitted.

Soloists and Orchestra

The controversy is not restricted to the predominance of music but extends to the singer's relation to the orchestra. The implication of this question must be considered in connection with the style of each opera and the presentation of it. Three very diverse types can be discerned: the Italian school, as being *vocal*, the French, *lyric*, and the German, *instrumental*. Mozart and Verdi certainly offer the singer more opportunities than Wagner, whose orchestra sometimes seems to overflow and suppress the vocal interpretation; the French composers usually take a happy medium. Today the different schools have more or less merged into a single form with variations. Debussy, Puccini and Strauss are still representatives of their national predilections, but Milhaud, Hindemith and Menotti can hardly be claimed by their native lands. While there still exists a vestige of national peculiarity, leading composers now strive more and more to develop a style of their own, related but not subject to their nationality.

Conductor, director and singer should discern the basic difference, since the style of production must agree with the respective school. The singer has the right to be heard and understood, but he must also realize that he is part of a large and complex group. Conductors, on the other hand, sometimes accord too much freedom to the orchestral tone waves, and thus, aside from preventing the singer to be understood, they destroy the balance intended by every good composer. The pit must be attuned to the stage no matter whether a work by Mozart, Verdi, Wagner or Debussy is produced. The best of conductors have tamed even Wagner's and Strauss' orchestras. And Toscanini, in turn, magically elicited, without drowning the voices, more brilliance from the scores of *La Traviata* and *Rigoletto* than Verdi's rather simple orchestration seems to promise. In *Otello* and *Falstaff* Verdi forsook the earlier style in favor of a subtle and complicated instrumentation. Yet no predominance of the orchestra is perceptible and the perfect balance of stage and pit is everywhere preserved. This happened not long after Wagner almost overpowered the singer with his orchestra.

FOREIGN OPERA IN ENGLISH

Belief among experts is growing ever stronger that, if anything obstructs the popularization of opera in America, it is the presentation of foreign works in the original language. During the past twenty years recognition of this opinion

15

has induced several professional and semi-professional and most educational organizations to produce musical drama in English. Some foreign operas have been performed in English for decades; a few of them for so long that they are hardly thought of as being translated. *Martha*, for instance, the comic opera by Flotow, has rarely been heard in German; a few times it has been sung in Italian, but more often than not in English. Humperdinck's charming fairy tale, *Hansel and Gretel*, has been enjoyed in English for a long time. *The Bartered Bride*, a favorite in the field of comic opera, is known to the majority of patrons only in English translation, although it has on occasion been rendered in Czech. Some years ago the Metropolitan Opera experimented with Verdi's *Falstaff* in English; a few arguments were voiced after the performance, but even ardent fans of Italian opera took the innovation in good grace. Mozart's operas have been tried in new translations which have become part of the official repertoire. Tchaikovsky's *Eugene Onegin* has been produced in various languages, seldom in the original, which gives the connoisseur artistic delight but means hard labor for soloists and choristers who have to learn Russian. But all this is only a beginning. Convention still requires that most Italian operas be performed in Italian, French ones in French, and German works in German.

Social Background

What are the roots of the custom to produce a musical drama in the tongue of its origin, and what are the reasons for adhering to it in the United States?

Opera, an indigene of Italy, was introduced to the rest of Europe and to England by way of *stagiones* of Italian artists. Stubborn efforts on the part of the French to develop an operatic art form of their own in competition with the Italian creation were quite successful, particularly in Central Europe, where French operas were favored by many connoisseurs. The European custom of having Italian and French ensembles present opera in Italian or French respectively prevailed until about the end of the 18th century when the common man was admitted to the Court Theatres. Slowly foreign troupes were then replaced by native artists who sang foreign operas in translated versions. At the same time opera written in the vernacular, hitherto well-nigh ignored as an art form, secured a place in the repertoire. Eventually, under the growing influence of the citizens who on their own supported many municipal theatres, opera performed in the tongue of the particular country became common all over Europe.

Only the Royal Covent Garden Opera House in London retained the arrangement to divide the season into Italian, French and German *stagiones*. The latter was included after the success of the Wagnerian music-dramas. When American society began to promote opera it was the tradition of Covent Garden which was adopted. Immigrants from Germany and Italy who settled in New York and who were great opera-lovers undoubtedly welcomed the opportunity of hearing the masterpieces of their native lands in their vernacular. This condition prevailed also in other cities where operas were occasionally presented. Once this custom was firmly established, those members of society who have always claimed opera as their privileged domain considered it a matter of prestige. Many of them understand foreign languages, yet even those who do not would rather follow the fashion than stand apart or admit that they do not understand the words.

In the meantime Great Britain abandoned the haphazard *stagione* system in favor of a well-prepared long season. The first step in this direction was taken in the 1930's by Sadler's Wells in London, where every opera was produced in English. When, after the last war, Covent Garden was taken over by the British Government, it too turned largely to English versions. This policy helped win new opera friends, as the box-office receipts show, and deeply impressed American visitors who attended these productions. An influential member of the Metropolitan Opera's board of directors confessed after a performance of the English *Der Rosenkavalier* that, for the first time, he had been able to understand and to enjoy the charming details of the action. Edward J. Dent, the eminent British musicologist, offered excellent reasons in favor of English versions when he wrote the author:

> Translations are made, not for critics or conductors, not even for singers, and least of all for those who are thoroughly familiar with the opera in the original language, but for the ordinary Englishman who goes into the Opera House, perhaps never having seen any opera in his life before, wondering what sort of a show it is, and whether he will enjoy it or be bored. The translator hopes to help him to enjoy it, to make him see that opera is as reasonable and as intelligible as a spoken play, and in any case, to want to come to the opera again as often as he can.

Among critics and experts in the United States some have already manifested their preference for translation. The main question is not, however, whether a few cognoscenti will be convinced and converted, but, whether, by removing the language barrier, thousands of new patrons will actually be attracted. Articles and informal statements alike report the growing interest, particularly outside New York, in operas performed in the vernacular. Most of the educational institutions follow this trend as do many civic companies. But several companies aspiring a professional status still adhere to the original versions; their policy is caused by the fact that they often engage foreign singers who are not accustomed to singing in English. Performances in foreign languages are prevalent in New York although new translations have occasionally been introduced at the Met. Generally speaking, it can be concluded that English is the preferred language. An evaluation of box-office receipts adds little clarification to this problem, since there are manifold reasons for attending an opera. It is all the more interesting to learn that in specific cases at least performances in English drew better crowds than those in the original language in spite of better known singers in the latter.

17

With reference to the discussion about the presentation of an opera in the original or in translated form, the opinion of singers and other artists involved carries some weight. Naturally the Italian, the French, or the German singer prefers his native tongue. But we must remember that there are also singers from Scandinavia, Poland, Russia, Spanish-speaking countries and elsewhere. Their own language is of no value to them in the United States; as they are obliged to perform in a language strange to them, they may as well be expected to master English. Lastly, a crop of young American and British singers are coming into prominence in ever greater numbers. There can be no doubt that English versions are a boon to them. It will be easier to teach every young singer the correct use of his native tongue in a perfect diction instead of having them superficially acquainted with three foreign languages. A singer from abroad should be expected to sing in English just as his American counterpart is requested to sing in French, German or Italian if he wants to become a member of an opera house in these European countries. Exceptions will be made of course on the occasion of festivals and for outstanding foreign guests.

The request for opera in English translation is supported by many singers and other experts. *Musical America* published a series of statements which can be summarized thus: opera can only become really popular if the average theatregoer understands the words. Among those whose opinion was offered were Astrid Varnay, Lawrence Tibbett, Lotte Lehmann, Brenda Lewis, John Gutman, Herbert Graf, John Crosby, Boris Goldovsky, Jerome Hines, and Douglas Moore.

Those who defend the presentation in the original language sometimes forward the view that the sung words cannot be understood anyhow. This criticism has some merit and should be considered seriously by the singers whose duty it is to have precise speech habits. It is moreover the responsibility of the stage director to insist on clear enunciation and of the conductor so to subdue the orchestra that the words remain intelligible except in ensembles and climactic passages.

Problems of Translating Opera

Proponents of opera in the original language emphasize the loss in artistic value through the translation *per se,* citing poorly adapted passages in present translations. In rebuttal to their assertion it can be pointed out that the original librettos are not always very good. Listeners who insist on hearing their favorites in French, Italian or German will be surprised when they read the often silly and unintelligible sentences of some texts. As already mentioned, our great composers with a few exceptions have not been very fastidious in the choice of a libretto. They have been more intent on dramatic action and sentences suitable to their musical conception than on literary quality. Their aim was to write melodies, not to judge a contest in playwriting. Anyhow, experience in Europe has shown that translated versions enhance rather than

18

impede the enjoyment of operatic performances. The second point cannot be denied. Some operas, to be sure, have been rendered in slipshod translations; in others, passages and even scenes have become almost ridiculous. At times this has been the fault of the translator, but more often than not it has been due to the specific fashion of the era in which the translation was made. Here thoughtful corrections could accomplish great improvements. It is not enough for the adaptor to translate well and truthfully; his responsibility also is occasionally to revise the original text.

If we agree with the purists that *Carmen* ought to be performed in French, *Tristan and Isolde* in German and *La Bohème* in Italian, because they do not sound well in English, then we should also prefer to have the great European dramas produced in the original. Really we would be far more justified in opposing renditions of the great plays of the world literature in translated form. But then the majority of Americans would be deprived of the privilege of enjoying the best in world drama. But Moliere, Ibsen, Chekov, Pirandello, Anouilh and many others have been staged in English with great success. At intervals foreign acting troupes have come to the United States presenting plays in their own tongue in special performances staged by famous directors, but this has always been an exception, a sort of festival. There is no doubt that operas, too, should be offered as originally conceived on special occasions.

However, to deny the possibility of an adequate translation means a lack of confidence in the English language, as Edward J. Dent pointed out to the author:

> If translations are to be used at all, we must make up our minds firmly that English is just as good a language for singing as any other, and we must never allow anyone to say to us that such and such an opera is simply untranslatable. We must also try to convince English singers that English is a vocal and beautiful language, and that it is their first duty to speak it clearly and correctly.

In fact, during the last twenty or thirty years translations have improved so far that English versions of German, especially Wagnerian, operas can be called adequate. Because of the close affinity of the two tongues, renditions from German involve fewer difficulties than from any other language. Some Italian works have also been expertly translated; opera companies, television corporations and educational institutions have commissioned or accepted new versions. This gives us hope that eventually we shall have fine adaptations of all the foreign operas.

The mentor in the field of English translations, Edward J. Dent, has translated twenty-three foreign operas, most of which have been published and successfully staged in their new form. Thus his ideas about the problems of translation are of particular interest. The following paragraphs are taken from an extensive memorandum sent by Mr. Dent to the author:

The translator's first duty is to make the story of the opera as clear as possible. He must therefore make it clear to himself, and for that purpose must go back, if possible to the original book, play, or legend, on which the libretto was based. A librettist, adapting from a play, is often led to leave out important factors in the plot, thus causing much obscurity, which the translator can generally clear up.

Language: The translator needs to know the language from which he is translating, but it is more important that he should know English and be saturated with English poetry and literature. Every opera demands its own literary style. For Handel, we must base it on Dryden, Pope and Gay; for Mozart's operas on Sheridan; for Weber on Planche, for the romantic operas on the romantic poets. Even operas by the same composer may demand different styles; *Rigoletto* demands the language of Shakespeare and his contemporaries, *Il Trovatore* the full-blooded romanticism of Byron and Scott, *La Traviata* the refinement of early Victorian poets and novelists. *Eugene Onegin* presents a curiously difficult problem of style, for Pushkin is not only "the Russian Byron" but "the Russian Jane Austen" as well. Here we come across another almost insuperable difficulty, for every poet's style is dependent on his own particular metres and rhythms, and these are often quite different from the metres and rhythms of opera. The translator must study every libretto as a drama, and try to visualize it in imagination as he would see it, presented on the stage.

In his choice of words the translator must always aim at clearness and simplicity of language. "Poetical" and unfamiliar words must be avoided as a rule; when they are sung they do not reach the intelligence of the audience. There is no reason for a translation to be literal or exact, unless this is vital to the sense and the dramatic situation. In certain places exactness is indispensable, and it often happens that the musical note-values have to be changed. This generally happens in recitatives, but sometimes also in more "musical moments." In lyrics, especially as in early Verdi operas, exact translation is impossible, and if possible, would be ludicrous.

Rhyme: Some translators think that rhyme is unnecessary; but this is mere laziness and want of ingenuity. The great difficulty of English is the shortage of feminine (double) rhymes, which are innumerable in Italian and common in French and German.

In French the accent often shifts from one syllable to another, and in lyrics a musical accent often falls on unaccented syllables, especially in older composers such as Gounod. In fact throughout most of the nineteenth century almost all composers, French, German, Italian and English, seem to have adopted the general principle that in recitatives words are all important, but that in arias the melody is the only thing and the words do not matter (Bellini is a striking exception). But for the English stage of today a higher standard of correct accentuation is necessary, and it must be secured as far as possible. A translator needs an expert knowledge of musical analysis, and of harmony and even of composition, so as to observe the difference of accentuation which may occur, e.g., whether a word comes on the first or the third beat of a bar of common time.

The harmony of the accompaniment will often determine the exact emotional sense of a phrase or a word, and must always be considered, especially in Verdi, Massenet, and other composers with a sensitive feeling for shades of emotion.

A great difficulty for the translator is to guess the exact speed at which the music will be sung. Modern conductors, especially Germans, always tend to hurry, and to concentrate their entire attention on the orchestra and on the general "symphonic" effect, ignoring the singers entirely.

The chief drawback of English for opera is that it is for the most part a light and rapid language. This is a great advantage in comic opera, such as those of Mozart and Rossini, which go much better in English than in German. But English resents the excessive prolongation of vowels characteristic of Wagner and Richard Strauss, and Wagner presents exceptional difficulty because his German librettos require a very Germanic type of English, avoiding words derived from Latin, and in practically every case the English word corresponding exactly to the German is light, while the German is heavy, e.g. *Brot*, bread, *Bruder*, brother.

As a general rule any libretto can be translated satisfactorily into English if it is a good libretto in itself and if the composer has treated it with due respect; difficulty occurs when the composer (early Verdi) treats his words as nonsense. The great advantage of English is its elasticity; all Russian and Hungarian rhythms can be reproduced in English, whereas some are impossible to reproduce in German.

Most librettists tend to write meaningless lines here and there for the sake of rhyme; the translator must seize these chances wherever he can of putting in something in English, which will help the drama along; for this reason especially he must have a clear conception of the whole drama before he starts to translate.

Such little touches may not be very noticeable, but they have a cumulative effect.

If we have to translate strophic songs with two or three verses, we must take care that the interest increases as the song proceeds. Verdi often repeats an entire aria with the same words; here I think it is best to write a new second verse, expanding the poet's original idea, and taking care to make the second more dramatic than the first. Since the repetition is often cut in performance, the translator should be prepared for this and indicate which verse is to be sung.

After World War II two young Americans took up the fight for opera in English. Ruth Kelly and Thomas Phillipp Martin approached the task in a fresh and modern manner and have already had great success with some new versions. Conductors, singers and critics as well as audiences have accepted their adaptations wholeheartedly. These are their principles as they described them in *Opera News:*

1. The music remains untouched.
2. The accent of the declamation is strictly observed, even in ensembles.
3. All forced methods of making lines fit by means of abbreviations, twisting of phrases, or contractions like e'er, you'll, he'd, etc. have been avoided except when typical.
4. The number of syllables in a phrase is never augmented or diminished.
5. The organic breathing points are accurately preserved. No phrase is distorted by an inorganic splitting. Nor do false connections alter the original phrasing.
6. The original vowel is maintained to the greatest possible extent at all exposed places where the nature of the vowel is part of the musical effect.
7. To insure clear enunciation and good diction, words which are difficult to pronounce are not crowded, especially in passages of rapid tempo.
8. Throughout the entire opera, the translation endeavors to follow the original as closely as possible in the conviction that the further a translation digresses from the original, the less it will preserve the unity of words and music.

Whether the example of the Martins has furthered the general trend or whether it was in the air is difficult to decide, but during the past ten years several outstanding musicians have devoted much time to translations of standard and little known operas. Walter Ducloux and John Gutman have been particularly active in creating successful English versions.

It can be conceded that the presentation of a lyric drama, as conceived and created by the librettist and the composer, will always be more artistic. Yet when the goal is to popularize this art form, it must, of necessity, be offered in such a manner that the layman can understand and enjoy not only the music but the story as well, hence in words which interpret the action and the mood of the characters. The intricate details of the plot are lost without the intelligibility of the words. The average opera-goer should be able to follow a performance without resorting to a description of the plot in his program or a recheck of a translated libretto.

THE STAGING OF OPERA

Before specific production problems can be enumerated and discussed, the task as a whole must be examined briefly. Staging opera is both similar and dissimilar to play production. The most striking dissimilarity is the supreme importance of music. It takes intimate knowledge of and feeling for musical styles to transform the printed score into a wealth of sound, dramatic action and pictorial beauty. Only people who deeply love music should attempt to participate in an operatic production. Certainly the conductor and singer, but also the director, designer and chorister, even the electrician and stage hand, ought to have a sense of music. A lack of empathy among these participants adversely affects the performance. Mere technical accomplishment without true musicality is a shortcoming, to say the least; it can lead to catastrophe if it involves the conductor, the singers, and the stage director.

Main Problems

A drama can, under certain circumstances, be produced with intuition, imagination, and improvisation. But opera, imposing an extremely complex task, artistic and technical alike, can never be improvised. On the contrary, the most exhaustive and thorough preparation is required. The leaders need comprehensive training and experience, and the other participants must at least have a solid schooling. Disregard of this prerequisite results in sloppy and dragging productions. Play productions have reached a high level of accomplishment in numerous civic and college theatres. It is unnecessary that operatic productions be imitations or parodies of spoken plays. They need not be inconsistent with the music, negligently, artificially or sloppily staged. Surely artistic and technical intricacies render productions of opera more susceptible to convention than those of plays. But to adhere to a tradition that makes no sense is a sin against the living theatre; convention is to be blamed for many an inferior performance which sometimes resembles more a stuffy museum or panopticon.

Snarls and traps can be avoided when both basic and specific points are thoroughly clarified before they are executed. Even more than in drama, artistic and technical questions are closely related. They are so interwoven that it may

23

be opportune to enumerate them together, but it must be stressed that each item implies technical and artistic prerequisites:

1. Opera is a synthesis of all the arts, combining musical, dramatic and scenic elements, in a theatrical production.
2. The musical element exercises a definite influence upon the presentation of opera.
3. It is therefore imperative that every participant understands or, at least feels, music.
4. Large groups have to be trained and handled.
5. A vast technical apparatus must be managed.
6. The synchronization of all elements is a complex task.
7. Cooperation and collaboration are intricate and vital.

For all his experience in staging drama, the director who uses a score for the first time to prepare the production of an opera may be at a loss. He may be accustomed to the ready-made copies of plays sent out by agencies to little theatres. These acting versions contain so many details of technical and artistic matters that there seems little to do but to execute the "assignment." An imaginative director of course will re-evaluate all printed requirements. In operatic scores not many directions are written down, not even by punctilious librettists and composers. The conductor, the director, the singer and the designer have to find out for themselves how to interpret the often sparse remarks. Almost the entire stage business, scenery and lighting, and many musical details have to be clearly and firmly established. The student, of course, can learn from watching performances of other companies, but this can easily lead to mere imitation, including the bad along with the good. In the score a general mood, not a specific action, is delineated. Contemporary composers have described their musical ideas in the most minute detail, but it still seems difficult to execute them. Stage directions, however, are meager indeed. The further we go back in history, the less we find marked in the score. Wagner, the theatrical genius, called his score a "technically fixed model (Vorbild)" of a perfect dramatic production. Another time he called it merely "a plan." He insinuates that the artistic leaders ought to interpret music and action according to their own empathy, although here a director has certainly less liberty than he has in staging a play. An operatic production is always subjected to the style of the music and the technical limitations imposed upon it by the omnipresence of the music. Aside from the question of style, the director and the designer ought to realize that scenic and acting requirements are not always printed at the proper spot.

It is a misconception to consider grand opera more difficult to stage than light opera. Basically the problems are the same, but emphasis may be on different elements, either on the singing and the orchestra, or on acting, settings, et al. A good performance of either type takes talent and, even more, hard work. One is mistaken in assuming that the staging of any opera or operetta is an easy task.

Nevertheless the beginner should not let himself be discouraged. For one thing he has an advantage over his colleague in drama. A good play (in a literary sense) does not in itself carry success, because a false basic conception, inadequate acting or directing, for that matter, quickly causes misinterpretations and missed effects, and thus stultifies a great tragedy or comedy. This is also somewhat true of many operas. A delicate piece, as for instance *The Marriage of Figaro*, or one with its almost superhuman requirements, like *Tristan and Isolde*, offers problems of a scope which can be satisfactorily solved only in exceptional cases, even by a professional company. But there are operas whose success can hardly be impaired by mediocre presentations. *Il Trovatore*, *Carmen*, *Faust*, *The Tales of Hoffmann*, to some degree even *Aida* and *The Valkyrie* belong in this category. Their own dramatic impetus and superabundance of melodies are so strong that they overcome almost any imaginable weakness of their productions.

Since librettos are often based on dramas and novels, it is advisable for all concerned to become acquainted with the source. Prosper Merimée's novel *Carmen* and Henri Murger's *La Bohème* ought to be read carefully. In *Eugene Onegin*, much material of Pushkin's work has been used; for *The Barber of Seville* and *The Marriage of Figaro*, the comedies by Pierre Beaumarchais should be read. From Goethe's *Faust* the love story of part one is taken as the plot for Gounod's opera. These books underwent considerable alterations before they were set to music. On the other hand, *Salomé*, and *Pelléas and Mélisande* were only slightly changed, as a reading of the plays by Oscar Wilde and Maurice Maeterlinck, respectively, shows. Verdi selected as subjects among others *La Dame aux Camélias*, *Le Roi s'amuse*, *Don Carlos*, *Intrigue and Love*, *Macbeth*, *Othello* and *Falstaff*. In each one of them it is interesting and instructive to trace the deviations in order to learn more about the characters and their background. This knowledge could be utilized to good advantage in the production, since some librettos are vague and superficial.

The staging of opera is subject to the principles which guide the directing of plays except that the style of the all-powerful music must be grasped and expressed. Theoretically the opera may be staged in as many styles as are known except in the extremely realistic one; there can be no naturalistic setting or acting, for music is never naturalistic. During the past decades experiments were made to present lyric drama in the style of the composer's day. A spectator could thus witness Handel's *Julio Cesare* dressed in Baroque costumes and Mozart's characters in *The Magic Flute* in those of the late 18th century. From an educational point of view this was enlightening. Some producers went even a step further. For festivals not only scenery and characters but also conductor and musicians appeared in "original" costumes, which created a surprisingly pleasant and artistic atmosphere. The repertory theatre has not been affected by these notions, patrons of today having outgrown the mere historical enjoyment of a production. Modern dress, on the other hand, has seldom been worn in opera. At times, *La Traviata, The Bat (Rosalinde)* and a few others have thus been offered. The current fashion is rather toward producing these operas as conceived, that is, in the costume of the middle or end of the past century, respectively.

There is one mode of staging which is possible only in exceptional cases; it is that of the large protruding apron stage. The theatre-in-the-round or arena stage, which has become popular in recent years, should not be applied to opera for the simple reason that conductor and orchestra must remain a stable factor. Singers must be able to keep contact with the musical director; and the arena staging requires of the performer to sing and act to an audience on all sides, and to move continuously, so that the contact with the conductor is necessarily lessened. This difficulty arises also on the apron stage when singers face an audience sitting on three sides. Nevertheless, it is possible to use this kind of theatre very profitably, as was demonstrated in Max Reinhardt's presentation of *The Tales of Hoffmann* in *Das Grosse Schauspielhaus*. The orchestra pit was built in the center in front of the apron. Reinhardt succeeded so well in arranging complicated scenes that, with the liveliest of action, the conductor was able to lead the singers. Later, other directors effectively used the same scenic set-up for the production of operettas.

Leadership

In a good theatre there are neither superiors nor subordinates. This does not mean that every participant may do whatever his whims tell him to do, but rather that there shall be no star who can dictate the repertoire, the staging, or the like at the expense of the ensemble spirit. Not a boss, but a leader who is *primus inter pares* is needed. Leadership in opera is even more essential than in drama. Ten good actors are somehow able to work out the interpretation and stage business with very little supervision and still achieve an impressive performance. Yet the number of artists necessary for an operatic production make true leadership imperative. The organization is complex indeed, since different experts are handling groups such as singers, choristers, dancers, musicians, technicians under the supervision of an artistic director. Collaboration must be more than just a slogan in order to obtain a performance of even quality. Richard Wagner who, when necessary, could be quite dictatorial and autocratic, realized this requirement very well. After the premiere of *Parsifal* he was asked how he had achieved such astounding cooperation in every aspect, musical and scenic. His reply was that this had happened "by anarchy," by which he meant that every participant understood his assigned task as part of a whole and, thus did the "right thing."

To obtain "the right thing" from so many and so diverse artists is a complicated process. It begins with the delicate relationship between conductor and stage director, orchestra and singer, and between technical and artistic questions of every sort; it touches upon every detail of rehearsal work up to the synchronization of all components during the last rehearsals. Each group has its proper place and so has each artist. Their functions will be discussed in the following chapters.

At this point a few general remarks may be of service. After World War I, it became an axiom that singers must also be actors. This demand concerns not only the singer, but also has a bearing upon the conductor and the director. The conductor must be ready to follow the singer's action and to give him a cue whenever needed. To develop a clear characterization is the director's task, but he cannot proceed without a solid basis created by the conductor in previous coaching. To achieve acceptable acting in opera is far more demanding than in drama; it takes more patience and more effort. To keep an individual or a group from becoming too static, or to build up a climax, is much more complicated than in a play. In opera there is grave danger that action will move from one tableau to another instead of in a cycle of logically and dramatically connected motions leading to brief moments of pictorial positions. Conductors and directors will agree that, in certain situations, complete absence of movement can better express a mood than poorly executed gestures. Sometimes total absence of action can be expressive especially when the orchestra describes and develops the mood of the scenery as well as of the characters. Pantomime, on the other hand, often plays a greater part than in drama. Musical preludes, interludes or postludes take up a few bars or a whole page. In most cases they have to be filled with action as a means for unfolding a character and the plot. Opera demands of the singer not only crossings and general stage business but anything in the way of bodily expression, including the most exasperating dance (as in *Salomé*). Freedom of interpretation is highly restricted by the time duration of the music. There may be too much or not enough music for the director's ideas, but he must subordinate his own wishes to those of the composer. To find an artistic balance, not just a compromise, is a challenge. Action and music ought to be treated like relatives, not enemies.

Conductor and director face crucial problems whenever the tempo, the rhythm, the key, and the volume change. The most vexing problem of a smooth transition occurs in those works in which musical numbers alternate with recitatives or dialogue. The same delicate task arises in the romantic operas which are composed throughout but in which one number follows another. It may seem easier to the neophyte to prepare an operetta, an old comic opera or *singspiel* with considerable dialogue, but the fundamental difficulty lies precisely in linking together the disparate elements of music and dialogue. Tempo, inflection, rhythm, key, pitch and volume are endangered at each transition from singing to speaking and vice versa. To achieve an effective and smooth transition requires a keen ear from conductor and director. In such pieces like the *Story of a Soldier, Midsummer Night's Dream, Preciosa* and *L'Arlésienne,* the particular style must first be determined. Stravinsky's work may be called a dramatic ballad while the other three works are plays with much incidental music, and it is the romanticism of their music which decides the style of the entire production. Music in these works overgrows the dialogue to such a degree that there is even an inclination to place them into the categories of *singspiel* and comic opera, respectively. This is particularly the condition when a part of the dialogue is eliminated, thus making the musical scenes still more predominant.

The Relationship of Conductor and Director

It seems impossible to find an artistic director who can fulfill the double task of staging and conducting. Therefore it is customary to separate the work, dividing it between two personalities, the musical director and the stage director. Upon the perfect collaboration of the two leaders, equally gifted and experienced, and equally willing and able to cooperate, rests largely the high quality of a performance. If conductor and director are true artists in their respective fields and sincerely seek to execute the composer's intentions, they will forget their personal rivalries and possibly produce the finest in art.

Briefly the task is divided in the following manner: the conductor is responsible for all strictly musical matters as the playing of the orchestra and the singing of soloists and choristers and under his supervision the chorus master rehearses with his group, and the coach practices with the soloists; the stage director is charged with all visual aspects of the production in addition to directing the dialogue; he arranges the acting of the singers and choristers and he is also responsible for the settings, the lighting, the costumes and properties. The details of these matters, however, are left to his collaborators, the designer, the costumer and the technical director. As to the ballet, the conductor determines the tempos and other factors of the music with the ballet master while the director discusses with him the floor plan and the general outline of the required dances.

It is obvious that such a division of authority contains the germs of friction. It takes a good deal of tact and self-control on the part of the two leaders to avoid potential tensions. Gradually, conductors and directors have learned to cooperate by prudently remaining within their own province. Occasionally one of them dominates in the artistic directorate. Conductors who, as a rule, receive more notice by critics and opera fans, sometimes misuse their more ostentatious position and interfere in the staging, thus transgressing the unwritten law of separate departments. On the other hand, there have been directors who, ignoring that tacit agreement, usurped predominance in the organization to the detriment of the production.

Collaboration in this delicate set-up is based on the assumption that both parties have an equally good background and experience, artistic taste, sympathy with each other's ideas and consideration for their frailties. Whenever one of them abuses his position the entire group will be adversely affected and consequently the performance itself. It cannot be denied that this separation of artistic

28

authority violates one of the fundamental laws of art, namely unity of purpose and execution. But opera in itself is such a strange hybrid that it virtually invites this violation. Nevertheless, the ideal will always be a single personality in full charge of the entire production; so far, this ideal has been reached rarely; Richard Wagner, Gustav Mahler and Arturo Toscanini are the outstanding examples.

From an artistic viewpoint the dual authority is a precarious compromise, but on practical grounds it is almost a necessity. Every operatic production needs an elaborate organization for rehearsals; it is well-nigh physically impossible for one person to attend to so many matters. The preparatory work with soloists, chorus, and orchestra takes up much time; the same applies to stage rehearsals and the supervision of technical details. It is a superhuman task for one man to be burdened with so much responsibility even if he has a staff of associates and assistants. This becomes at once evident during the last rehearsals. Conducting demands full concentration on the orchestra and the singing, leaving little if any time to spare for watching stage business and scenic effects. Only under extremely favorable circumstances can the ideal ever be approached.

Since the twenties several stage directors have been hailed for their fascinating achievements in modern staging. Yet others have been denied recognition and artistic freedom which they needed to accomplish their vision. It is taken for granted that the director of a classical drama uses his imagination to the fullest in order to effect an original production. He will even be criticized sharply for failing to do so, or for merely repeating what his colleagues have done or are doing. In opera, however, audiences and critics alike seem to accept without complaint a performance unaltered for a generation. It is no wonder then that the imaginative director faces great obstacles in attempting a reform. Fortunately this conservatism has given way to a more progressive spirit. Educational institutions and some civic companies have begun to rejuvenate the staging to the delight of their patrons. Lately the Met has thoroughly broken with tradition by putting great weight on modern ideas and this example may provide more authority to directors all over the country.

Conductors, limited by the orchestra score in their imaginative interpretation, are in a similar predicament. Errors and misconceptions crept into performances and were passed on as tradition. Only a few outstanding artists like Arturo Toscanini, Fritz Busch and Bruno Walter have been commended for their courageous work of purifying and "detraditionalizing" conventional performances. On the average, all the credit a conductor receives refers to keeping everything "running smoothly."

If the conductor and the director truly cooperate during the rehearsals they have gone a long way toward success. They will be helped in this by mutual understanding of and respect for their work which, in turn, will derive from an indispensable knowledge of each other's field. Felix Weingartner in his book *On Conducting* said poignantly: "In my opinion no conductor should be appointed to

29

a theatre who has not proved that he can stage an opera, and no stage director who cannot rehearse the musical part of the work."

Operetta Is Not a Separate Art Form

Perhaps the operetta and her younger sister, the musical, ought to be dealt with more extensively in this book. A case can be made for such a request. There are good reasons however for considering these forms as basically a sort of opera, related to the Italian, French and German type of comic opera. Out of a mixture of diverse elements grew the strange, but often entertaining and fascinating operetta and its related forms. As a rule it is lighter, funnier, more sentimental and more farcical than opera. Plots and characters are often more stereotyped; scenery and dances play a far more important part. For these reasons it has an immediate appeal to a large audience. Some of its outstanding specimens make it almost impossible to draw a straight line between the operetta and the comic opera. This has been recognized by leading opera houses in Europe and the Met in our country which have included in their repertoire works by Johann Strauss, Jacques Offenbach, and Gilbert and Sullivan. Fortunately some of our civic and college groups are not too blasé to schedule these operettas.

Since the operetta borrows elements from a variety of sources, its staging has to take these into consideration. The book may be based on the tradition of the *commedia dell'arte,* the comedy of manners, or the romantic comedy. The English masque and the Viennese fairy play contributed the emphasis on spectacle. In this country a new movement created a specific American type which based on modern plots is less sentimental and more dramatic. The trend culminated in *Showboat* by Oscar Hammerstein and Jerome Kern and in *Porgy and Bess* by DuBose and Dorothy Hayward and George Gershwin. The definite turn came with the now legendary premiere of *Oklahoma* by Oscar Hammerstein and Richard Rodgers. Another high point was reached with *West Side Story* by Arthur Laurents and Leonard Bernstein; this musical has no really comic scenes, though it contains some ironical and biting humor.

Here too the artistic leaders of the production must base their approach on the style of a particular work, a style which is related to the music and to a smaller degree to the libretto. The main attractions of operettas and musicals are infectious melodies, splendid dancing, admirable settings and costumes. The singer's stage presence, his personality, is often more essential for a successful presentation than his vocal prowess. Consequently it is understandable that a slight shift takes place in the relationship between the conductor, director, designer, and choreographer. Particularly the latter gains prominence at the expense of the other artists; in recent years he has sometimes assumed the task of staging the entire production, a welcome solution if we witness the increasing importance of dancing in the contemporary musical. All the artistic leaders need a very "light hand," a sense of humor and a great talent for all kinds of scenic effects. Whether the plot is believable or not, the staging has to make it convincing. Characters who are often only slightly sketched have to be made dramatically fascinating. And the singing should be neither the operatic kind nor degenerate into speaking (which, unfortunately, it sometimes does with stars who have no voice at all). Mastering of the *parlando* is imperative for participation in these productions.

THE INCEPTION OF MODERN OPERA PRODUCTION

Richard Wagner

Adolf Menzel, the great artist, made a sketch of Richard Wagner directing a rehearsal on the stage of the Bayreuth Festival House. The composer is sitting at a small table with a score and lamp in front of him. Why is he not standing near the piano or in the pit? Why does Wagner choose to be immortalized as a stage director and not as a conductor? We know that Wagner staged *The Ring* as well as *Parsifal*. Obviously he considered directing so important that he, an experienced conductor, preferred to give the baton to a favorite disciple while he concentrated on the staging of his music dramas. Through his ideas as well as his deeds he became the originator of the modern opera director, giving him a position equal to that of the conductor. He has explicitly pointed out the essential role which acting and designing play in every production.

Richard Wagner wrote the librettos to his own operas. He was a conductor who became a stage director. He was extremely interested in every phase of opera production. These talents, combined with his revolutionary mind and his conception of opera as a factor of education, enabled him not only to devise the *Gesamtkunstwerk* (collective work of art) but also to execute it. He thus accomplished a nearly perfect unity. That he did not succeed in every detail is not entirely his fault. Although he was a product of his generation his ambitions were far ahead of his time. His designers did not always grasp his ideas, but adhered too strongly to the conventional romantic style.

Years of working in various opera houses gave Wagner a dislike for the traditional, which he still had to accept to some extent. But he never ceased to be a revolutionary. Well-remembered are his words: "Children! Create something new! Something new and ever new! Should you hang on to the old the devil of unproductivity gets you and you will be the most miserable of artists." The years of apprenticeship helped him in molding his own ideas of reform. While he wrote mainly about his own works and conceptions he did not refrain from criticizing frankly the conditions of his day. Wagner loathed conventional staging methods and he rejected effect for effect's sake. He was so disgusted with some of the conventions that he called the chorus a "scenic machinery made to walk and to sing."

31

Despite his general condemnation of events around him, Wagner readily and gratefully appreciated true art. It was his good fortune to know and to collaborate with Wilhelmine Schroeder-Devrient, one of the really outstanding dramatic singers of all times. He frankly confessed that he owed all his knowledge about the nature of the art of acting to her who excelled as Iphigenia, Euryanthe and Leonore (*Fidelio*). He especially admired her "incomparable dramatic talent" and her "inimitable and individual characterization" of her roles. While he was a conductor at the Royal Opera House in Dresden he also met Eduard Devrient, Madame Schroeder's brother-in-law, a renowned actor, stage director, manager and author, whose cooperation Wagner valued very highly in the production of his first operas. Long after their roads led them to separate cities, Wagner sought the advice of this fine artist for the staging of his music dramas. Wagner's concept of staging was further affected by the style propagated by George II, Duke of Meiningen. He shared the Duke's horror of the star system and his preference for a closely knit ensemble. From the Meiningen productions he also learned how a crowd scene can become an integrated part of the action, and he applied this method to his chorus scenes in Bayreuth.

"The mute splendor of scenery transformed to moving noise" is the description Wagner gives the conventional performances. He had an intimate knowledge of the Parisian Opera and was well informed about methods used in London. Despite his sharp criticism, which was mainly directed against Meyerbeer's works, he was not above borrowing from that composer's superficiality. It must be conceded, however, that through completely integrating the variegated elements in his productions, Wagner achieved a far more artistic and unified whole. In his works the emphasis was usually on the superlative. There were more ships, more phantastic beasts, more phenomena of nature employed than by any of his predecessors and contemporaries. The effects he adopted had been known before his time; even the impressive *Wandeldekoration* of his *Parsifal* had been seen in the dramatized fairy tales in Vienna and London.

A revolutionary innovation in Bayreuth was the sunken invisible orchestra, "the mystic gulf" as Wagner called it. He held that the conductor and the musicians, by their very presence, would distract the attention of the audience from the music and stage. In addition, he intended to restore the balance between stage and pit by lowering and partly covering the latter, since the orchestra of his music-dramas was extremely large. Wagner thought of music as the immediate expression of feeling; for him the inner life of the drama was reflected in the orchestral music whereas action and words unfolded the outer development.

Insofar as speaking and acting were concerned Wagner approached these phases of directing with his customary thoroughness. He did not entrust this important duty to anyone else and devoted much time to the staging of his music dramas. We know that, on the whole, Wagner tried to achieve a combination of two styles: on the one hand he stressed the importance of the "picturesque"; on the other, he was most anxious to accomplish "verity of gesture and movement." His assistants and friends who had watched him during rehearsal admired the masterful way in which he himself played every role. Hitherto it was left to the singer, as a rule, to work out the dramatic action. Occasionally composers and conductors would give them bits of advice. But the stage director, who was merely a manager, had to efface himself and was not permitted to "interfere" with the whims and wishes of the singers. Now Wagner took over the task of explaining every nuance of the characterization in the most minute detail.

In the execution of his duties as director Wagner emphasized the great value of clear diction. This problem seemed to be so important to him that he called on some of his associates to coach the singers. Friedrich Schmidt and, later, Julius Hey fully understood his wishes and developed a system in which the singing tone was derived directly from the spoken word. Wagner himself coined the term "*Sprechgesang*" which means "speech-song," stating: "My song is speech and my speech is song." His *Sprechgesang* was specifically conceived to fit the presentation of his music drama. Experience has shown that singers, following his advice, have no difficulty in being heard and understood even when the orchestra is quite powerful.

A thorough study of Wagner's writings is essential not only for the conductor but also for the stage director and singer, who will profit tremendously from reading his several essays in which he deals with problems of opera in general and those of staging in particular. These writings, such as *Actor and Singer*, *Music of the Future* and others in which he delineates his directions for *The Flying Dutchman*, *Tannhaeuser* and *Parsifal* are extremely interesting not only for the musicologist but even more so for all the participants in an opera group. Wagner was a unique phenomenon who combined creative and interpretative faculties. No one after him attained the same degree of authority; he had some excellent pupils who were his assistants in Bayreuth and who in later years became leading conductors, such as Hans Richter in Vienna, Hermann Levi in Munich, and Felix Mottl in Karlsruhe. As to the staging of operas, these former pupils were at least in a position to preserve the best of Wagner's intentions.

After Wagner's death his widow Cosima took over the reins in Bayreuth. Only too quickly the great revolutionary spirit disintegrated, the slogan was "preserve" and not "develop." Some innovations, nevertheless, were introduced, as in *Parsifal*, where the rather poorly devised costumes were replaced by better ones when Ludwig Thoma, the famed painter, became the adviser of Madame Cosima. Although the festival house was officially opposed to the conventional production of grand opera, eventually some proscribed elements of this style crept in.

Today when we refer to the now historic "Bayreuth Style" we refer above all to a thorough training of singers and choristers. This particular school includes the acting as well as the singing. While the spirit of Wagner, the reformer, was no longer noticeable in Bayreuth it is true that every visitor was impressed and fascinated by the thoroughness and accurateness of the rehearsals. As to settings, costumes and special effects, Bayreuth was for many years a model of precision but it contributed nothing of lasting artistic value. Its *mise en scène* followed the trend of the time; it did not lead a way into the future, as Wagner himself had done. It is all the more gratifying that Wagner's grandsons are making every effort to modernize Bayreuth, imbuing it with a revolutionary artistic spirit.

Adolphe Appia

When Wagner, the great reformer, died in 1883, there lived an artist who understood him so well that he succeeded in the field in which Wagner had failed, the scenic reform. He was Adolphe Appia, a Swiss born in Geneva, who remained almost unknown during his lifetime except to a small group of admirers. For a long time even many experts neglected to pay official recognition to the tremendous impact of his ideas, to the influence he exercised on the development of the art of the theatre. The reason is that Appia was less a practicing designer than a theoretician. It was left to others to adapt and transfer his visions on to the stage. Because Appia played the decisive part in the revolutionary change from extreme realism to symbolic and stylized staging, it is necessary to examine his conception closely. He himself described his principles extensively in books and essays which should be read and studied by all those interested in a modern production of plays and operas.

Basically Appia was a romanticist but he did not define his style as it was accepted by his contemporaries. He did not strive for elaborate settings, costumes and properties, but on the contrary wished to simplify all these external elements. He was a purist and in his later years was called a "Calvinist" when he limited his scenic effects to a bare minimum. His simplicity leaned toward the monumental style of the classic Greek era, yet it was also affected by impressionism, which taught him the importance of light. A combination of so divergent styles can easily result in a lack of any style, but Appia's genius succeeded in moulding a truly unified conception, in which music formed the source and the foundation. His style seems to be the realization of Friedrich Nietzsche's dictum in *The Birth of Tragedy*: "Music is the soul of drama, drama the body of music." Of this basic question Appia wrote in his *Music and the Art of the Theatre*: "The soul of drama, music, bestows life upon the entire body and determines, through the beat of the pulse, the relationship and sequence of the movements of the entire body."

Appia rejected the conventional setting with its wings and backdrop, painted realistically, aiming instead at placing the three-dimensional performer within a truly three-dimensional environment which he called "spatial setting." In all his plans the living moving actor stood in the center. For him Appia devised the spatial setting consisting of platforms of different levels, stairs, ramps, pillars and simple flats; drapes of neutral color surrounded the wings and often the upstage area, unless he expressly requested a sky drop. Other designers had previously discarded some of the flimsy set pieces substituting plastic trees, pillars and similar pieces, but Appia was the first who created a simple unified spatial setting. Appia re-examined lighting, because he despised the conventional border and footlights which destroyed plasticity. He divided lighting into two parts, general illumination and special effects. These became eminently important, for by means of spotlights, which touch the performer from the rear, the latter can regain his plasticity. Prior to 1900, long before directors and designers ever used a slide projector, Appia explained how to utilize this device. While he eliminated most of the decorative element in the setting, he applied light elaborately as a means for creating a dramatic atmosphere. In the theatre of today, lighting is regarded as the unifying element which gives life and sense to the settings. Appia initiated this revolution. During the years before 1910 he discarded the last traces of romanticism when he experimented with settings which were even more simplified; he called them "Rhythmic Spaces" and they are the forerunners cf the cubistic movement.

In order to give the performer the dominance he deserved Appia considered it imperative to have him more thoroughly trained. Instead of the conventional, often meaningless gestures and actions he recommended the initiation of a special "choreography" for the actor. Appia rightly felt that, as in ballet, music must be used as the basis of every move; ot course he did not want to have the singer "dance," but to discover a notation which could enable the stage director and the performers to execute the stage action in precise and dramatic synchronization with the musical score. Appia's ideas in this field remained unfulfilled until he met Emile Jaques-Dalcroze, the inaugurator of eurythmics, who became his congenial collaborator. In their productions of Gluck's *Orfeo* in Helleran near Dresden in 1912 and 1913 they came close to their ideal. Here the rhythmic movements of soloists, choristers and dancers were completely integrated with the settings and lighting. In these performances Appia accomplished for the first time the hierarchy which he had established: the performer, the spatial arrangement, the lighting, and the color. Based on this success he expounded his theories, whose goal was the true *"Work of Living Art,"* the title of his last book.

Appia never deceived himself about quick acceptance of his revolutionary principles. Thus he wrote: "A convention as deeply rooted as that of our stage cannot be brought down with one stroke." But his ideas did penetrate the theatre eventually. Modern directors and designers take it for granted that imitation of reality is unnecessary and an imaginative transformation of reality is essential. They all realize that lighting plays an all-important role in a production. Appia stated the basic problem when he inquired with reference to Wagner's *Siegfried:* which element is more important in act two when Siegfried appears in the forest? is the spectator of this music drama primarily interested in seeing the forest through which the hero is walking or is he interested in a man who wanders through the forest? The answer is self-evident. With the new emphasis on the performer's role, Appia's recommendations on acting have also been widely accepted though much must still be done to perfect it.

Gustav Mahler

About the same time as Adolphe Appia published his first two books, almost unnoticed by the public-at-large another artist seized the opportunity to rejuvenate the production of opera. In 1897 Gustav Mahler became director of the Opera House in Vienna, a position he held for ten stormy years. Although he was, nominally at least, the subordinate of a courtier who administered the Imperial Theatres, he obtained almost unlimited authority soon after his arrival. Mahler is highly regarded as a composer and was also revered as a conductor from the time he was engaged at the Metropolitan Opera House. In Vienna he was able to present performances that were not merely outstanding in their day but which became models for succeeding generations.

Mahler was an uncompromising personality, but his biographers agree that he did not abuse his authority for personal reasons. As the artistic director of his opera company he was ruthless whenever he met pettiness; sarcastic when he was confronted with tradition which he defined as *Schlamperei* (slovenliness); impatient when he discovered intrigues and indolence. His was a purity of purpose. His aim was a unity of work achieved only by Wagner before him. Years of apprenticeship in small and middling theatres of Central Europe increased his dislike and distaste for the conventional methods. Even in Hamburg he was dissatisfied with the rehearsal work. When at last he obtained complete authority in Vienna, he thoroughly changed the prevailing system. Nothing escaped his brilliant mind. His attacks against long-sanctioned conventions made him enemies among a privileged group of singers and their friends. But, at the same time, he acquired many devoted followers who supported him in every crisis, because they believed wholeheartedly in his ideas.

Mahler was primarily a conductor but, fortunately, he was also an excellent interpreter of dramatic action. Furthermore, he examined the *mise en scène* in every detail before he permitted its execution. His interest extended also into the field of management. Almost everything he introduced in Vienna shocked the conservative audience as well as the members of the ensemble. Instead of leaving the auditorium in semi-darkness he decided to have it completely darkened during an act, an innovation virtually unheard of at the time. He did not permit patrons to go to their orchestra seats or to enter the galleries any time they pleased. With the overture the doors were closed and only holders of boxes were exempted from this regulation. The claque system was abolished and at the same time the traditional repetition of favorite arias was eliminated, notwithstanding the protests of some stars.

These details may seem rather unimportant, almost trivial, but each represented a vital step in establishing artistic integrity, since patrons, coming late, disturbed other opera-lovers, as did the members of the claque who noisily required a *da capo*. Of greater significance, of course, were the abolition of cuts and the restoration of original notes and words. Outside Bayreuth, for example, it was nearly impossible to hear a Wagnerian music drama as originally created, because in many cases important passages were omitted. Mahler gave the same care to many other composers, restoring the true value of music and action—in all his deeds he completely ignored the tradition. Henceforth these operas were performed as conceived by the composers. Every passage was checked and rechecked for faulty holds that crept in and for words that had been changed in disregard of the original version. Thus during the ten years of Mahler's activities in Vienna many operas of the standard repertoire and of modern composers were given a true, rightful presentation through the selfless insistence of a great personality.

Opera-goers were accustomed to hearing an admirable musical interpretation, but now there was a conductor who also demanded impeccable acting, something well-nigh unknown outside Bayreuth. Just like Wagner, Mahler aimed at a coordination of the two elements, music and drama. When he conducted he did not forget the acting; when he was in the orchestra pit he observed the stage where nothing eluded his keen eye. A question frequently discussed is whether Mahler himself directed the performances he conducted. Bruno Walter, for many years his pupil and friend, who became a renowned interpreter himself, settled the argument in a letter to the author with the statement that "Mahler never staged an opera." August Stoll was the stage director in Vienna when Mahler assumed his position there and he remained in that capacity until Mahler's resignation. But, as Bruno Walter declares, Mahler very carefully informed the director of his wishes in the most minute detail, before and during rehearsals. Often he was carried away by his enthusiasm, Walter reports, and he actively intervened in Stoll's directing during the first rehearsals and even during the orchestra rehearsals when he instructed the soloists as well as the chorus through words and gestures. Thus he was actually the director of the scenic events in all their aspects.

In examining Mahler's work one gains the certainty that a good many singers cooperated with him and that the stage director too was at least willing to help realize the new concept. Mahler had the good fortune to find a congenial collaborator in the designer Alfred Roller. Although this artist was not a revolutionary like Appia, he was an outstanding man, thoroughly aware of the shortcomings of the conventional system. Taking up the growing trend toward simplification, Roller so well captured the atmosphere of many operas that his magnificent settings remained excellent examples for about a generation. Being versatile he was not committed too firmly to any style, although he seemed to have a basic preference for impressionism. He was completely understood by his contemporaries who widely acclaimed his innovations in the monumental spatial settings for Wagner's music dramas and the brilliant unit setting for Mozart's *Don Giovanni*. His reputation as a leader in his profession soon grew beyond the borders of his country.

Under Mahler's management the Vienna Opera came as close as it is possible to Wagner's idea of a festival house. Mahler's concept of the duties of the artistic director had been realized in his own personality and work. He held that the artistic director should understand everything connected with the production and should be able to inject his thoughts into the performance. He himself was the true and actual interpreter of the lyric drama, both conductor and director, although he relied on collaborators for the decorative aspects of the *mise en scène* and, to some degree, for the acting of the singers and choristers. His approach was so extraordinarily modern that his style remained intact for many years after his resignation, but the gap he left at the Vienna Opera was not filled for many years, because his overwhelming personality, his irrepressible energy, his dramatic imagination and artistic integrity were irreplaceable.

Constantin Stanislavsky

When Constantin Stanislavsky extended his interest beyond drama into opera he was internationally the acknowledged leader of a movement. His productions in the Moscow Art Theatre were studied and described by directors, critics and other experts. This was true also of his dramatic studios, the training ground of the younger generation which turned out many gifted actors and directors who themselves became protagonists of a younger generation. The old master was no newcomer to opera, since in his youth he had studied operatic roles with the elder Komissarjevsky. In addition, he was well acquainted with the conventional system of opera productions. Besides he had the opportunity to observe one of the outstanding singers of the early 20th century, Feodor Chaliapin, who combined the rare gifts of a phenomenal voice with great acting ability.

The Opera Studio was founded at the end of 1918 and began its work early in the following year. As Stanislavsky indicated, its aim was to place the dramatic side of the operatic performances in Moscow on a "higher footing". The turbulent months of the post-war and revolutionary periods were certainly not favorable to so daring an enterprise. Yet Stanislavsky with his immense energy and authority succeeded in overcoming most of the difficulties confronting him. He was assisted by singers and other artists who, braving the hardships of those trying months, came to practice and to rehearse with him. He set a limited goal and never pretended to search for a completely new operatic style. Fundamentally he tried to apply to the lyric drama what he had discovered in his productions of the spoken play. He discussed his theories and experiences with the singers who thus became fully conscious of the importance the psychological background had on a character and of the tremendous effort that must be spent to make every bit of dramatic expression and stage business clear.

In addition Stanislavsky introduced classes in subjects which hitherto had been neglected in training Russian singers. He concentrated all his energy on the problem of rhythm, a concept he evidently based on the eurythmics of

Jaques Dalcroze. Stanislavsky was anxious to use rhythm not merely to improve the execution of gestures and movements but primarily to develop an inner feeling for an understanding of the characters. The principles he employed for many years in his play productions were now widely applied to operas. Just as he was extremely eager to elicit the most intimate emotions from his actors, so he strove to make his acting singers visibly express their inner intensity. In his book *My Life in Art* he made this significant statement: "All is ready-made by the composer; all you have to do is to sing what has been written. And it is easy to understand what is necessary." We may be sure that not all his cast members grasped the composer's and librettist's intention as quickly as he did, but we may also assume that, in training experienced as well as inexperienced singers, he applied patience and perseverance, qualities for which he was well-known, to achieve his aspirations. The works he prepared in his Opera Studio were mostly Russian, like *Eugene Onegin* and *Tsar Fjodor*, but he also selected foreign operas such as *The Girl of the Golden West*.

Unfortunately this eminent director did not delineate his concept of operatic staging as extensively as he dealt with his ideas on and observations of his previous achievements. Consequently we have to rely largely on reports by experts who attended his rehearsals or discussed operatic art with him. From such reports and his own writings these conclusions can be drawn: first, all singers were imbued with the principle to act naturally, to probe deeply into every trait of characterization and to think of themselves as part of an integrated whole; secondly, these principles can be materialized only through many intensive rehearsals. An essential part of the overall preparation for the rehearsals was the practicing of all factors involved in them, particularly of rhythmics.

Although Stanislavsky was musically gifted and, to some degree, trained, and thoroughly understood the essence of opera, he evidently approached the new task from the one-sided viewpoint of the director. This necessarily led to a slight neglect of the musical phase as the conductor perceives it. The result was an over-emphasis on the staging problems as against the musical part. In his specific field he succeeded in eliminating all remnants of the conventional and often superficial acting and in devising settings which marvellously expressed the mood of the music, although we are inclined to regard them as too realistic. There can be little doubt that his basic principles are still valid, yet contemporary directors and designers modify his desire for extreme naturalness.

Vladimir Nemirovitch-Danchenko

While Stanislavsky's work brought about great improvement of the existing system, his friend and collaborator, Vladimir Nemirovitch-Danchenko, decided on a clear break with the conventional staging and on experimentation with the new styles of Central and Western Europe after World War I. He was also influenced by Dalcroze's eurythmics but he used this method to have the performers trained in absolute rhythm which involved everyone and everything on stage, as he envisioned a pure, theatrical performance in which all resemblance to the traditional concert-like staging was erased. Therefore his singing actors had to learn to make the most intricate steps and gestures and to execute them in strict synchronization with the music in a complex spatial setting. His followers called his style "The Synthetic Theatre".

His principles, taken separately, were not completely original, but molded into a unified system they greatly helped rejuvenate the staging of opera. Regular courses in eurythmics were introduced to train all members of the company. True to the fundamental concept, all realistic elements were removed and the music was materialized on the stage in a strictly rhythmical manner. Experienced singers were unwilling and frequently unable to give up their conventional acting. The director tried to persuade and convince them, but his demands for total subordination to the ensemble spirit were not entirely to the liking of old-timers. Hence the core of his groups consisted of young singers who flocked from all over Russia to Moscow eager to participate in the new venture. As in the Stanislavsky studio, extremely demanding rehearsals and outside work were part of the regular program. No individual singer was permitted any privilege. Roles rotated, as did the repertory, primarily some French operettas of the 19th century, and, among others, a musical version of Aristophanes's *Lysistrata*, the famous Russian opera *Boris Godunov*, and *Carmencita and the Soldier*, adapted from Bizet's *Carmen*. In the presentations of these works Nemirovitch-Danchenko in his capacity as artistic director as well as stage director demonstrated his theory—to accentuate the psychological background of the characterization through rhythm in gesture and movement.

Settings and costumes, simplified and highly stylized, were of vital importance in the productions. The scenic arrangement was usually a unit setting consisting of platforms of various levels, galleries and towers, often connected by ramps or stairs. Light was employed to define acting areas as well as to create mood. Isaac Rabinovich, the designer of this group, succeeded in building amazingly simple, yet very impressive settings. His *Lysistrata* was acclaimed wherever it was presented, and so was the staging of the French operetta, *La Perichole*, and *The Daughter of Madame Angot*. *Carmencita*, however, received some criticism, although this production too fascinated the spectators. Audiences accustomed to the traditional version were bewildered by or displeased with the adaptation of the opera (the role of Micaela, for instance, was eliminated) and with the "newfangled" interpretation. Outside Russia reviewers acknowledged the immensely dramatic impact of the acting, the interesting scenic solutions, and the colorful costumes, but adverse criticism was trained on the musical phase, above all on the lack of first class singers and the retouching of the orchestra score.

Contemporary Conceptions

The great artists whose ideas and achievements in the field of opera have been presented in the preceding pages are the initiators and the protagonists of contemporary staging. Each of them contributed essential principles, but none of them succeeded in fulfilling all his dreams. Their writings and books should be studied and their accomplishments analyzed in order to gain an overall impression of the several trends affecting the lyric theatre of today. To obtain a well-rounded picture of their influence it is imperative to check also the achievements of the past generation. Books by and about leading conductors, directors and designers offer very instructive material.

Since the end of World War I, a good number of conductors, directors and designers have fought for a scenic reform, a rejuvenation of all staging aspects, but only a few have made a lasting impact. An obstacle to complete success was the diversity of experiments. Praiseworthy as this variety has been, in the end it confused the average opera-goer who was unable to make a choice between one new style and another, with the result that for a long time he cautiously remained rather neutral. Another difficulty lay in the fact that no artistic leader possessed the many talents and the full authority of a Wagner or a Mahler. As a consequence, experiments were sometimes not executed as they were conceived, when powers behind the scene interfered; or the experiments had no strong basis from the beginning and thus remained unconvincing in their execution.

In Central Europe before 1930 a growing interest in modern staging became noticeable. Audiences and critics began to welcome the new principles so that directors and designers occasionally received as much credit as had been accorded conductors and singers in the preceding period. The musical phase of productions admittedly maintained at that time a very high level in the leading opera houses, and lesser companies also aimed at and achieved fine performances in many cases. This was by no means true of the staging. Here these smaller theatres were more daring than their big brothers. In Moscow the fascinating experiments of Stanislavsky and Nemirovitch-Danchenko were not emulated by the metropolitan opera houses, which under the influence of the Stalin regime, fell back into the conventional pattern. Arturo Toscanini put his great prestige behind a new production of *Tristan and Isolde* in 1923 which he entrusted to Appia. The disapproval of this unique *mise en scène* by the conservative opera lovers in Milan discouraged Toscanini from making another attempt in this direction. Paris and Vienna were slow in offering a new approach. The Kroll Opera House in Berlin became the acknowledged lodestar for daring productions; some of them were conceived in Appia's spirit while others went to the extreme of the Bauhaus style. In England admirable modern productions were offered in the Glyndebourne Festivals inaugurated in the middle thirties. In the United States the professional companies adhered to the tradition with few exceptions while educational groups, unburdened by convention, contributed much to a scenic reform.

The changes involved all phases of staging. Attacks were launched not merely against production methods, but also sharply against theatre buildings. Indeed the old form, inaugurated in the Baroque era, cannot be entirely ignored. The arena stage as well as the open stage are hardly suitable for operatic presentations. Yet plans to eliminate the disturbing proscenium frame, seriously projected since the twenties, did not materialize until after World War II. In new theatre buildings every effort is now made to de-emphasize the sharp break between auditorium and stage, and to bring audience and singers closer together. The current attention given to modern staging is carrying over to good acting. The training of many singers embraces both the voice and the body in contrast to the period before 1914, when the voice was considered all important and the acting significant only in exceptional cases. The present experience is that singers can be highly successful if they are fascinating actors though their voices may not be the first rank. It is impossible today to succeed with a performance in which the chorus is slovenly rehearsed and the ballet indifferent. These groups have undergone a thorough rejuvenation.

The style of operatic acting is entirely subject to a unified overall conception. No director still adheres to the old Bayreuth style, but some accept the often oratorio-like picturization of the present Bayreuth Festivals. Some are intrigued by the captivating productions staged by Walter Felsenstein in East Berlin, who promotes a strange mixture of dramatic stylization and realism. Others follow the extreme simplification of scenery demonstrated in Bayreuth. Still another movement makes use of rhythm as the dominant element in acting, thus almost transforming the action into a dance composition. Finally, there are artistic leaders who refuse to impose one style upon all operas; they are anxious to re-create each work in keeping with the style of music. Common to all is the aim to bring the score to life on the stage in a modern interpretation.

THE ARTISTS

THE SINGER

The attention of the audience in any opera house is concentrated on the singer, especially the "star". This fact alone justifies beginning this discourse with him. Despite all theories propagated and promoted by a comparatively small group of experts and friends of opera, the situation has not changed to any measurable degree since the beginnings of opera. Gluck, Wagner, Verdi, and Debussy certainly contributed much to the development of the musical drama. Their place in the history of opera is secure, but the public-at-large goes to the theatre to hear the singer. The vocal interpreter of opera plays a more important part than its composer. Of course, there have always been times when the work itself, its musical or dramatic interpretation, was the center of interest, or when the settings fascinated audiences. Yet on the whole, it is the singer who draws the crowds to the theatre.

We may regret that sometimes he is too dominating a factor in the performance and in the repertoire, but we have to accept this condition as a fact and reckon with it. Just as plays cannot survive without good actors, so operas cannot exist without good singers. Occasionally great operas have had to be dropped from a repertory because there were no singers available who could execute some difficult passages in certain roles. It is true that the artistic standard of many performances has suffered when singers were permitted too much freedom. And still they cannot be denied a certain pre-eminence, since the singer is, after all, the visible executor of the ideas, words and melodies laid down by composer and librettist.

Prerequisites

It is difficult to define clearly the art of operatic singing, for it has changed with the customs and habits of a period. At its initiation opera had a style which differed strongly from that of Handel's era. Mozart wrote for one type of singer while Wagner certainly needed another. There is often little resemblance in taste and customs among various countries. Experts and opera lovers in Italy rarely admire the same type of singer as do those in Russia or Germany. Just as each country developed its own national opera so did it develop its own style of singing. There is more emphasis on pure singing in one country, more on acting ability in another, or the requirements may be balanced in a third. Even the technique of singing varies in a certain measure. The timbre of a voice may enthrall audiences of one nation, but leave the people in another land almost unmoved.

An inquiry into the reasons for the success of many famous singers reveals that it is founded on a series of principles: good voice training, hard work, patience, perseverance, imagination and personality—in addition to an innate quality of the voice which may, however, not always be recognized before training has started. And, to be sure, a bit of luck! There are few who were able to climb to the top without these requisites which, as a matter of fact, are the elements of a successful career in other professions too. In this connection the young singer may be advised to test certain traits in his character such as extreme shyness or overconfidence, both of which may affect the development of his voice and also his performance on the stage. Recognizing these short-comings in time gives him an opportunity to overcome or suppress them.

Before deciding on a career the student should carefully judge himself and ask advice about the following factors: good, or at least adequate, stage appearance, since only exceptional voices can balance this handicap; strong health, since the training and the career are strenuous; musical and dramatic talent; a voice basically with a wide range and with a fine timbre. If possible, he should acquire a college degree which includes courses in music and theatre. And he should have no illusion about quick success. Both the student and his teacher must be patient. To present a young singer too early can do more harm than to start a career a little late. No definite statement about the required length of study time or the right age for a debut can be made. The latter decision should await the individual's maturity of body and mind, for without it he will be unable to bear the immense strain of performing operatic roles. Although many singers have been quite successful without a thorough preparation, the following subjects ought to be included in the studies, apart from an efficient voice training:

piano	acting (pantomime)
music literature	fencing
opera literature	eurythmics (dance)
diction	foreign languages

The student will further benefit from participation in activities of dramatic clubs, opera workshops and church choirs. These requirements may sound too extensive. They will, however, afford the singer the possibility of manifesting and developing his talent and knowledge on a broad foundation.

Some students show from the beginning an inclination and a natural gift for certain parts such as heavy dramatic; others will tend more toward lighter roles. Voice, body, acting ability and personality as a whole will determine in the end to which field the young artist will turn.

Exacting demands are made of a singer who prepares for roles in grand opera. A voice should be perfect and the student should show obvious talent for acting, particularly for pantomime combined with dramatic intensity. If the student has a light voice and is an agile actor, light or comic opera will probably be his aim. He must however not overlook the fact that a light voice can change. For operetta and musical comedy the requirements are high too, although of a different nature. Here the accent is more on appearance, agility, and ability to characterize. But "classical" operettas, like those composed by Johann Strauss and Jacques Offenbach, are often vocally so demanding that opera singers are usually engaged for these works.

It is of no great concern where and how a singer takes his first steps on stage—experience is all that matters. For this reason the young singer is advised to accept roles in operettas and light operas even though his voice indicates the future heavy tenor or soprano. Such a "training period" offers the beginner the opportunity of developing stage presence without putting too great a strain on his voice.

Formerly actors were able to take parts in both plays and operas and vice versa. During the 18th century a separation of the two art forms scarcely existed, although there were renowned singers who specialized in coloratura soprano, lyric tenor, and so on. Many actor-singers were engaged at smaller court and municipal theatres in Europe to play in a classical drama one day and to sing an operatic role the next evening. This custom, which held into the end of the last century, afforded the artists a versatility rarely attained by present-day singers, who often tend to specialize too early in a small field.

The Voice

Since the voice is the supreme tool of the opera singer, it has to be treated with the greatest care. But, at the same time, teacher and student must beware of considering it all-important. Operatic singing means more than merely exercising the vocal cords. After all, the training of the voice is only one step, the first and most vital one though it may be. It is not always possible at the beginning to predict the particular sphere of the young singer. Extreme types are easy to recognize but it is often difficult, even for the expert, to classify the majority of untrained voices. There are many bass-baritones and mezzo-sopranos: they could develop into true basses or baritones, into sopranos or contraltos; they may even gain an extremely wide range. Frequently a young voice does not show any definite character during the early period. Under certain circumstances the tone character may not be perceptible until much later; many times it emerges after years of studying and experience. These "in-betweens" are best left to develop and settle in a natural way, without the use of force to fit them into one type or another. Sometimes voice teachers add artificially a few notes to the lower or upper register and thus make the student believe he is a bass, a tenor or the like. Such forced training will usually harm the voice; it is far better to wait and let nature and experience do the job of maturing.

Provided the voice is of good and promising quality, the teacher ascertains that the pupil practices only with the voice correctly placed and projected.

Above all the beginner must avoid any use of force. If the voice has a definite character there ought to be few difficulties, but if it has not, as indicated previously, the development will proceed more slowly. As a matter of fact, voices can tend toward the lower or upper register even years later. A lyric tenor can develop into the heavy Wagnerian type, a lyric soprano change over to the dramatic field or a baritone to a bass. If such a transition is carefully watched by teacher or coach the voice will settle unharmed. If the change is too great, it may become necessary for the singer to give up professional singing for several months. Two reasons should persuade him to do this: to rest his voice and to study his new repertoire.

At what point in his training may a student safely take up the study of an entire operatic role? This question has often been asked. Disregarding the essential factor of maturity of body, voice and mind, we may say that it can be started after two or three years of proper voice practice. This does not imply, however, that every student is ready for it after this period; strictly speaking, it should seldom, if at all, be attempted before that time.

The teacher ought to be assured that the voice is healthy and natural, without obvious defects such as breaks or too narrow a range, before he encourages any student to embark on an operatic career. It is furthermore advisable to have him examined by a medical expert, a nose and throat specialist, to check the resonance cavities and the state of his vocal cords. If these organs are somewhat under-developed and need exercising, or if there is any malformation or unusual condition which could be improved by an operation, as in the case of obstructing cartilage or contortion of the nose bridge, the physician can easily detect and correct the situation. At any rate the future singer should be cautioned.

Other prerequisites are the same for all singers aspiring to a professional career. The voice must be "placed in the mask," so that the tone can be produced without forced pressure of throat muscles. The passage of the throat must be open and not block the flowing tone. The transition from one register to another should be smooth. This principle is generally accepted, although some Italian voice teachers do not believe in inconspicuous transition from the heavy chest to the middle register.

As soon as the voice is well-balanced, and every tone placed right so that the student does not have to pay any (or very little) attention to the technique of voice projection, he may begin the musical study of roles. Tutor and student will then be able to judge whether more training is needed or whether the pupil can proceed to act his part after having memorized it. During this period he should try to sing his role in a hall of medium size where experts can find out how his voice carries. If an orchestra instead of a grand piano is available, such a try-out will be even more instructive. The singer who is accompanied by an orchestra for the first time is faced with a new dilemma caused by the multitudinous sounds of the instruments. A well-placed voice will have no difficulty in penetrating through a medium-sized orchestra. It is the matter of pitch and adjustment of the voice that takes some experience. The problem of singing in action will be discussed in a later chapter. It should be kept in mind, though, that singing an aria without action is quite unlike performing it on stage and there is an even more remarkable difference between doing a role in a relatively small studio and playing it in an opera house.

How to Execute Dramatic Effects*

Unlike the art of concert singing, opera, especially the Italian and French genre, permits the use of a series of technical tricks in eliciting emotion in order to achieve certain theatrical effects. Some are marked in the scores by librettists and composers, others originated in the interpretation of singers or conductors. Such effects as "laughing, crying, sighing, weeping, and screaming" can injure the voice unless they are executed with proper technique. They should not be left to the singer's temperament; uncontrolled, these emotional outbursts can turn out to be melodramatic and thus ludicrous. They may result in irritation of the throat, thus jeopardizing a performance. In a more serious case a singer with little experience and inadequate training might even lose his voice altogether. If, however, the proper amount of support is being given, and the breathing technique is functioning in the right way, it should be possible to execute these effects without damage to the voice. But they have to be practiced by the young singer with utmost care, and under the supervision of his coach and director, long before the performance of the role in which they occur.

The Treatment of Recitatives

The execution of lyric or dramatic passages has to be mastered; the recitatives also require a style of their own. There are two kinds to be studied: the *secco recitativo* which is accompanied by the conductor at a harpsichord or, if this instrument is not available, at a piano; the *recitativo accompagnato* which is played by the orchestra.

The first is written in a conversational style, and is executed without strict adherence to the length of the notes—in fact notes are mostly short, little inflection being used. It differs from dialogue only in so far as the word is spoken on a definite pitch laid down by the composer. The singer must have his voice under complete control. The tone must be produced in front with ease. A minimum of it, *parlando*, is all it takes. No forcing or outpouring of tones in big volume should be heard. Furthermore, not only the vowels but also the consonants must be so distinct that the words can be understood in the far corner of the theatre, even when the tempo of the recitative is very rapid, as it mostly is. Mozart made splendid use of the *secco recitativo* in his operas, as did Rossini and Donizetti. The recitative may be light and comic or serious, sentimental or heroic.

° See Appendix II for examples.

47

The *recitativo accompagnato* was originally devised as an introduction to an aria or ensemble. The style of singing, therefore, approaches the style of that particular piece of music and describes the character's thought and emotions, thus forecasting the mood of the subsequent piece. In *Aida, The Marriage of Figaro, Fidelio,* or *Don Giovanni* the style and technique in the recitative must correspond with the style and technique of the arias or ensembles succeeding it. As opposed to the *secco recitativo,* the singer will use his full voice. The introductory recitative can be, like the *secco recitativo,* in any mood or color, and is designed to prepare and lead into the next aria or ensemble.

Acting

For too long a time the importance of acting has been overlooked by too many. There has been too much admiration for vocal prowess regardless of a noticeable lack of dramatic expression. And yet, whenever a great singer has also been a fascinating actor he has captivated the spectators. The neophyte will do well to take to heart the words attributed to Mary Garden: "Take care of the dramatic line, and the musical line will take care of itself!" For all its exaggeration this statement indicates the significance of dramatic interpretation. The young singer must be able to demonstrate talent in both fields. Instead of the previous complacency, an almost rigid standard seems to be forming. The stereotyped gestures and movements of yesteryear are unacceptable in our theatres. There are already opera productions in which acting is valued as highly as in play productions. Listeners are now rarely satisfied with a performance in which poor acting destroys the dramatic mood. It has always been the custom to join a group, to be a cooperative member of an orchestra. Not so on the stage; yet here too the ensemble spirit is indispensable and becomes increasingly one of the leading principles. The individual singer as well as the entire ensemble is being measured with a new yardstick.

Before condemning the opera singer, however, one should remember that a good deal more is required of him than of the actor. A brief glance at the repertoire of our leading singers shows that many must master a far wider range of characters than their counterparts in drama. Rarely is an actor, except for some character players, asked to personify such a variety of types as the average singer has to represent. Few singers have the good fortune to play only themselves. A young coloratura soprano may, with good luck, be cast as Rosina, Zerlina, Susanna, and similar roles exclusively. The majority have to take on young and old, sweet and vile personalities.

This variety warrants flexibility of body and mind. Influenced by the modern trend in general and the movies in particular, opera-goers have become critical of a singer whose physical appearance is not in keeping with his characterization. As a result singers have to watch their diet, lest they become too corpulent. It does not mean that they must remain slender under all circumstances. They have the advantage of performing usually in large theatres and on big stages where they need well-developed lungs and a solid foundation for a big voice.

A beautiful voice combined with an attractive figure will always be the ideal. But many fine voices are placed in bodies inappropriate for roles indicated by these voices. A young woman of slim figure can possess a dramatic soprano. She will probably never play Isolde or the Marshallin, but she can concentrate on roles like Butterfly, Mimi, Elvira, Salomé and some parts in Verdi's operas which do not require imposing stature.

Even so, the career of some excellent and successful singers proves that this handicap can be overcome. There are a few well-known remedies, such as built-up shoes, a high hair-do or wig for the short figures. Sometimes the position on the stage and other technical tricks help. A singer who is too tall may wear flat shoes and keep hair arrangements and wigs low with emphasis on horizontal lines. Further, it is not always the question of how tall Don José is but how tall he is in comparison to his Carmen. Right casting can thus promote the success of a young undersized singer. Once he has established himself his figure will probably be overlooked. This is especially true of the tenor, who is such a rare songbird anyway.

The singer is also at a disadvantage as regards mimical expression. An actor is free to use his eyes, mouth, or face when interpreting a character. But a singer's first thought belongs to the projection of his voice; this interferes in a large measure with his facial expression. Besides, most of the time he has to see the conductor, another fact which obstructs natural acting. These impediments are quite conspicuous in highly dramatic scenes where the use of the full voice is necessary. In recitatives and light lyric passages the singer is more independent and, therefore, has more possibilities to express himself freely.

Yet in no case should singing strain throat or arm muscles. Limbs and head must be relaxed. The singer should be able to gesticulate freely and turn his head without affecting his voice. When he can do this, he may concentrate on the most momentous feature of his acting—the synchronization of gestures with music and words. The student who has learned to time his movements with the music has achieved something of the utmost importance. What is left to accomplish is an artistic task rather than a technical one: to project the vocal expression of every mood and situation.

There are still singers who believe that sweeping gestures support the emission of the voice. This opinion is erroneous; rather they weaken it and they are unnatural. Often such gestures have no relevance to words or music and hence fail to convey any meaning to the audience. Having become stereotyped they express nothing.

Many opera houses are large and thus demand, above all, a good characteristic make-up. If the eyes vary in expressions, arms and hands move convincingly, they will support the interpretation sufficiently. Poise and countenance are often more impressive than many details of acting. To keep in character is essential; details and subtlety in acting will eventually be attained. If the young singer tries to do everything at once he can become confused and sloppy in his performance. But long before rehearsals begin, he ought to practice facial expressions in the preludes to his arias, in the interludes, and postludes and whenever he does not have to sing. This practicing can be done in front of a mirror, so that he can scrutinize his expressions, learn to control them and to make transitions from one mood to another.

Every student is able to learn the fundamentals of acting. It takes much more to become a good actor. The beginner must bear in mind that poise and a pertinent movement are more eloquent than vague gestures or poorly timed movements. Gesturing with hands and arms close to the body remains ineffective. It is not enough just to indicate an action, on the contrary, it is imperative that everything be executed accurately and clearly. Gestures depend not only on the particular role, but on the size of the stage and auditorium as well. Generally speaking, they must be broader and larger in opera houses. The proscenium opening of the average American theatre is 30 to 40 feet; that of opera houses or auditoriums 40 to 50 feet and more. The capacity of legitimate theatres is 800 to 1,500; singers may face an audience of 3,000 to 6,000 in opera houses and municipal auditoriums, and many thousands more in open air theatres.

Synchronization of gestures with words and music is extremely important. This is also true of actions such as crossing, turning, kneeling, running and handling of properties. A course in eurythmics and practice in pantomime will be very beneficial. Great weight ought to be given the manipulation of swords. At one time or another, most singers have to draw a sword, fight a duel, or wear just a weapon. To be prepared for these events, the student should take lessons in fencing. Operas make use of all sorts of foils and swords; yet it suffices to master one kind, because then the student can rather easily familiarize himself with other types. The wearing of swords with period costumes should certainly be practiced during some rehearsals. For that purpose the director will give the singers swords or sticks in a bandelier and have them also wear cloaks or long robes. The sooner the young singer tries out his proper costume, the easier he can make it part of his character. Ladies have worries of their own; long dresses, hoopskirts and the like should also be worn in several rehearsals. Women seldom use swords (Octavian being an exception); mostly they carry daggers and pistols which are easier to handle.

An actor learns comparatively fast to execute most kinds of stage business. Not so a singer who faces a more complicated task; he should therefore be schooled in the fundamentals of acting as soon as feasible, that is, he should study the acting right along with the vocal study of a part. It is not difficult to teach a beginner the proper use of his arms and his whole body, but it is almost hopeless to undo poor habits once they have been ingrained. The student will profit from a course in eurythmics in the natural use of his limbs and torso. This practice will also improve his sense of rhythm. He will also be well-advised to take some work in pantomime and to become acquainted with the fundamentals of ballet.

Enunciation

Diction is sometimes dealt with less than is permissible in the interest of operatic art. It certainly is a superhuman task to master not only English but three foreign languages besides. To be sure, the general adoption of English versions would simplify matters immensely. Nevertheless, acquiring a clear diction in his native tongue is the student's first obligation. This will enable him to enunciate correctly all words while singing and to handle the dialogue and recitative in operas and operettas. Richard Wagner's concept of the close relation between speech and song can, in a modified way, be applied to other compositions. Before the opening night of *The Ring* in Bayreuth, Wagner addressed his cast with the admonition: "Enunciation! the long notes will take care of themselves; the short ones and the text are what matters."

It is also interesting to read in the preface to *Intermezzo* what Richard Strauss has to say about the difficulties and errors of modern productions:

> "Now may I remind the singer in particular that only the well formed consonant will penetrate through the very loudest orchestra, while the strongest vocal tone, even when the best vowel "a" is used, will be drowned out without effort by an orchestra of eighty to one hundred musicians who may be playing only mezzaforte. The singer has but one weapon against the polyphonic and indiscreet orchestra; the consonant. I myself have witnessed, especially in Wagnerian musicdramas in Wotan's story, and in the Erda scene in *Siegfried*, for example where singers with big voices but with poor enunciation have been swallowed up in the orchestral waves, while artists with smaller voices but with sharp enunciation and with distinct phrasing were able without difficulty to uphold the author's words against the tonal floods of the symphonic orchestra."

We would understand an opera far more readily if our artists had better diction. In particular would this improve the performance of operas with dialogue; there is too often a discrepancy between good singing and poor speaking and it is gratifying to see the younger generation apparently as much interested in good dialogue as in excellent singing. Strange as it may seem, it is difficult to persuade singers to accept the good advice of Dr. Arne, who, about 200 years ago, counseled them to memorize the text before studying the music. Old Arne had probably heard of this principle from an Italian. Alas, singers as a rule start with the melody, neglecting the clear enunciation of the words.

As mentioned previously, the quality of the singer's voice counts most, but some acting talent should be perceptible before a decision is made to choose an operatic career. Long and hard work are imperative in order to reach even the first goal. Perseverance in the pursuit of the studies, willingness to spend several years of preparation, and understanding the need for cooperation with artistic leaders and colleagues build the foundation to success.

THE CONDUCTOR

"There are no poor orchestras, only poor conductors" Gustav Mahler once said. Even if we take this statement with a grain of salt we must admit that an outstanding conductor can spur a rather mediocre orchestra to amazing achievements. Substituting opera for orchestra we may apply Mahler's words to this art form too. Although the conductor shares the responsibility with the stage director, success or failure of a production depends to the highest degree on the musical leader. A director can do much harm, but so long as the musical performance is excellent, the production can still be impressive. Should, however, the conductor bungle his part even the best director cannot save the evening.

The conductor catches the eye of the audience during the performance; he has the great advantage of being visible, and gives the impression of supervising everything. People moreover are still accustomed to think of an opera as a purely musical creation, disregarding the fact that it is a drama set to music. The apparent predominance of the conductor should not tempt the beginner to abuse his position. There are on the concert platform as well as in the theatre pit conductors who seem to be of the opinion that their work will not be appreciated unless they gesticulate rather wildly, sometimes ostentatiously disapproving of a mistake made by a musician or a singer. Thus they succeed in attracting unwarranted attention to themselves. Berlioz describes the situation pertinently when he said: "A poor singer can spoil only his own part while an incompetent or mediocre conductor spoils everything."

The stage is the center of the performance and the good conductor will do everything in his power to keep the audience's attention focused there. The aspiring conductor must realize that he is to synchronize stage and orchestra and to interpret the work to the best of his ability, but he is not expected to be conspicuous himself. The true artist is so involved in his task, so conscious of his responsibility to the composer that he will not develop any distracting and irritating mannerisms which hurt the ensemble and, in the end, himself. Therefore every gesture that is unnecessary and non-essential should be avoided or, at least, restricted to a minimum.

It is rather easy to define the basic task of the conductor—to recreate the orchestra score together with the singers and musicians whose work he moulds into a unified whole. This sounds simple, yet the materialization of this task is complex since even with all the technical problems solved an artistic interpretation is by no means assured. Such an accomplishment presupposes not merely musical talent, but a dramatic vein as well as thorough knowledge of opera and a gift of leadership. The utmost concentration is required of the musical leader from the first playing of the score for his group of singers until the performance is over. He must realize that conducting an opera is far more demanding and exasperating than conducting a symphony. A seasoned orchestra can play a symphony under almost anyone who is somehow capable of giving the downbeat and of keeping rhythm. But even the best opera organization can go to pieces under inferior leadership; there is such deep interdependence between orchestra and singers that any wavering or lack of clarity will affect the entire ensemble.

The mere technical phase of conducting includes a great variety of matters. Some students observing the masters in the pit may believe that beating time and giving cues is all that needs to be done. These young aspirants may also be impressed by the glamour that surrounds great conductors, not realizing that the road to fame is long and paved with hard work. They will be surprised to read the list of items, such as pitch, rhythm, tempo, length of notes, volume, cues, and, most essential, dramatic interpretation, which every good conductor must be able to supervise and correct, not only during three hours of performance but also during the preceding rehearsals. In his charge are singers and choristers in addition to a large number of musicians in the pit. The conductor must never lose the image of the dramatic beauty of an ensemble while supervising its precise execution, the shades of tonal volume as well as the balance of instrumental and vocal groups. As if that is not enough, there are actions on stage calling for sharp attention on his part.

Prerequisites

The mere technical skill expected of the musical director is great and accordingly the prerequisites are extremely demanding. It is possible for a young singer, designer or even stage director to join a good company without much experience. Yet a conductor-to-be has to go through a long and hard training period before he will be offered a baton to take over an operatic production. The basic requirements include adequate piano playing which means playing at sight complicated piano scores and if possible orchestra scores. Of course a thorough knowledge of operatic literature is indispensable. In addition to the piano he must be acquainted with the various instruments and should possibly play an instrument of each group (string, woodwind, brass, percussion); this will give him the solid foundation he needs when he has to advise the musicians. Above all, he must have a keen ear. Perfect pitch may not be one of his gifts, but it can be developed through training. An understanding and feeling of the several musical styles is indispensable for the conductor. Lastly, he should be well versed in the theory of the art of conducting and also in the achievements of the outstanding masters of the baton.

One of the student's first steps should be to obtain a thorough knowledge of opera; coaching and accompanying will offer him this opportunity. He will learn much if he serves as assistant in rehearsals with experienced conductors. In his music school or college he should participate in every musical production: there is work to do backstage, such as giving cues to the curtain puller, to the stage manager who has to fire a gun, to a singer, to the electrician who has to execute a black-out or a difficult transition. After some experience he may apply to function as conductor backstage for the chorus or band. Another good method is to help the conductor correct the orchestra parts, a tedious but necessary work. Prompting in rehearsals and performances will add to his knowledge of operas and of the problems faced by singers. The student must make tireless efforts to attend operatic productions and to listen to good recordings. As soon as he is well versed he should ask to be allowed to conduct a chorus rehearsal or an ensemble. Each of these activities requires a vast amount of knowledge and understanding; each includes also the element of responsibility. The fundamentals can be learned in every good conservatory or college, yet very few institutions can offer an opportunity to gain experience in all these aspects. If feasible, the student should serve as an apprentice in a professional company in order to undergo a training in every phase of his work. To take charge of a small group and to handle everything will show him how to manage the divers hazards and problems involved in every opera. If and when he thinks he is ready for the big step he must know intimately a good number of works, almost knowing them by heart.

Obviously musicianship, including reliable pitch, is the *sine qua non* for anyone who intends to conduct opera. In addition he must be endowed with a good memory, a light hand and dramatic inspiration. Other skills can be acquired through experience. There are several that concern every conductor, but all are prerequisites for an operatic career. Theory, clear baton technique (operas should not be led without a baton!), quick reaction to trouble, making cuts and corrections, and again playing the piano. These are the requirements for any kind of conducting, but in opera, conducting an ensemble in motion takes a still more precise baton technique. Furthermore, the art of executing *rubato* passages has to be mastered and foreign languages ought to be studied. The opera conductor needs some knowledge of acting, scenic and light effects in order to appreciate the singer's and director's problems and to adapt himself to them. Understanding the technique of singing is also imperative since, during the period of coaching and stage rehearsals, the conductor ought to be able to counsel the singer. Such broad knowledge will be of immense aid in balancing pit and stage.

All these requirements for technical as well as artistic interpretation serve the one purpose of transforming the printed score precisely and dramatically into sound. It takes more than a knowledgeable technician to make music live and speak eloquently; this demands a personality sincere and honest toward himself and capable of materializing an artistic conception.

Dynamics (Rhythm and Tempo)

The beginner in operatic conducting is in a far more difficult position than his colleague on the concert platform. Any experienced symphony orchestra adjusts itself quickly to the beats of a conductor; even peculiar mannerisms do not affect the playing to a point where it would necessarily injure the performance. But the conductor in the pit must always be aware of the fact that there are also singers and choristers and that the coordination of stage and orchestra is a basic law.

The student of symphonic music knows already that terms like *andante*, *allegro*, and so on, do not have the same meaning all the time but are to be understood in relation to previous or following markings. This is certainly true of the old masters. Since the middle of the 19th century composers have marked tempos more and more precisely, either by modifying the general terms through indicative adjectives, by using their native language rather than the traditional Italian, or by giving every tempo the exact measure of the metronome. There should be little disagreement concerning the works of the last generation. Puccini, Strauss and others have been extremely thorough in marking their orchestral scores. The conductor, however, must be able to read these remarks, to understand them and to execute them by means of his beat. Yet various examples prove that the composers themselves did not adhere to their own printed markings. Fritz Striedry relates a story about Richard Strauss who answered his inquiry about the interpretation of *Salomé* as follows: "For God's sake, conduct it exactly as it is printed and do not bother about compromises which the composer-conductor was forced to make to have his peace of mind." This statement suggests that Strauss, a famous composer, had to give in to the whims of some singer. In his preface to *Intermezzo* Strauss expands his views:

> May I, at this point, refer to my very specifically marked orchestra dynamics which are no longer restricted to the degrees pp, p. f, ff, for the orchestra as a whole, but which require different degrees simultaneously for different groups, even for single instruments within a group. To follow the markings accurately— the prime requirement for proper execution of my scores—presupposes a discipline on the part of the orchestra which is still somewhat unusual today; but the important thing to remember is that the scores should really sound as I intended. Special attention is demanded for a meticulously executed fp, or, for that matter, any expression mark which would give preponderance, however slight, to some single instrument as against minor parts. Only thus can delicate web-like polyphony be properly heard. One noisy part can upset the balance, destroy important subordinate episodes. The more polyphonic and complex a score is, the more

essential it is that every musician, unmindful of the volume of his neighbor in the orchestra, play exactly as his part demands. . .

It is self-evident that the beating of time should not be executed with machine-like precision, but on the contrary should be carried out with a light hand that will readily accelerate, hold back, or indicate little rhythmical accents within a measure. This is chiefly true in French and Italian music. But even in the very precise German compositions there are passages demanding a faster or more restrained treatment. The following words by Richard Wagner illustrate the difficulty in determining the right tempo: "It is unnecessary to mark the exact tempo because a talented conductor will find the right tempo anyway; and the untalented conductor will never grasp the tempo even if it is printed in the score."

Celebrated conductors who disregarded the composer's markings have usually been sharply criticized, but sometimes they have been acclaimed for their boldness. Such a success, however, is the work of a towering personality which, overshadowing these violations, integrates them meaningfully into the whole. Arthur Nikisch, for instance, took the overture to *The Flying Dutchman* rather slowly; his intention was to underscore the tragedy of the opera, yet Wagner had marked this piece *allegro con brio,* so as to describe the sea storm. Another significant example is offered by Hans von Buelow who conducted the Toreador's song and march in *Carmen* more slowly than was customary. He meant in this way to show the character of the proud Spaniard, rather than to follow the more effective French tradition of playing the music in a somewhat quick march tempo.

There is a "too slow" as well as a "too fast." Felix von Weingartner defines this problem with the pertinent words: "No slow tempo must be so slow that the melody of the piece is not yet recognizable, and no fast tempo so fast that the melody is no longer recognizable." Every musician of good taste knows that a shift toward either extreme can distort the melody almost to the point of absurdity. Not only the melody but the mood and meaning may be lost. A few examples will illustrate this point: If Sarastro's aria, "*In diesen heiligen Hallen*" is played too fast, as has been done by a well-known conductor, the serenity of the atmosphere undergoes a change detrimental to the original meaning. A similar case is Sparafucile's entrance music in *Rigoletto,* which should suggest his sinister character; if, however, the orchestra plays the melody too fast or too slow, Verdi's intentions are lost. An accidental difference in tempo or an ill-chosen tempo can cause discomfiture to everyone during a performance.

In his requests for fast or slow tempos the conductor must be realistic about the resources of singers and instrumentalists. In the Nile aria of *Aida,* in the third act the tempo is quite slow, as the composer wrote down *andante mosso;* but a renowned conductor forced his leading lady to draw out the tempo to a point where she lost her breath and the wonderful aria lost its lustre. Going

56

to the other extreme, if Figaro's *"Bravo, bravissimo"* which is marked *stringendo* is accelerated to a racing speed, the singer is unable to enunciate distinctly and even to sing it. This is true of many a *stretta* passage.

The warning against exaggerations does not mean that the young conductor should cling religiously to the conventional tempos, provided there is any acceptable convention at all. Many great composers and conductors have spoken frankly against too strict adherence. Wagner, for one, was in favor of experimenting since without it there is no vitality.

The reader of this book is expected to be familiar with the fundamentals of conducting. Here the specific problems of opera will be delineated. The student must first visualize his position in the orchestra pit where the musicians are spread far to the right and left but few are in front of him. He will have trouble in supervising the stage, since too many pits are built without the necessary consideration that the conductor must be seen by everyone on stage and that he must see everyone. If the pit is deep, a higher platform on which he can stand will somehow remedy this condition; but he must not stand too high as this makes it impossible for the musicians to follow his beat. Experimentation with different levels will bring about the most satisfactory position. The conductor must realize that whenever singers must follow his beat he is obliged to keep his arms higher than on a concert platform.

The eyes, the prominent feature in facial expression, can be most effective in controlling the best apparatus of an operatic team, keeping contact with singers and musicians by giving them little cues, stimulating and inspiring them. The function of the hands in conducting a concert differs somewhat from that of opera. In the pit more than on the platform the young conductor must be careful not to make the same motion with both arms. Each hand must make independent gestures. The right arm and hand with the baton are used for the broad line of rhythm and melody. Our leading conductors often seem to beat exclusively; but on close observation one can see the wrist indicating accents and details of a complex melodic pattern. The left arm and hand play an especially important part in conducting opera. With the left hand cues are given for the pit and for the stage, and little errors of singers or instrumentalists, such, for example, as coming in before their cues or missing them are amended. The raising of a hand will hold or lead the erring person. A singer who is off key can also be corrected in this way: the finger held up or down will indicate whether he is too high or too low. On certain occasions both hands can be used in the same pattern—a strong *crescendo*, a sharp chord, important cues for the chorus, difficult ensembles, can hardly be managed with one hand. But the conductor should be mindful that this procedure is the exception, not the rule.

The Beat

The beginner· faces some difficulty in deciding how to interpret a given rhythm and tempo through his beat. Let us say he has a signature of 3/4 or

3/8 while beating time of one. He has to be extremely accurate in his technique though not pedantic, for too many details can slow down the tempo. A consensus of many renowned conductors would be about as follows: if a piece in 3/4 or 2/4 can be conducted in one, do so by all means! 4/4, 9/8 or 12/8 can be simplified in the same way by beating two, three or four. The procedure is clear when *alla breve* is printed in the score. There are, however, instances where this marking appears to indicate only the rhythmic nature of a piece, as in *Don Giovanni* in the *terzetto* before the first finale. It is marked *alle breve* but the beat in four is considered too hazardous by some conductors who therefore prefer a beat in eight. The *larghetto* in the first finale of *The Magic Flute* and the prisoner chorus in *Fidelio* are indicated *alle breve* but conducted in four. In many cases tempo and rhythm have to be weighed carefully. As a rule the smallest unit for the beat is the best choice, yet this kind of beat need not be continued throughout the entire number. In Italian and French operas in particular, but in German ones as well, one may rightly take the liberty of changing the beat within each number. Mozart wrote the *arietta* of Figaro *"Se vuol ballare"* in 3/4; a good solution is to begin with a beat of three and to change over to one after a few measures as soon as the tempo is clear to all participants. Yet other conductors prefer to keep the beat in three on account of the *pizzicati* and the horns. In order to avoid a hurried performance it may be wise now and then to go back to the beat of three for a few bars. The march in *The Mastersingers* is fairly broad and obviously requires a beat of four. And yet Karl Muck, one of the great Wagner conductors, changed in the middle of the march to a beat of two, succeeding, nevertheless, in keeping the tempo *"durchweg breit und gewichtig"* (sustained and weighty throughout).

For an inexperienced conductor the risk in beating too many unnecessary fourths and eighths is that this method retards the tempo too much. Only a light hand, the faculty of using the wrist for these fast little beats, plus experience can help him develop the technique which allows him to be very exact while at the same time keeping his tempo. The girls' chorus in *Carmen*, *"Dans l'air nous suivons des yeux,"* is written in 6/8 divided in two parts; the previous passage of the basses *"Voyez-les"*! has the same rhythm and is marked *andantino*. Even if the conductor begins with a beat in six the girls' chorus should be conducted in two (although in many vocal scores the 6/8 beat is subdivided in two 3/8 beats). It may be necessary to indicate each quaver in a few bars; yet thorough rehearsal work should make this superfluous. A waltz rhythm is best conducted in one; the first bars can be taken in three and even in between an indication of the first and second or of the third crotchet may produce a more lucid performance. As a rule, the tempo drags when waltzes are conducted in three; most of them require quite a fast tempo. The beat in one is possible for the overtures of *The Abduction from the Seraglio* and also *The Marriage of Figaro* although with inexperienced musicians a beat in two is advisable. In *The Masked Ball* Verdi requested *allegro agitato e prestissimo* for the *terzetto* No. 5 *"Che v'agite cosi?"*. It is in 3/8 and certainly has to be conducted in one. An example for cutting up a 4/4 or other rhythm into smaller segments is the great finale in Traviata; the conductor begins with a beat in four but every so often changes to 12 to prevent the ensemble from disintegrating. A similar situation arises at the end of act three in *Otello*. A case of a 9/8 is found in act three of *Martha*; the larghetto ensemble is to be conducted in three but, here again, some bars require a beat in 9 to hold singers, choristers, and orchestra together. In *Mignon*, on the other hand, the greater portion of the ensemble in act one is beaten in 9 with but a few bars in 3.

Quite a problem is created by different patterns of rhythm (beats) within a single passage and more than technical skill is necessary to master such pieces. The conductor must be very sensitive and capable to keep each rhythm pattern in the ensemble clearly identified, while apparently directing just one group. He ought to rehearse with each group separately so that its particular rhythm is established when he conducts the whole orchestra. In the first finale of *Don Giovanni* Mozart's score indicates three string ensembles playing on the stage. Even in some leading theatres number one is placed in the pit, the other two on stage. Group one plays in 3/4, group two begins in 3/4, but changes later on to 2/4 and 3/8, and group 3 plays in 3/4 and 3/8. Theoretically, this seems almost too complicated to be done even by the most seasoned conductor. Actually it is quite simple; the conductor, after having practiced with each ensemble separately, conducts in 3/4 (the beat for group I); the other elements—singers and groups two and three—with their variegated rhythm are fitted into the basic pattern.

Another interesting, if less involved, situation is found in act two of *Tosca* while Scarpia leads a conversation with Cavaradossi and others in 2/4, Tosca herself joins with the chorus backstage in a *cantata* written in 4/4. The conductor in the pit watches his 2/4 and an assistant synchronizes the *cantata*. In the first finale of *The Mastersingers* the main movement is 2/2 but the apprentices are singing in 6/4. Such overlapping of two rhythms should be no problem, the main beat being identical. The smuggler quintette in *Carmen* is composed in 6/16, but some soloists and orchestra change occasionally to 2/8. In the subsequent duet of Carmen and Don José the *allegretto moderato* is in 6/8, both singers, however, having a few measures in 2/4. At first glance Richard Strauss sets a difficult problem in the last act of *Der Rosenkavalier* (number 267). The orchestra plays in 3/4, Sophie and Octavian sing also in 3/4, but the Marschallin in 4/4. The composer himself made the decision by marking the passage: to be beaten in one. A little further the situation is similar when Sophie's melody is to be sung in 6/8 while the orchestra plays in 2/4 as well as in 6/8.

Cuts and Other Changes

One of the most delicate tasks is to decide on cuts and other changes in a score. This requires good judgement based on knowledge, delicate taste and sense of style. To make a cut does not simply mean to eliminate a repetitious passage or another which the singer or conductor or director dislikes. Since this is such an intricate procedure, the outcome has been all too often the reliance on conventional cuts which are open to criticism. The conductor who is primarily responsible for this task should realize that no cut is sacrosanct however traditional it may have become. It is up to him to determine in every case whether a passage can be omitted or should remain. Good conductors have an aversion to senseless cutting. Some even insist that an opera be performed as composed. This view may sometimes be carried too far, for it is an acknowledged fact that even the great masters occasionally composed weak passages or made unwarranted repetitions. Other conductors in turn feel compelled to improve at any costs upon the original version. They are liable to omit passages and entire scenes at will and also tamper with the orchestration. If a composer has left his opera unfinished, certainly a friend and pupil may be able to complete and edit it, as was done in the case of Puccini's *Turandot*.

Here not the broader aspect of a thorough adaptation but rather the more limited assignment of preparing a score for a particular production will be discussed. The questions which arise should be reviewed by both the conductor, director (and in some cases the choreographer) with the musical, dramatic, technical and financial situation in mind. Suggestions can be made by either of them, but the final word about the musical changes belongs to the conductor, about the dialogue to the director. In cutting the dialogue the director may proceed as in a play, but he has to consider the transition from the preceding and to the following music. The cutting of musical portions takes a slightly different approach. Here mere omission does not suffice. Words or notes of singers and musicians may have to be altered to harmonize the loose ends. Often a cut ends with a chord of the eliminated passage, especially when it is only a matter of dropping a repetition. Otherwise, as indicated, minor alterations are necessary.

Generally speaking, before any modification is made the conductor has to decide whether a passage is really weak or repetitious or too difficult for the singer. The director determines whether an interlude or a postlude is to be repeated, shortened or omitted in order to achieve a more effective staging of a scene. Both artists have to agree on the elimination of an extra chorus or a stage band, of recitatives and ballet scenes. The most complicated problem is that of abbreviating lengthy operas such as those by Wagner which in their original versions last four hours and longer. Not even the Metropolitan Opera can ordinarily afford such long renditions because of the tremendous expenses connected with overtime pay for rehearsals and performances. Although the uncut (or nearly uncut) version should be the norm with leading opera companies, under certain circumstances the choice of an abbreviated form of *Parsifal*, *The Mastersingers* and *The Valkyrie* will be prompted by the alternative of no production at all.

Acceptable cuts are marked in some printed scores or can be discovered by listening to recordings and broadcasts of operas. They can also be found in the orchestra material which an opera company receives on loan from agencies. Inquiries addressed to professional conductors, directors and singers will supply further instruction. The sometimes conflicting opinions must then be examined and weighed against each other. For instance, notwithstanding the puritans' objection to the removal of any passage, a few cuts are generally admissible. *Carmen* may serve as an example to show what is right and wrong. One conductor eliminated the wonderful interludes between the acts on the ground that presumably the patrons would chatter during the music. Similarly unmotivated cuts are to be found in the *Habanera*, the duet between Micaela and Don José and other scenes. But the following cuts can be retained if so desired (Schirmer edition): from page 222 to page 228, 4th bar; from page 287, 2nd bar to 292, 3rd bar. The opening chorus of act four is often omitted; a ballet with music from the *L'Arlésienne Suite* is substituted. If the chorus remains, a cut to be recommended goes from page 343 to 346.

Even some ardent admirers of Mozart concede that the last act of *The Marriage of Figaro* is lengthy in spots. Hence, the arias of Marcellina and Basilio are often omitted. In a few productions even Bartolo's aria in act one is not sung either. For *Don Giovanni* Mozart composed two arias each for Donna Elvira and Don Ottavio; the conductor, after consulting with the singers and the director, selects those to be included. In *The Barber of Seville*, Rosina may have her own idea about the song to be inserted in act two. A prudent conductor makes sure, however, that this piece does not violate the style of this opera. In the same comic work two arias are often dropped; one is aria no. 9 for Don Bartolo, the other Bertha's aria no. 13. A gavotte is taken from one scene and included in another in Massenet's *Manon*. Often the entire scene in act two, *Cours la Reine*, is eliminated, but Manon's charming song became so popular with singers and listeners alike that it is now heard in the subsequent act where it does not belong at all. If the men's chorus is not very strong, the backstage passage in act three of *Otello* may be left out without any consequence. The last ensemble "cries" in *La Traviata*, *The Masked Ball*, *Otello* and *Lohengrin* can be omitted without any ill effect to the musical part. As a matter of fact, these scenes gain dramatically if the characters express their sorrow through their attitude and facial expression rather than overstressed exclamations.

Studying the Orchestra Score

The true conductor has a tone image of all the instruments and voices. He "hears" the entire opera within himself. A music student can pretty rapidly gain experience in reading and playing the score of a classic symphony, yet an opera contains new and intricate complexities. Scanning the orchestra parts alone will lead to a misconception. The eye should first glance at the singer's part and then at the accompanying instrumentation in order to obtain the impression of a lyric drama. Overtures, orchestral preludes, interludes, and postludes are treated like symphonic music, yet the action as arranged by the director should be taken into account. Conductors, most of them anyway, have a special technique of piano playing quite different from that of a concert accompanist. During the coaching sessions it is advisable to help the singer by playing his melody while the printed piano part can be simplified. As soon as the singer feels safe in his role, the piano score should be played as written. The young conductor should acquaint himself thoroughly with the orchestra score and acquire the facility needed to play it for coaching. The use of orchestra scores should commence with comparatively "simple" scores of Mozart, Beethoven, Rossini and Donizetti to be augmented by the more complicated romantic scores; then the most demanding works can be studied and coached. As to the polyphonic orchestration of scores by Richard Strauss and other contemporary masters, the student, in despair of transcribing them satisfactorily, may console himself with the fact that very few conductors can play these scores at sight.

Two methods may be employed in acquainting oneself with intricate orchestra scores; one is to use the piano transcription before attempting to play the full score itself. Thus the musician can recall the desired sound while glancing at the instrumentation to compose his own transcription. The second procedure is more strenuous but brings better results. The student himself makes a piano transcription after a careful examination of the orchestra score. A brief training in this method is so instructive that the reading and playing of the most involved scores becomes fairly easy.

A troublesome problem for the young musician is the lack of opportunities to attend performances regularly. Only in a few cities is it possible to hear a good number of operas every season. And not every music student will be permitted to attend the rehearsals in which he could follow the music with the score in hand. A few seats, close to the emergency exit lights, will provide the opportunity to read the score during a performance. The other alternative has, to some degree at least, been given by science which brought forth the radio and the recording. The aspiring student is thus in a position to listen to the large number of operas which are broadcast from the Met annually. Television stations too include a lyric drama occasionally. An even better chance is offered by the multitude of recordings of standard and rather unknown works. These two substitutes of live performances should not be underrated or belittled. Recordings in particular are very beneficial since they can be played over and over again while the student can make notes in his score.

Radio and particularly recordings offer the beginner a great temptation to imitate renowned conductors. He should remember, though, that interpretation is a most personal affair and cannot be taken over indiscriminately, and also that errors can occur even under the baton of a great master. The student should therefore discern between mistakes and whims on the one hand and desired effects carefully planned on the other. Without becoming hypercritical the young musician, with the orchestra score in hand, ought to make sure that nothing is inserted which runs contrary to the composer's wishes, and, furthermore, that the particular conception fits his own personality. It is imperative for the neophyte to scan and study all operas as if he were the first to conduct them. His aim must always be to recreate the composer's ideas, not to invent new features for the sake of a short-lived success.

The careful examination of an orchestra score should never tempt the young artist to attend too much to details to the detriment of the whole. No single effect is unrelated to the preceding and succeeding passages. It is the conductor's skill to combine and unite all elements and effects within the frame of the basic style and his own interpretation. The overall tonal combination is more important than any fine effect of a chord or melody, in short than the balance of sound which includes the voices on stage as well as the instruments in the orchestra. Every musician comes to a different conclusion as to what is most essential in the score and how his interpretation can best be achieved. His own personality appears in the execution of the score. Gustav Mahler expressed this thought in these words: "The most important thing in the music is not written in the music."

A *forte* or a *piano* does not always mean just that. In the orchestra scores of the classic masters all instruments were marked *forte* if the composer wanted to have a considerable amount of volume, and vice versa. Though many follow the general markings, some sensitive conductors make fine distinctions by having each group or each instrument play with a different volume. Again, the question of *forte* and *piano* depends on the preceding and succeeding passages, for every marking is related to others. Of the greatest importance is the accurate observation of signs such as *crescendo, decrescendo, accelerando* and *ritardando*. Just as essential is the adherence to phrase markings that visually connect a series of notes, a melody. To dissect a phrase held together by an arch gravely violates an artistic requirement. Any disregard of such signs is painfully noticeable in an opera for it affects the relationship of stage and pit. For a while it was fashionable so to cut up the phrasing that it became well-nigh incoherent. Composers mark clearly whenever they wish to have a pause, a *caesura*, a *fermata*. Tradition has led to many insertions of this kind but unless the score indicates such effects they should be dropped. The conscientious conductor will not indulge in such arbitrary changes. Letters and essays written by great composers and conductors like Hector Berlioz, Karl Maria von Weber, Richard Wagner, and Felix Weingartner should be read scrupulously and reread and their ideas applied to the opera in preparation.

One of the conductor's chief objects must be to protect the singer against the tone waves of the orchestra. A Mozart orchestra is small and, moreover, the brass instruments play only a subordinate part. With the increasing number of musicians required by composers of the 19th century the problem becomes more acute until the orchestra is predominant in Wagnerian and Straussian scores. Puccini, mindful of the singer's voice, most of the time, employs the full orchestra sparingly as a rule; yet his operas contain passages in which the conductor must take extreme care lest his musicians cover the voices on the stage. The beginner has to be conscious of the task of keeping every accent exactly as it is printed for an instrument or a group. Effects must not be exaggerated or "shades become blurs and accents shrieks," as Berlioz complained. In a *piano* passage a slight *marcato* is sufficient to create an effect; in a *forte* piece a *fortissimo* or, at least, a *sforzato* might be necessary for a similar achievement. In other words the student must learn to express an accent on a single note or chord in various ways. It cannot be stressed too often that no detail may be considered and treated as a separate element; it is part of a passage, the passage is part of an aria, the aria part of an act and so on. Each accent, each effect, each melody must fit into the general pattern of the composer's style. If the conductor ignores this principle he will be unable to achieve an artistic whole; his ensemble will fall apart.

THE STAGE DIRECTOR

Prior to Wagner the position of a stage director in an opera company was thought of as so insignificant that almost anyone was entrusted with it. In some extraordinary cases composers who were also conductors advised the singers about their actions and dramatic interpretation, but usually the stage director was a singer of secondary roles or a former singer who supervised the technical details of the production. He knew the routine well and possessed enough authority to manage the external matters. Today, staging an opera has become an artistic rather than a technical task. In this new position the stage director is the collaborator of the conductor—he is his equal. If he is to fulfill all expectations, he must acquire a great deal of knowledge and possess moreover an innate sense of musical style.

The primary task of the stage director is dramatic interpretation which embraces all activities on stage plus scenery and all effects related to it. In directing singers he needs a thorough understanding of acting, especially acting in harmony with music. The director must þe able to instruct singers, choristers, and extras, and also to plan the ballet or, at least, to discuss with the choreographer the role played by this group. His responsibility for settings and special effects is much the same as in play production except that more complicated settings and more effects have to be considered and that each one of these has to conform to the style of the music. He must, furthermore, possess the qualities of leadership, tolerance and immense patience.

The diversity of the director's work necessitates a correspondingly broad training which should include:

1. Acting
2. Fundamentals of singing
3. Piano playing
4. Operatic literature
5. Fundamentals of conducting
6. Languages (pronunciation)
7. History of opera
8. Directing of soloists
9. Handling of large groups
10. Stage craft

With good reason acting is mentioned first. The singer on the stage is the most arresting personality of the entire production and it is the director's responsibility to train him or to improve his art. Thus the young director will lean heavily on his experience as an actor, or at least on his extensive knowledge of acting problems, in particular of those which apply to the acting singer. Some practice in singing is likewise helpful; he who has had voice training and has even sung a few roles can far better sympathize with the troubles and tribulations of his soloists.

A director should be able to play the piano score of an opera, though not necessarily as well as a conductor. He should also be capable of reading the orchestra score if not playing it. His musical training ought to give him a sound knowledge of styles and operatic literature. Studying the fundamental technique of conducting will greatly improve his appreciation for the work of his associate in leadership. The other requirements listed above indicate the extent of studies which must be undertaken and the kind of opportunities which every student must seek. Above all, the guiding principle must be an understanding and knowledge of music, as the style of music is the determining element of his art.

The Director and the Soloists

Since the director deals primarily with singers he should thoroughly understand their problems and difficulties. He must realize that every gesture and every movement is to be executed in accordance with the rhythm and the mood of the music. This is not as easy as it looks to the outsider. It is one thing to hear that Verdi's operas are not written in the style of Mozart's; it is quite another, to know how to translate this difference into action. In order to accomplish this it is advisable to listen assiduously to the music of these and other composers. Their style, as expressed in rhythm and orchestration, must be studied and grasped. The pure perspicuity of Mozart's music for instance calls for a similar lucidity, and an almost serene equanimity on the stage. Nothing should be harsh or hard, a divine harmony lies over every expression and move. Verdi's dramatic verve, on the other hand, and his fervor must radiate from the action which is vibrant with passion. Wagner's broad pathos, in turn, has to unfold on the stage as in the music. And veristic operas like *Tosca* and *Louise* demand almost the same treatment as realistic plays. Modern composers present new problems. The rhythm of some opera by Carl Orff calls for an interpretation that approaches dance. The monumentality of Igor Stravinsky's *Oedipus Rex,* on the other hand, needs an arrangement which resembles an oratorio rather than a lively drama.

Further, each aria and each ensemble must be dealt with differently within the frame of the style of the work as a whole. Tempo, rhythm, key, instrumentation and volume determine the stage action. A 2/4 is not the same as a 3/4, an allegro is faster than an andante. A minor key suggests another mood than does a major key. Most musicians will go a step further by insisting that a piece composed in the key of C expresses an entirely different mood from another written in G. A thorough knowledge of instruments and their color is essential for the interpretation of the score, not to mention the question of volume and any sharp accent. An understanding of all these matters tells the director what is essential and how to transfer the meaning of a passage into action on the stage. For every detail the director depends on the score, which provides the necessary clues if he can read and interpret them.

Gestures and movements as a rule, are executed more slowly than in a play because the music develops a mood and an emotion at a slower pace. Of course there are numerous exceptions in the animated recitatives, arias and ensembles of the comic operas. Following the trend of realism toward the end of the 19th century operatic acting became natural, indeed so much so in some productions that the original style of some operas was entirely disregarded. These characterizations did not only violate the style of the opera but they gave the appearance of nervousness to the point of being almost jumpy. The Wagnerian school, on the other hand, fell into the opposite extreme; movements frequently resembled a procession, a slow motion film rather than a dramatic action.

It is the director's task to teach the singer how to use his body as a means of expression. To be sure, the young singer is expected to be familiar with the art of acting. But remembering his music, thinking of voice projection, and at the same time concentrating on his stage business are a tremendous challenge. He will succumb to superficial, meaningless gestures unless he is constantly cautioned by a watchful director.

The Director and the Ensemble

Librettists and composers are rarely satisfied with a plot based on just a few soloists. The staging of opera therefore usually includes the management of large groups on stage and off, and while getting on and off. Handling numerous choristers, dancers and extras is an exacting job and quite different from directing a few individuals in a play. It implies the ability to think in terms of these groups, to organize rehearsals for them, and to lead them during the rehearsals. Many a play director, accustomed to stage intimate dramas, has failed when he faced this task because he was unable to deal with large groups.

The necessity to understand the musical style of a work must be emphasized again; but in addition it takes great patience to project this style through forty and more choristers. Since the director must give his full attention to the chorus, it is appropriate to rehearse its important scenes without the soloists. The treatment of the chorus suffers much more under conventional ideas than the work with soloists. The director should avoid arranging ensembles in a straight line or in a semi-circle. It is amazing to see how often this principle is broken; in many productions, professional ones not excluded, the soloists stand along the curtain line with the choristers and others building a conglomeration farther upstage, or the leading roles are lined up in a semi-circle with the choristers forming another behind them. Directors, tolerating these positions, apparently mistake an opera for an oratorio. There are exceptions of course, such as some works by Orff and Stravinsky, which can be staged almost without action; this is also true of certain scenes of older works, as in the great finales. In general, opera is indeed not an oratorio, and dramatic action, composition and picturization are the very essence of its production.

Yet, in his effort to transform words and music into action, the director must not ignore the vital part of the conductor. He cannot arrange singers and choristers in such a manner that the conductor is unable to control them. It is unnecessary to have everyone look at the conductor all the time; in fact, our greatest masters of the pit have shown that they can very well hold the ensemble together without having singers stare at them. In dramatically important scenes it is enough for the singer to see the baton from the corner of his eye. But there are scenes which would suffer musically if soloists and choristers were turned toward the wings. Thus during ensemble scenes, as in the finales of Verdi's and Wagner's operas, the picture inevitably becomes static; every singing person must face the audience to project the full tone volume. It is up to the director to place the leading voices in such favorable positions that they easily penetrate through the ensemble, that is, to find the effective solution between a meaningless arrangement and a purely dramatic staging which might wreck the musical execution. Inherent good taste, understanding of all artistic and technical problems, and experience will guide him toward the right solution. Two examples may be of help in clarifying this point: in the great ensembles of *Aida* and *Tannhaeuser*, the leading soprano stands rather near the footlights, center stage; but in *Mignon*, act one, Filina, who leads the ensemble, is placed on a veranda or balcony, and should not come downstage, since if she does, the dramatic tension is lost—she must remain in her original position.

Style of Acting

Disregard of the music leads to misinterpretation in the action. With the exception of a few veristic operas the musical rhythm should be expressed in gestures as well as movements. And even the exceptions do not permit the singer to proceed according to his own feelings. Precise timing is indispensable. Individual singers may interpret certain passages or effects in various ways; the director must then forge these different views into one. He must clearly perceive the composer's style, and make the ensemble express it in every detail.

As stated previously, gestures are slower, but most of the time they are also broader than in drama. Large opera houses with their wide proscenium openings require more of an *al fresco* style of acting than do more intimate playhouses. As words are not always understood, gestures and motions must assist in elucidating the dramatic situation. Even in operas sung in English the enunciation is obscured in an ensemble or through the volume of the orchestra. The performance of an opera in a foreign language makes it imperative to illustrate the events. Therefore, each move or, for that matter, any stage business must make sense according to the action it is supposed to explain.

Through relentless though not inconsiderate discipline a director can be of great service to the audience. But in his struggle against carelessness he must beware of going to the other extreme by unreasonably insisting on irrelevant details. Directors have sometimes gone too far in instructing singers and choristers. If every step and every move is rehearsed in the most minute detail, the performance will look more like a ballet. Such meticulousness is based on the misconception that each note of the score is so essential that it must be interpreted by steps or gestures. A young director may have the notion, when studying a score, that every agitated passage requires commotion on stage. This is right for the opening scenes of *Carmen* and *Otello* and the arrival of the mail coach in *Manon*, but it would be a mistake in the first act of Gluck's *Iphigenia in Tauris*. Here, for all the excitement of the Priestesses and their frequent changes of positions, there should be intervals of rest.

A well-balanced interplay of action and repose is a criterion of the stage director. It calls for close scrutiny of text, music and the dramatic situation, besides a sense of esthetics. Stereotyped movements do not support the singer's characterization. "Gesture means not a physical but a mental manifestation" emphasized Chaliapin. This is true of every phase of stage behavior, be it gesture, movement, facial expression or handling properties. It is the factor of contrast that promotes dramatic efficacy.

No singer ought to be afraid of standing or sitting virtually motionless. The inner intensity, as expressed in dramatic poise (not pose!), will transmit his interpretation across the footlights. Desdemona and Elizabeth, while praying, need no gestures; their countenance reveals their emotions. The same is valid for des Grieux in his "dream aria" in *Manon*, for Traviata in her "*Addio del passato*", and for similar airs of a contemplative mood. In the lively scenes of *The Marriage of Figaro* or *Carmen*, the action can largely be restricted to small indicative gestures and facial expressions which tell the story better than unmotivated running around and arm swinging. Since the orchestral music lucidly describes the atmosphere, this curb on movement is all the more appropriate. Problems of a different nature await the director in many scenes of *The Barber of Seville* and *Gianni Schicchi* where wild gesticulating and rapid changing of positions are the essence of the comic spirit and its projection on stage. At any rate, each phase of either action or repose must be properly performed and integrated into the whole.

A chord marked *sforzato* or *forte* often suggests a gesture or a move. The passages leading to such a chord and succeeding it indicate how the motion is to be prepared, how a gesture or a turn is to be carried out, and how to behave afterward. A pause preceding or following the chord can mean to stand still, slowly to prepare the execution of the action. To state it briefly, pauses are signals for a transition. Typical examples are in *Carmen* when the leading lady throws a rose at Don José in act one, in the entrance scene of *The Flying Dutchman* (act two), in the pauses of Aida's arias, and the duet of Violetta and Germont. Some directors seem to believe that a pause or a *fermata* should be just that; thereby they overlook many dramatic possibilities. Generally speaking, the director should avoid presenting a "tableau." He must envision the dramatic expression called for by the music; then he will know through empathy what to do with a pause or chord with a *fermata* sign.

Planning the Production

Studies in history of theatre, operatic literature and designing, in addition to impressions received from operatic performances, give the young director the background for developing his own ideas. But observing and reading do not suffice, for practical experience which can be gained to some degree in an educational institution is invaluable to the aspiring director. Again the ability to organize and to handle large groups must be stressed as of prime importance. The best method for the beginner is to start with a small ensemble of two, three or four singers. The chorus he will face for the first time should preferably consist of not more than 12 or 16 members. An exact promptbook should be prepared for these rehearsals, not to have the actions pedantically executed as he wrote them down, but to obtain a very clear picture of the stage business as a whole. This necessitates virtually memorizing the music and the planned business.

Only a person who can control the complicated machinery of an operatic ensemble is capable of freely using his imagination and intuition. During initial rehearsals the beginner becomes acquainted with the fundamentals of his profession. A first step is to familiarize oneself with the traditional staging of as many operas as possible; the next is a critical review for potential changes of prevailing methods. Great understanding and knowledge are needed when altering even minor details of a conventional production. Both Wagner and Mahler, who may be called the first modern operatic stage directors, had labored several years in the traditional set-up of European opera houses before they began their reforms. If an impetuous director dismisses in a new production everything that has been done before, he probably succeeds in improving one scene but, by the same token, he is likely to make grave mistakes in others, unless he has pondered carefully every planned change. Experimenting is welcome and salutary but it should not lead to violation of the composer's ideas. Nothing must be read into the score that is not in it; nothing should be overlooked. Potential changes have to be considered for their effect on the production as a whole.

Details of stage business which have slipped in by routine, yet are not explicitly demanded by the librettist or composer, can be altered if not discarded altogether. It is more difficult to modify required actions. Technical plans may be readjusted if a desired effect cannot be achieved on the particular stage. This also applies to the number of choristers and extras. If the available groups are too small for the opera under consideration, the director should either object to the choice of the work or he must adapt the demands to the special circumstances. To be sure, it is of little concern whether doors, windows, pieces of furniture, or trees are at their "conventional" place or whether they are arranged in a different way, as long as these pieces are not the focal point of action. If they are, the consequence of the change on acting and singing must first be examined. This consideration is still more important when any piece of furniture or setting is to be moved upstage. King Henry in *Lohengrin* can have his seat on stage left or right in act one, but not in the upstage area which is needed for the arrival of the hero. In *The Mastersingers* (act one) or in *Tannhaeuser* (act two), however, chair and throne respectively can be placed more center upstage than is customary. A window in act two of *Tosca* is necessary for the clarification of the plot, yet basically it does not matter whether it is located right, left or upstage, as long as all movements can be adapted to the alteration.

In dealing with the interpretation of style and the conception of the entire production the director must show wisdom as well as good taste. Much harm has been done through overacting, which has turned charming comic operas into farcical operettas and dramatic masterpieces into melodramas. The director must not invent gags upon gags for every scene and character just because of a few comic ingredients in a light opera. A Mozart, Rossini or Donizetti has to be treated with a delicate touch, and grand opera can be spoiled through unwarranted exaggerations. The fact that certain passages of *Tosca* approach melodrama induces the director of fine perception to bring out all possible effects, but at the same time to underplay the gruesome scenes.

Gian-Carlo Menotti, one of the most successful composers of our time, should be heard, for he is not only the creator of effective masterpieces, but has also the eye and ear for frank observations of the work done on the stage. The following quotation from a lecture he gave at a meeting of the National Theatre Conference will serve to make clear his views as well as the duties of the director:

> People often ask me 'Why do you want to be a stage director?' My answer is that as long as there is not a Society for the Prevention of Cruelty to Authors, I advise almost any author to become his own stage director. The relation of the author to the stage director is very much the same as the composer's relation to the conductor. The more famous the conductor or stage director, the more the author has to fight against the distortion of his works. As the late Richard Aldrich once said: 'The trouble with conductors is not that they are paid so highly, but that they try to earn it.'
>
> The stage director's attitude is invariably the same: 'There is something wrong with the play; I must improve it.' So, disregarding the author's intentions he fashions the play to satisfy his own

taste, and the mangled version that results is hardly recognizable by the author himself. We had recent examples of such disfiguration in the productions of *No Exit, The Duchess of Malfi, The Eagle Has Two Heads,* and of course, even more recently, *Red Gloves*. But if we are to consider the theatre as a form of art, and not merely a form of entertainment, if we can see that it has a cultural value—we should fight against such degradation.

If we accept art as a form of expression we must accept the expression in its entirety. Let us re-establish genuineness in the theatre. Let us realize that Shakespeare does not need Orson Welles, or Bizet, Billy Rose.

I shudder every time the newspaper announces a revival. The word itself, 'revival', indicates the attitude which will be taken: an old play is something dead which has to be brought back to life. Even critics without realizing that the message it brings out of its own period and culture is precisely the quality which should most interest and move us!

This is a very important point in establishing an imaginative theatre. The main trouble with Broadway is that it is constantly 'leveling' every play to a conventional success formula, killing everything that seems (to them) excessive or arbitrary in the original script and thus destroying the artistic physiognomy of the play.

In my own case if I had listened to the Broadway know-it-alls, my two operas, *The Medium,* and *The Telephone,* would have been very different. *The Medium* might have had a greater popular appeal if I had stressed in it, as everyone suggested, the horror. But I did not intend *The Medium* to be a show of *Grand Guignol,* but rather a poetic play with certain philosophic implications. For that reason I avoided many obvious realistic details, which might have added to its naturalism. I asked that the room be designed without windows, so that time be kept ambiguous; and I requested lighting effects completely unmotivated from a rational point of view.

As for *The Telephone* everyone begged me to insert a few Noel Coward-ish lines in order to make the audience laugh. But I, as the stage director, knew that I, as the author, had never intended to laugh in that particular way: that in an opera bouffa the laughter must be in the orchestra rather than in the audience, and its humor completely self contained. When I see the way in which Rossini is staged at the Metropolitan I think of the remark attributed to him: 'I know I'm not Bach—but I also know I'm not Offenbach.'

Timing

Because of the predominant part played by timing it is advisable to discuss this term in a separate chapter which makes it possible to unite the several indications which have been made previously. In all his work the director must keep this essential term in mind. The score often contains minute directions in musical matters but rarely clear ones for the action. Particularly it is not always obvious on which chord or passage stage business should be executed.

Five factors, enumerated before, determine the dramatic interpretation; they are rhythm, tempo, key, volume and instrumentation. All five have to be analyzed carefully in order to define their influence on the staging. A great deal is left to the director's imagination who must feel and understand the music and action to detect the composer's intentions. To correlate music and action the director must pay special attention to floor plans, orchestral passages and holds.

The floor plan depends on the size of the stage and the auditorium, the number of settings, the general action and, very considerably, on the music. The often large number of participants necessitates a careful examination of the passages allotted to entrances and exits. Doors and platforms must be rather wide to facilitate all movements of such large bodies. In the first finale of Mozart's *The Magic Flute* only four and a half measures of an *allegro moderato* are designated for the entrance of the chorus. In big opera houses the director is obliged to employ more choristers for this opera than the composer had in mind and used in the premiere. In order to have the chorus on stage for its first cue the tradition is to have the men and women enter through wings left and right and a center door. It has even happened that they began to enter during the preceding recitative, a decision not at all suggested by the score. A proper solution for this scene depends on the width of the main door through which forty or more choristers can enter during the brief passage assigned to this movement. *The Marriage of Figaro* shows that the problem remains even when a small group appears on stage. In act one, two and a half bars are provided for the exit of the chorus. In this case a somewhat shallow setting is advisable. In addition the choristers should stand rather close to the door, usually upstage center, which will allow them to disappear without disturbing the succeeding recitative. Verdi in the third act of *La Traviata* wrote just four measures after Alfredo calls his friends to witness his accusation of Violetta. There are two possibilities: the conductor agrees on having half the choristers on stage for their cue which can easily be arranged; if the entire chorus has to be on stage, it is mandatory to have not one but two doors available for this fast entrance.

To elaborate on the relationship of floor plan and score would transgress the problem on hand, but one can at least point out the influence which musical passages exercise on dramaturgical ideas. Act three of *The Marriage of Figaro* is sometimes performed in two settings, and each act of *Der Rosenkavalier* has been played occasionally in two settings. Scenic solutions of this kind are

72

strictly related to the musical interludes available for shiftings; a few measures more or less can decisively affect the staging.

Orchestral passages, a term which refers to preludes, postludes and interludes, sometimes take up only a single measure, yet in other cases they fill entire pages of the score. Marches and dances also belong in this category. In romantic and veristic operas the dramatic interpretation is mostly related to the mood of such a passage, to a lesser degree to its rhythm. Yet in the works of Mozart, Gluck and other composers the rhythmical element should be examined first. They also pose the problem of finding the right transition from a recitative or dialogue to the aria or ensemble.

Passages to be danced are fairly easy to execute. It is almost impossible to fail in the entrance scene of Zerlina, Masetto and their friends in act one of *Don Giovanni*. The director should have no trouble moreover in finding the suitable rhythm for the last scene of Papageno and Papagena in *The Magic Flute*. The task is more complicated in a good part of act two of *I Pagliacci*, where certainly Nedda but also Tonio and Canio should move with dance-like steps and gestures. A typical example of an aria with an extremely extended prelude is Constance's *"Martern aller Arten"* in *The Abduction from the Seraglio*. Directors have given much thought to the interpretation of this overlong introduction. There have been attempts to relate the solo instruments (violin, violoncello, flute and oboe) to the characters of Constance and Selim respectively, a charming idea which however has no relation to Mozart's style. Perhaps we should be satisfied with Edward Dent's recommendation to eliminate nearly the entire prelude instead of trying to perform it as a pantomime. It is not simple to execute appropriately the passages at the end of act one in *La Traviata*. Violetta has a rather long recitative before her aria. The brief orchestral passages may serve her to make a gesture or take a few steps, but she must by all means avoid exaggerating realistically or to give the impression of getting ready for her bravura aria. She must not try moreover to move downstage soon; on the contrary she can remain upstage for quite a while, even during the *andantino*, played very softly by the orchestra.

The question of when to raise the curtain belongs to the topic of timing. Although the curtain sign in act one of *Carmen* appears on the fifth measure, some directors have waited until briefly before the male chorus sings, probably to save themselves the trouble of finding suitable business for the introductory music. Yet the hurrying passage is precisely needed for setting the mood of the opening scene as it provides the cause for the soldiers' first phrases. Another controversial curtain cue is found in *The Masked Ball*. In the scene where Amelia meets Riccardo near the gallows the curtain usually opens after about twenty bars, but it is more dramatic to open it with or after the first bar of the prelude and to use the music for slowly bringing up the lights and thus to create the mood for Amelia's entrance.

As to holds, we are concerned here with their value for the dramatic interpretation, not with their purely musical execution which prolongs a chord or a pause. For a precise synchronization of music and action, the passage leading to and that following the *fermata* must be analyzed in accord with the five factors previously listed. A *fermata* may denote the maintaining of a mood or a transition, either slow or fast, to a different one. If a transition is indicated, it is usually preferable to keep the mood unaltered for the duration of the hold and to begin the transition with the succeeding passage. It is theoretically impossible to determine the accurate length of a hold. In general this sign will double the basic value of a chord or pause, yet under extreme conditions it can be tripled or quadrupled. This matter must of course be discussed with the conductor lest uncertainty affect all concerned on stage and in the pit. A mere interruption of a mood is suggested in Osmin's aria, "*Solche hergelaufenen Laffen*", in the *Abduction*. A transition is delicately inserted in Figaro's *Se vuol ballare* in the change from an *allegro* to a *presto,* a transition sometimes neglected even in otherwise praiseworthy performances. One of the best known effects in *Carmen* is the scene in which the leading lady throws a flower at Don José. Whether the brief dialogue is spoken or whether she exclusively mimes her flirtation is of less importance. The main task is that Carmen raises her hand in tune with the music to throw the flower exactly at the end of the *fermata* so that Don José is hit and reacts on the following sharp chord. The success of Puccini's delightful comic opera, *Gianni Schicchi*, depends considerably on the right timing. Twice relatives believe they have found the will of a deceased man, twice there is first jubilation and then disappointment. In each case a hold offers a splendid opportunity for a quick transition. When later in the scene all characters are reading the will, the growing excitement and disillusionment are excellently illustrated in the orchestra. They all freeze in their expression with the last measure and pose during the hold until the orchestra suggests increasing anger and fury.

To explain verbally how to synchronize music and action is almost impossible. It is to be hoped, however, that the examples and explanations given in this brief delineation will suffice to guide the earnest student when he is confronted with this intricate problem. The main conclusion should be that important as the libretto is, it is more essential to probe into and to understand the musical score. A consideration of all the elements involved is needed to bring the dramatic action into perfect harmony with the music.

THE DESIGNER

The Basic Task

Many outstanding designers have worked on opera productions. Only a few can resist the fascination of this medium. Some of the latter are interested in opera but feel handicapped by the special problems involved and fear they will be frustrated in the exercise of their own artistic skill. It has also happened a few

74

times that designers have tried their hand at musical drama, notwithstanding their intellectual and emotional indifference to this particular field.

Any artist who intends to design settings for an opera must comprehend music as expression of mood, meaning that he must be sensitive to a musical atmosphere. There is a saying that "architecture is frozen music." Stone stands still; it is motionless. Music too has its straight lines, ornaments, volutes, curves, lights and shadows like architecture. But music is perpetually in motion. Unless the designer feels the difference of style in the music of a Gluck, a Mozart, a Wagner, a Debussy, a Verdi and a Rimsky-Korsakov, he should not attempt to mount their works. The interplay of word, movement and picture is the fundamental consideration for planning the settings for a drama; in opera, music is to be added as the predominant element. Feelings expressed in music and executed through action in space must be clearly conceived by the designer.

Of course, a thorough knowledge of all practical matters related to stage craft is a prerequisite. As lighting plays a great, often a decisive role in modern productions, this art and craft must be mastered. If the designer wants to be in charge of costuming and make-up, these fields must be studied too. Above all the artist needs a sense of style, sharpened by thoroughly probing into theatre history. Sketches and photographs of old and modern settings will give guidance to further studies. If the young designer has a preference for one or another of the contemporary conceptions, he ought to select works suitable for that particular concept. To submit all operas, no matter how different their styles, to the same treatment can bring the production into conflict with the work. Due to the emphasis on spectacle, inherent in the nature of opera, some designers still adhere to a modified version of romanticism. Others, disciples of the opposite extreme, eliminate almost all ornamental details and often come close to cubism. Yet music, even in its most abstract form, has an emotional appeal which must not be ignored. After some years of experimentation these designers have changed their views; their former bare platforms and stairs made room for more elaborate colorful designs.

There is no reason whatever to hold religiously to Victorian procedures. Since the turn of the century several new styles have been tried under the impact of principles propagated by Appia and Craig. Impressionism, expressionism, cubism, and constructivism have been applied to the lyric drama— alas, sometimes without the least discrimination and thus with fatal results. Yet all these concepts demonstrated definitely that, on the whole, opera can be visualized and staged in several ways. Mainly they discredited the two dimensional wings and backdrops which have definitely lost their function and should be discarded for good, a few exceptions notwithstanding. The approach should be to create a spatial setting, and this obliges the designer to think and to plan in terms of the architect and sculptor rather than in those of the painter.

In creating the environment for operatic action the designer like the stage director has to submit to special circumstances. The intimacy of the play production gives way to the spaciousness required by crowds of choristers, dancers and supernumeraries. Even operas without large groups can rarely be staged in smaller settings because of the largeness of the average auditorium and stage. Wide space is also needed for the singer's extended movements as against concentrated areas for actors. Changes of settings must indeed be executed within the given time of an interlude, as for instance, in *Tales of Hoffman* between the prologue and act one, and between act three and the epilogue.

These considerations, while limiting the artist's free creativity, at the same time point the way to imaginative use of simplified settings, color and light in a manner seldom offered in plays. The spatial form as expression of music becomes a most valuable factor of the artist's inspiration, and so does the variety needed for costumes and their ornaments.

The designer can indeed make good use of studies and experience in stage-craft and lighting for play production. Yet he must be fully conscious of the influence exercised by the musical style of a given work, which will demand some incisive deviations of principles that dictate the design of settings for the spoken plays. An appreciation of the following four points will help the young artist find the right approach:

1. Perception of the musico-dramatic atmosphere
2. A feeling for the dramatic beauty of spatial settings
3. A feeling for the symbolic effect of light, color and movement
4. An understanding of the functional distribution of space for the grouping of soloists, choristers, dancers and extras.

Some plays, and not merely those of the Elizabethan era, can be conceived with a modicum of scenery, even without any scenic effects, but most operas demand a visual materialization which expresses the mood and style of the music. The emphasis on spectacle should not induce the designer to consider himself the center of the production. His work is still subordinated to the over-all approach to create, in collaboration with the stage director, an environment for the singing performer. Besides, the settings must be related to the score and must never be an effect for effect's sake.

The usual procedure is that the designer studies the vocal score (not the libretto!) and then discusses the entire production with the director who basically determines the style and the floorplan. The designer needs accurate information about the number of participants in the chorus, the ballet and the group of extras, since these data determine his plans for the settings. The director should delineate, though perhaps only in general terms, the light plot. The properties should be discussed early. If the designer is in charge of costuming, more data about the style and number of costumes must be given. The designer needs a large amount of information before he can start drawing sketches—the more information he receives, the more it will enrich and facilitate his demanding work. It is advisable at an early stage of the preparation to invite the technical director and lighting designer to attend meetings with the stage director. If a specialist is engaged to devise the costumes, he too must participate in the planning from the beginning, as it is impossible to separate the various phases. As a matter of fact, all of them are subject to the general staging idea and its scenic realization which, as one cannot repeat enough, must conform to the musical style.

Mounting an Opera

On the basis of artistic requirements and technical possibilities the artist draws his plans. The exigencies include large acting areas, wide entrances, platforms of different levels. If the particular opera consists of scenes following each other with musical interludes, the time limit of this music also has to be considered. Since opera settings are, as a rule, rather high and complicated, their mounting ought to be planned in such a way that shifting takes the least feasible time. Very often the audience could be spared unnecessarily long intermissions during scene changes if designer and director had understood how to combine artistic and technical demands. In the provincial opera houses in Italy, settings of the overdone realistic period are still in use, causing sometimes intermissions of almost 45 minutes. Such extreme cases are no longer known in the United States, yet in some theatres intermissions are unduly long under the assumption that they are welcome for social reasons. Managers might as well realize that there are surely as many opera lovers in the audience as there are socialites who want to be seen rather than see a performance. One can safely assume that the audience in general enjoys the performance more if the atmosphere of a work is not destroyed by extended intermissions.

If an opera house possesses a good sized stage, equipped with all the modern paraphernalia such as a first-class fly system, a turn table, many wagons, a complex lighting set-up and a large crew plus strong financial backing, the most elaborate *mise en scène* can be devised. Yet technical luxuries are not synonymous with artistic achievements and they are seldom found in our civic and educational theatres, which must quite often do with inadequate means. These groups are fortunate if the available space is satisfactory. The lack of magnificent technical equipment makes it imperative to rely on dramatic imagination and technical ingenuity rather than gimmicks. Grandiose ideas alone give no assurance of great results. To adapt beautiful images to the means available in a theatre proves the artist's versatility. This does not compel the artist to compromise his integrity, it just means the elimination of frills and ornaments and a concentration on the essentials of a production. The expert proves his worth in designing artistic and, at the same time, efficacious and practical settings.

Platforms or perhaps a raked stage are an essential device to create the plasticity indispensable for an artistic presentation of opera. Platforms facilitate the arrangements of groups, they support the action and they help the singers, standing farther upstage, keep contact with the conductor. Through the use of several levels street scenes such as those in *Faust, La Bohème,* and *The Mastersingers* obtain a far more impressive picturization and movement, and garden and forest settings such as in *Faust* and *Martha* certainly look better and offer a greater variety for action. If a stage is equipped with a large trapdoor or an elevator in the upstage area, the designer has even more possibilities to create interesting settings. He can build an exit by means of a low platform or ramp in front of the trap with a staircase on the elevator itself leading to the lower level. Such a solution allows soloists and choristers to enter the stage from below and leave it going down. This dramatic effect can be arranged, for instance, in *Cavalleria Rusticana, Madame Butterfly* (act one), *Aida* (act three) and *The Masked Ball* (last scene).

Many of our civic auditoriums have a proscenium width too wide for intimate operas. Mozart's delicate works, except for *Idomeneo* and *The Magic Flute,* can be staged more effectively on a limited acting area which has a width of not more than forty feet. The usual opening of fifty and more feet is appropriate for works requiring a multitude of choristers and dancers. The unfavorable condition of so many stages should prompt the designer to narrow the opening by a second (false) proscenium frame containing doors or by placing low platforms and stairs left and right close to the curtain line. Let us hope that new theatre buildings will provide a movable second proscenium frame for widening and narrowing the opening in accordance with the designer's ideas. Low level platforms, covering the entire center area of the stage, will bring about the desired intimacy for light operas like *Don Pasquale* and *Cosi fan tutte.* Stairs may lead from the platforms to the downstage area so that arias and other scenes can be arranged close to the curtain line. Another method to restrict large acting areas is to build corners and to jog the flats. Thus act one of *Der Rosenkavalier* can be divided into two areas, a rather shallow alcove with the bed for the opening scene and a large and deep area on the opposite side. The last act of *Otello* gains more privacy by adding corners left and right; in one are a table and a chair, in the other a praying bench.

Quite interesting is the mounting of exterior settings in a modern manner. During the last two or three decades the use of square or rectangular acting areas has been more or less abandoned in favor of an irregular shape. This kind of contour permits the construction of appropriate settings on shallow stages. Streets can lead off stage at an angle or rooms can be erected in an almost triangular shape. The stages of most of our auditoriums being fairly wide allow the action to develop from one side to the other; but it is difficult to plan for the entrance of large crowds from center upstage if little or no space is available backstage. Here the designer can assist the stage director with a diagonal setting. Good opportunities for such a solution, either with or without additional platforms, stairs and ramps, are given in *Rigoletto, Martha, Faust, La Bohème* and *The Mastersingers.*

Rigoletto, in particular, poses an interesting challenge, for the two settings must include two sharply separate acting areas. On one side of the stage in act two the audience must see the garden and house of Rigoletto separated by a rather high wall from the street outside. The action changes from one area to the other through a little door and directly across the wall. Designer and director are in a dilemma: the garden is more important since most of the scenes are played in it. On the other hand, the street cannot be too narrow because there the appearance of the male chorus has to be seen by every spectator. Separate spotlights must be thrown on each area. In the last act two floors of Sparafucile's house and the embankment of a river, possibly with a bridge leading across it, are called for in the libretto. The second floor of the house may be omitted if the technical equipment or the height of the proscenium is unsatisfactory, but the dramatic effect is impaired if the spectators hear the Duke singing without seeing him in the room upstairs. The lighting problem is quite trying: the lower room is brightened by a lamp or candle while it is dark outside; hence an adequate set of spotlights and a good light control system are necessary.

As exterior settings are frequently required, a white painted canvas cyclorama is almost a necessity. This device, equally suitable to realistic and non-realistic settings, is also very practical as it allows the creation of marvelous pictures with a few set pieces. In our modern theatre the old-fashioned blue sky drop is unacceptable as is also the backdrop with a realistically painted landscape, or whatever is demanded, unless it is used within certain limits behind a portal or gangway. On the other hand, a large canvas filling the entire upstage line, painted in a stylized, even absurd and grotesque manner, can immensely enhance the effect of a specific production. If there is no cyclorama available, the designer must resort to known substitutes such as lowering the teaser, inserting borders, introducing faked arches. In a few cases it is possible to shift the open air setting to an interior: in *La Traviata* one scene is often played in a garden, but it is just as effective, even more so, in a large drawing room.

An effective simplification is easily achieved with a cyclorama consisting of drapes which mask the entire acting area. This method has been successfully applied to many plays, and it is equally impressive in operas. A few platforms and a few set pieces placed before the drapes create impressive symbolic interiors of a church and a castle, or a hilly landscape.

The designer and the stage director cannot expect to find all the modern marvels of technical equipment in their theatre. As long as the stage is large, which means there is sufficient space backstage left, right and in the rear, almost every problem can be solved through ingenuity. Space permits smooth and hence quick scene changes. Space makes everything clear and easy.

Lighting

Several special lighting effects are delineated in the comments on Staging Problems (see Appendix III). At this point the discussion is confined to a few general remarks. The basic conditions in college theatres are usually at least adequate, whereas those in our civic auditoriums are often unsatisfactory. The latter are provided with footlights and borderlights, but with few circuits, free for other instruments, which is an old fashioned arrangement utterly insufficient for modern purposes. In such cases it is imperative to bring in a series of spotlights and attach them to battens, light trees and other suitable solid places. As the switchboard is sometimes not equipped to handle these additional devices, it is necessary also to rent a portable switchboard. Borders and footlights may be used for general illumination but one should keep in mind that the latter can make faces flat and harm the painted flats and therefore should never be used at full volume.

The lighting designer or master electrician should rely mainly on spotlights of all kinds to brighten up areas and the performers moving in these areas. Every effort ought to be made to criss-cross the beams touching each area, and in order to create interesting effects and plasticity of the characters some spotlights should throw their beam from upstage (attached to a batten, or from a wing) toward downstage. As some books on lighting are still based on methods valid a generation ago, the designer and master electrician should acquaint themselves with recent productions in American and European opera houses.

The large acting area available for operatic productions makes the use of floodlights practical for general illumination and the use of spotlights for detailed effects. Great care must be employed to the lighting of the cyclorama which requires a special series of floodlights and possibly of strip lights too. Let us assume that modern theatres show a battery of spots installed in the auditorium; if this is not the case, spotlights should be attached to the balcony railing to help illuminate the downstage area. In operas as well as in musicals directors now and then like to have a spotlight follow the leading characters. Its handling is not easy unless a catwalk behind the proscenium is available. A light tower or high step ladder can be used in the wing but from such a position it is impossible to cover the entire stage. From an artistic point of view a follow spot should be employed most cautiously, for although it can intensify the dramatic mood, its perfect timing is a precarious task, since a slight deviation or too strong a volume will spoil a scene. The follow spotlight is very effective, if properly applied, when the Queen of the Night appears in *The Magic Flute* as she does not have to move much; it is more hazardous in *Faust* to follow Mephistopheles who never remains long in one place. In operettas and musicals this device can be rather impressive for the aria of a leading lady or man if it is not overdone.

Costuming

Mielziner's request that "no singer will bring his or her pet costume out of the wardrobe trunk" to his production should be taken to heart by all organizations, primarily those engaging guest singers. The designer, or the costumer, will thank him for this remark, for they certainly must loathe to see a good color scheme ruined by one or two costumes adorning the guest stars. This is by no means the only thing the costumer has to worry about; it is equally important that he insist on the selected style and shades of color for the costumes to be rented. Not all institutions can afford to have their own costumes made, because, unlike a play, which, on the average, requires 10 or 15 costumes or in some extraordinary cases up to 50, an opera with its choristers, dancers and extras may call for a hundred and more if a change of dresses is necessary in different acts, as, let us say, in *Carmen* and *Faust*. In the last scene of *The Mastersingers* 200 costumes are not unusual. No organization would spend so much money on a single production unless it planned to present, perhaps at a later date, other operas in which these costumes could be used again. Thus the events in *Faust* and *The Mastersingers* take place in the same country and at almost the same period of time. Similarly, some of Verdi's operas such as *Otello, Il Trovatore* and *Rigoletto* may be costumed. Many of the costumes used for the smugglers and common people in *Carmen* can easily be adapted to be shown in *Cavalleria Rusticana* and *I Pagliacci*.

The modern theatre has fortunately given up the verisimilitude for which the Duke of Saxe-Meiningen and Henry Irving were celebrated. An indication of a period is now artistically preferable to a copy of historic costumes. Greater leniency will also be a boon to the singer who needs more freedom than an actor. The latter can speak with a rather tight collar or vest; the singer, however, must be able to breathe freely and to obtain full support from his diaphragm. Some period costumes, furthermore, overload the character (heavy headgear, high boots, hoop skirts, high collars and long swords) and impair his singing in action. The designer can alleviate the singer's plight by taking off some weight from hats and crowns, widening collars and belts, and inventing other little tricks. Opera costumes should be so cut that they give the singer all the necessary body freedom. In designing them consideration is to be given

1. the style of the music
2. the period of the opera
3. the character of the role
4. the personality of the singer

Whether they are made in the shop of an educational institution or rented, care must be taken that every detail suits the character. The habit of dressing leading singers better than members of the supporting cast and choristers can still be witnessed. This is particularly true of guests who prefer to bring their own costumes. It is absurd to see Sergeant Don José dressed in beautiful riding boots while his lieutenant wears ordinary shoes with leggings, simply because the latter is a minor role. The same thing applies to leading characters who are either poor or are going through a change of fortune during the performance. Manon, in the last act of the opera, is a prisoner, supposed to be worn out and downtrodden; she certainly should not be as well dressed as in the previous acts.

The stage has a realism of its own not quite synonymous to the realism or the naturalism of the fine arts in general. Make-up has to be applied in keeping with the specific conditions in the opera and the particular character. Well-groomed wigs and beards are out of place in storm and prison. The designer should plan such details in connection with costumes and settings. He should also distinguish between various characters. Mimi, Gilda, and Susanna often look alike except for their period dresses; too little attention has been paid to hair-do and make-up. Dramatic truth should never be neglected for the sake of personal vanity or ornamental beauty. As the modern trend is against the use of wigs and beards, the make-up man and his immediate supervisor, the designer, should spend all the more time in planning the characteristic appearance of the singers.

DESIGNER'S NOTE

Each of the following twelve designs executed for this book is an attempt to illustrate some phase of simplified production. The first, *La Bohème,* Act III, is in the tradition of the Italian School of scene painting and relies heavily on the services of a highly skilled scene painter as well as a great deal of construction for its execution. The *Carmen* setting, on the other hand, could be constructed of simple frames covered with burlap and detailed with the application of shutters of slats of wood and bits of drapery.

The designs for *Tales of Hoffman* were developed to simplify the shifting of scenery and require only simple line drawings and large color areas for their visual effect. Their theatrical quality is further enhanced by the exposed scene shifts and simple effects simply achieved. The works of Wagner present problems of a different sort that must be solved by other means. The *Parsifal* design is of the simplest sort depending for its theatrical quality upon colorful banners and expressive light from the implied great rose windows off stage left. The scale of this design is enhanced by the unseen distances beyond the view of the audience.

The light operas, particularly those which are generally called "period pieces" present a problem of another kind. In the *Marriage of Figaro* sketch it is solved by the use of a false proscenium with simple inset pieces. This sort of setting magnifies the always present necessity to execute even the smallest detail with the greatest skill at one's command. A poor bench or badly scaled pot of flowers can destroy the entire effect of a well designed setting.

The designs for *Il Trovatore* approach the style of grand opera and its complications. Each scene is developed to use rolling screens and the introduction of one or two units used for that single scene. Steps, balustrades and platforms are used again and again in different combinations as can be seen by referring to the accompanying floorplans.

The final two designs for *Orfeo* are Appia-like in their simplicity. In the Act II design the dependence is upon light. The act begins on a darkened stage and as we hear the voice of Orpheus the orange and red light at the center back begin to glow. As the light of the concentric circles grows accompanying the music we see Orpheus descend the winged platform to the center as the shades and furies swarm about below. When at last his sweet voice is welcomed he descends to the center below.

The present day scene designer who approaches the problems of operatic production would do well to remind himself that music is the language of inner life. Its proper expression in visual terms develops from a pictorial idea, not a visual experience, and the excessive concern with the real world of "things" may defile his vision and thereby his work.

John R. Rothgeb

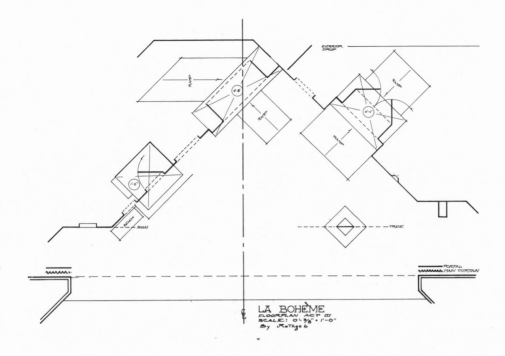

LA BOHÈME
FLOORPLAN ACT III
SCALE: 0'-3/8" = 1'-0"
By Rothgeb

LA BOHEME , ACT III

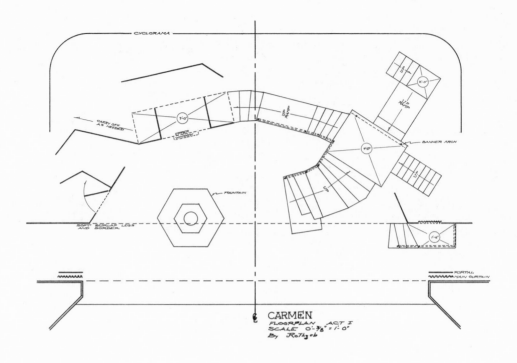

CARMEN
FLOORPLAN ACT I
SCALE 0-⅜" = 1'-0"
By Rothaycob

CARMEN ACT I

86

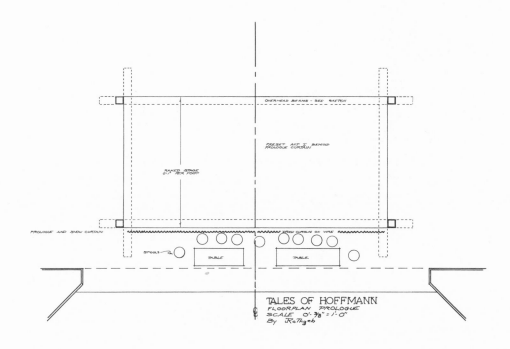

TALES OF HOFFMANN
FLOORPLAN PROLOGUE
SCALE 0'-⅜" = 1'-0"
By Rothgeb

<u>THE TALES OF HOFFMANN</u> PROLOGUE

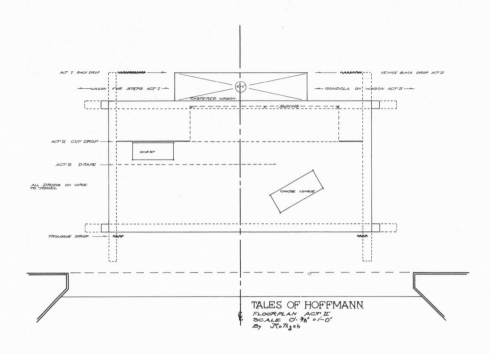

TALES OF HOFFMANN
FLOORPLAN ACT II
SCALE 0'-3/8" = 1'-0"
By Rothgeb

ACT I BACK DROP
WAGON FOR STEPS ACT I
CASTERED WAGON
ACT II CUT DROP
CHEST
ACT II DRAPE
ALL DROPS ON WIRE TO TRAVEL
CHAISE LONGUE
PROLOGUE DROP
VENICE BACK DROP ACT II
GONDOLA ON WAGON ACT II
AWNING

THE TALES OF HOFFMANN ACT II

88

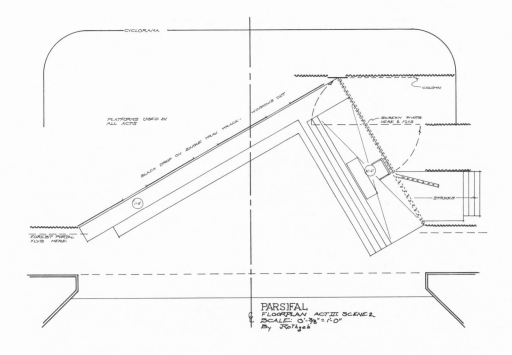

CYCLORAMA

PLATFORMS USED IN
ALL ACTS

BLACK DROP ON SINGLE TRAV TRACK

WINDOWS CUT

COLUMN

SCREEN PIVOTS
HERE & FLYS

STRIKES

FOREST PORTAL
FLYS HERE

PARSIFAL
FLOORPLAN ACT III SCENE 2
SCALE: 0'-3/8" = 1'-0"
By Rothgeb

PARSIFAL, ACT III, SCENE 2

89

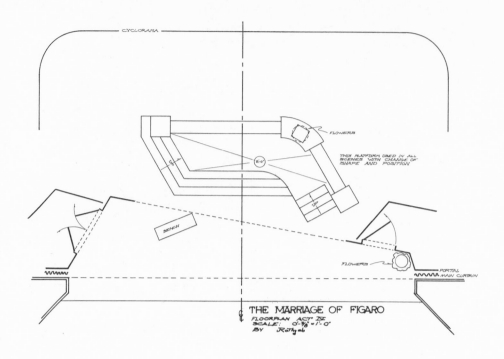

CYCLORAMA

FLOWERS

THIS PLATFORM USED IN ALL
SCENES WITH CHANGE OF
SHAPE AND POSITION

UP

BENCH

FLOWERS

PORTAL
MAIN CURTAIN

THE MARRIAGE OF FIGARO
FLOORPLAN ACT IV
SCALE: 0'-3/8" = 1'-0"
BY Rothgab

THE MARRIAGE OF FIGARO ACT IV

90

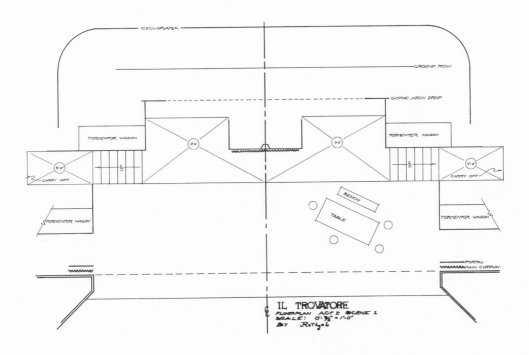

IL TROVATORE
FLOORPLAN ACT I SCENE 1
SCALE: 0'-3/8" = 1'-0"
BY R.Tigab

IL TROVATORE, ACT I, SCENE 1

91

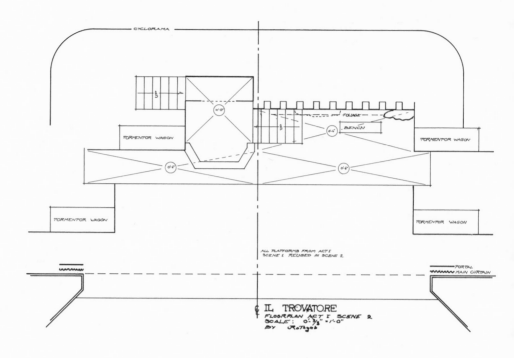

CYCLORAMA

FOLIAGE

BENCH

TORMENTOR WAGON

TORMENTOR WAGON

TORMENTOR WAGON

TORMENTOR WAGON

ALL PLATFORMS FROM ACT I
SCENE I. REUSED IN SCENE 2.

PORTAL
MAIN CURTAIN

IL TROVATORE
FLOORPLAN ACT I SCENE 2
SCALE: 0'-3/8" = 1'-0"
BY Rothgob

IL TROVATORE, ACT I, SCENE 2

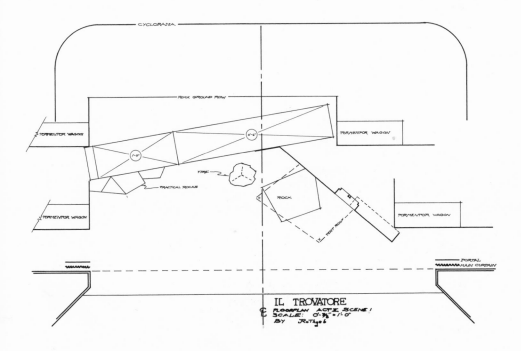

CYCLORAMA

ROCK GROUND ROW

TORMENTOR WAGON

TORMENTOR WAGON

TORMENTOR WAGON

TORMENTOR WAGON

PRACTICAL ROCKS

TYRE

ROCK

TENT ROW

PORTAL

MAIN CURTAIN

IL TROVATORE
FLOORPLAN ACT II, SCENE 1
SCALE: 0'-¾" = 1'-0"
BY R. Thjob

IL TROVATORE, ACT II, SCENE 1

93

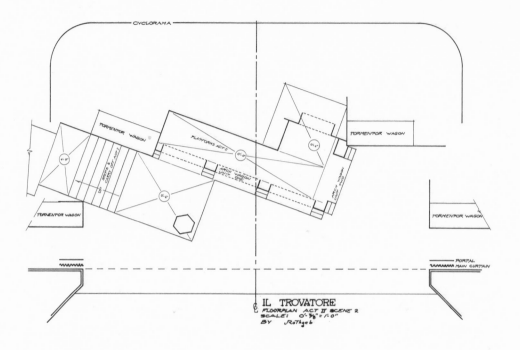

IL TROVATORE
FLOORPLAN ACT II SCENE 2
SCALE: 0'-3/8" = 1'-0"
BY Rothgeb

IL TROVATORE, ACT II, SCENE 2

94

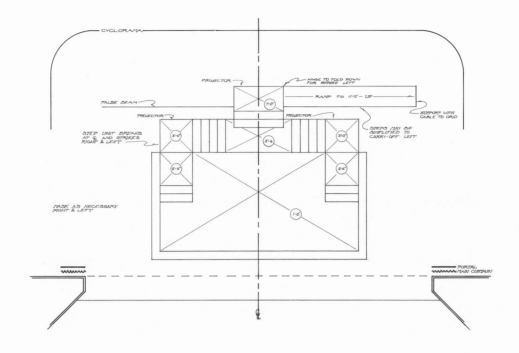

CYCLORAMA

PROJECTOR

HINGE TO FOLD DOWN
FOR STRIKE LEFT

FALSE BEAM

RAMP TO 1'-0" — UP

7'-0"

SUPPORT WITH
CABLE TO GRID

PROJECTOR

PROJECTOR

STEP UNIT BREAKS
AT ℄ AND STRIKES
RIGHT & LEFT

3'-0"

5'-6"

3'-0"

STEPS MAY BE
SIMPLIFIED TO
CARRY-OFF LEFT

2'-4"

2'-4"

MASK AS NECESSARY
RIGHT & LEFT

1'-0"

PORTAL
MAIN CURTAIN

℄

ORFEO ACT II

95

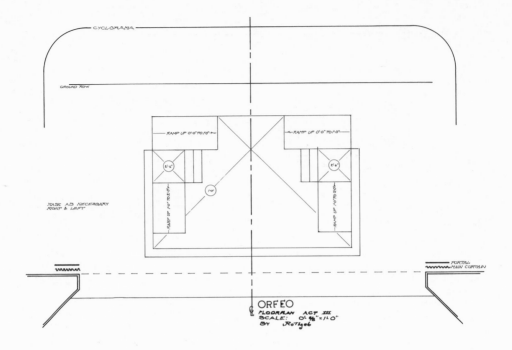

CYCLORAMA

GROUND ROW

RAMP UP 0'-0" TO 1'-0"   RAMP UP 0'-0" TO 1'-0"

8'-6"   8'-6"

MASK AS NECESSARY
RIGHT & LEFT

RAMP UP 1'-0" TO 2'-0"   RAMP UP 1'-0" TO 2'-0"

1'-0"

PORTAL
MAIN CURTAIN

ORFEO
FLOORPLAN ACT III
SCALE: 0'-¾"=1'-0"
BY Rothgeb

ORFEO, ACT III

THE GROUPS

The Orchestra

Among the groups, the orchestra ranks first not alone in importance but in difficulty of assignment as well. Upon the orchestra rests much responsibility for a successful performance. Beginning with Romanticism composers have more and more elevated the orchestra from the task of accompaniment to a prime means of expressing the mood. Consequently the orchestra members should be well trained and experienced musicians. In smaller cities it is almost impossible to procure enough experienced instrumentalists, yet this unfortunate condition should not cause the producer to reduce the orchestra to a great degree or to use a piano together with a few musicians. If a city is eager to have good productions, those in charge should try everything to organize and to develop a satisfactory orchestral body. The next step is then to mould all the players into an integrated whole, a task which takes much time and much effort.

One phase of this task is to acquaint the musicians with the problems involved in playing in an orchestra pit. Those accustomed to participating in symphonies and bands find themselves suddenly in a rather narrow and elongated space instead of the wide and deep concert platform. The player, unable to hear his colleagues farther off, depends far more on his nearest neighbors. Frequently the available space is insufficient, causing the desks to be cramped. Rare is the pit where musicians can sit and play in comfort. The light on the desks can be bothersome too, and sometimes it is difficult to see the conductor's baton clearly. Of greater consequence is the fact that the conductor has to watch primarily the ensemble on stage, since the singers, using no score, rely largely on him for cues. Hence he must be able to trust his musicians, who in the great opera houses are so experienced and sensitive that they sometimes straighten out an error on the stage before the conductor gives the signal to do so.

The conductor's preoccupation with the singers and choristers puts a strain on the players in the pit who have to watch with extreme attentiveness their score as well as the conductor. Furthermore, a slight change in a tempo, caused by nervousness on the stage, makes it advisable for every musician to take care of some cues himself instead of waiting for the conductor's sign. More difficulties arise when, for lack of experienced players, some instruments are eliminated. Although it is the conductor's task to prepare the orchestral material for rehearsals, drawing in two of four French horns or two of three trombones, each musician should understand this kind of work well enough to be able to advise about it, or even to do it himself. Not many conductors know all the instruments and their possibilities; often they lean heavily on the collaboration of their musicians.

Perhaps the most delicate task is the execution of a *recitativo accompagnato*.

Much depends on the clarity and accuracy of the conductor's beat, but each musician must be alert. In these scenes, more than in any others, mistakes are perceptible to the whole audience. Despite the most exacting rehearsals, the conductor for one reason or another may be obliged somewhat to modify his beat in the performance. In a newly formed group of instrumentalists each individual is expected to work hard and concentrate on his particular part. Consideration for the singer makes it also imperative that markings of volume and intensity should be interpreted with caution. It is to be stressed time and again that voices must not be drowned out by the tonal waves of the orchestra; singers should always be heard and even understood most of the time. Therefore the volume of the orchestra has to be held down. The limitation of the human voice, compared with the potentialities of massed instruments, places on orchestra and conductor the responsibility to keep within corresponding bounds. Dynamic indications in older scores should be played with a sort of consistent relativity, especially when the singer's portion is more essential than that of the orchestra. Thus *forte* becomes *mezzoforte*, as a rule *mezzoforte* becomes *piano*, *piano pianissimo*. Instrumentalists experienced in opera know this, and can correctly interpret the markings in the score. Some modern composers have taken the utmost pains in this regard; in their works the musician can execute the markings precisely as indicated in his part.

In conclusion it may be stated that it is the common lot of the orchestra player in concert and the one in opera to subordinate his artistic personality to the ensemble except in solo passages, which are few and far between. He is expected to be a master of his instrument, but not permitted to shine. Unless the instrumentalist is willing to suppress any false ambition, he cannot become a useful member of an orchestra. Playing in operatic performances puts additional strain on his nerves. Aside from general requirements of knowledge and experience he must

1. give utmost attention to the conductor;
2. listen to the singer when accompanying him especially in recitatives while, at the same time, watching the conductor;
3. grow accustomed to conditions peculiar to the pit which make it impossible to keep contact with some instrumental groups and which are sometimes so cramped that they further aggravate his playing.

In engaging musicians for an operatic production, it is wise to look first for those who have played symphonic music. Members of a band have to learn more before they are completely adapted to the new challenge of joining a string body. There is no doubt however that most instrumentalists are very eager to work in the pit where they acquire valuable experience in an exciting artistic venture.

The Chorus

To assemble a satisfactory, yes, a good chorus is hardly a serious problem. In colleges and other educational institutions the main trouble is to schedule the many necessary rehearsals so that they do not overlap with other activities. A workable solution is to form a special chorus which is free to concentrate on the task ahead. This can easily be arranged in the large universities, but smaller institutions also ought to try to organize a separate chorus for opera productions. Civic companies rarely have any difficulty in attracting good singers for their chorus. There are many young, middle-aged and older men and women willing and able to devote their free time to an enjoyable task. Usually these people are extremely cooperative and anxious to do their share in achieving an outstanding performance. Their lack of experience is balanced by good will and energy.

The choristers have different backgrounds. Some come from church choirs, others from glee clubs, while some are simply housewives or office workers without any previous vocal training. Some voice training is desirable but not vital. A voice, good in timbre and range, is satisfactory. Adequate stage appearance is an asset—this does not mean beauty. Stage people, like common people, may have all sorts of figures and faces; extreme types, though, either too tall or too short, too thin or too stout, can be at some disadvantage. It is important for the chorister to possess a good memory for words and music. Indispensable to participation in a chorus are ability to sight-read, to stay on pitch, and to keep rhythm, willingness to cooperate and enjoyment in the work.

These are the requirements for choristers in general, in educational and civic organizations. Standards are of course higher for a professional chorus singer, who must have proper voice training, if not as extensive as that of a soloist. In the choruses of our opera houses there are usually some members who joined in order to acquire stage experience, while preparing for a career as soloists. Many who do not succeed remain in the chorus, satisfied to receive a small role now and then.

In the civic and educational theatre, participating in the chorus rates highly in the young singer's training as a kind of apprenticeship; and the opera-lover appreciates the opportunity to become conversant with the music and many phases of the production and to observe from close range the soloists, in some cases, famous singers.

Great care must be taken in assigning the applicant to his correct voice group, for negligence here can damage both the individual voice and the quality of the choral tone. Mezzo-soprano and baritone are particularly prone to crop up in the high or the low part, where they do not belong. Striving for high notes strains their voice; in trying to force a voice down, they mar its timbre. Especially in a small group such mistakes are costly to the total effect. It is the one blunder which applicant and chorus master must beware, and indeed it is the only one of which they need be afraid.

A few well-trained voices will heighten the brilliance of tone, and an experienced chorus master can raise the quality of the singing in a surprisingly short period. His personality and the example of a few trained members will

99

stimulate the beginners who thus will quickly overcome their nervousness or timidity. A good chorus soon endears itself to the audience. The spirit of team-work and the knowledge of contributing to an artistic accomplishment gives deep satisfaction. For the choristers it is a feeling of pride to support a worthy cause and to share in its success. To strengthen this feeling it may be a good idea to encourage the chorus members to organize themselves so that they can meet during the "dead" season and moreover have a chance to discuss, through their officers, mutual problems with the leaders of the civic opera association.

The Ballet

A well choreographed and well danced ballet greatly enhances an operatic performance. As ballets are an integral part of many works and a charming addition to others in which they are of an incidental nature, it is essential for every opera group early to ponder the organization of a ballet group whose ef-forts are completely devoted to opera. Perhaps it is asking too much to aim at the highest standards, but those anxious to develop an opera company ought to realize that it is practically not feasible to discover many experienced dancers in an average city. Neither are educational institutions assured of a sufficient number of good dancers. Dancing is an exacting art form and many years of training are required to prepare girls and boys for the participation in public performances. The best approach is to engage a first-class ballet master or mistress who is also an imaginative choreographer. Under this guidance and leadership talented dancers could be pooled from ballet schools which exist in nearly every city. Some colleges may use the same procedure, but many of our educational institutions now offer courses in ballet or eurythmics, and a few even have a ballet division. With such a start the initiation and development of an adequate ballet can proceed. The young dancers will welcome the new challenge, and all opera aficionados will be highly pleased with the added attraction of ballet scenes.

Dancing in opera requires understanding and knowledge of various styles. So-called ballroom dancing is of little help except in operettas and in a few modern operas. Even a waltz is often danced in stylized fashion. Specific empha-sis is to be placed on folk and period dances, which should be part of the training. Scanning the list of operas we note that almost all countries and periods are represented. As operas are composed in divers styles, the dancers need an adequate background in both the classic ballet and modern (character) dance. Different styles of operatic works should not be subjected to the same treatment, which means that they should not all be danced in the same manner.

The brief dance scenes in *Rigoletto*, *The Mastersingers* and *Faust* give the beginner no particular difficulty. But *Aida* and *Carmen*, to mention just two works, demand an almost perfect technique aside from a sense of form and rhythm. Only an experienced ballet group should undertake the assignment to execute the dances in Gluck's *Iphigenia* or Handel's *Julio Cesare*. In some operas the director and the choreographer may want to expand the part of the

100

ballet. Successful experiments in which the chorus part was expressed by dancers have been accomplished since the twenties. Under such an arrangement the chorus is located in the pit or sits on platforms stage left and right. All actions are mimed by the dancers while the choristers sing. This solution provides much greater mobility since the dancers can move freely, whereas the choristers would be handicapped in their movements. Examples in which the ballet group can take over the chorus' action are Handel's *Acis and Galatea*, Gluck's *Orfeo* and Rimsky-Korsakov's *The Golden Cockerel.* Much depends on the talent and the experience of the choreographer. If he is moreover an excellent teacher he will succeed within a surprisingly short time to raise the standard of his performers. Hard work, long hours and increasing cooperation compensate for lack of experience under the direction of an outstanding ballet master. One additional hint may be given before the section on ballet will be closed. The artistic leaders of an opera group ought to ponder earnestly assigning the direction of an entire production to a choreographer. This has happened in leading European houses, and the success proved that if such a man or woman possesses the qualities described in the section on the director, he can contribute his sense of rhythm and apply it to his entire ensemble. It is an experiment worthy of consideration.

Dancing is above all a career for girls, although many young men have likewise been very successful in this field. A professional dancer has to begin her training at an early age. In general, parents have their children take dancing lessons as an educational occupation and as a means of developing grace and poise. A professional career should not be considered unless it is clear that the youngster is physically strong and healthy enough to endure the long and quite strenuous practicing required of a dancer. The more variegated the training, the better is the chance of securing a position with a professional group. If the ballet student intends to specialize she will do well to look for employment with a particular ballet company. Those who are anxious to dance in the modern musical must know more than the average dancer since they must be prepared to act and to sing in addition to dancing.

The Extras

Most operas need not only a chorus and a ballet but also a third group, the extras or supernumeraries. On occasion it is possible for choristers and dancers to take over the mute parts of the extras but, as a rule, a special group of men and women is called in for this task. Superficially the work of the extras seems to be easy; there is apparently no more to do than carry a spear, follow a knight, or simply stand around on the stage. And yet it is wrong to look at this sort of work only as a means of attending a performance free of charge, as it were. Any stage business properly executed needs concentration and some ability. There are swords and other weapons to be handled, a sedan-chair to be carried, drinks to be served. In many scenes extras really participate in the action as individuals, the only difference being that unlike the choristers they do

101

not sing. But they have to act so well that their movements are integrated into the particular scenes and their appearance is as inconspicuous as possible to the audience. Men and women with some experience in high school or college dramatic activities are best suited for this type of work.

The quality of the extras depends on the willingness of each member and their training by the stage director. All should consider the work essential. The extra ought to be conscious of the fact that any activity poorly performed on stage may very well spoil a scene otherwise beautifully presented. He should control any stage fright, as well as overeagerness. In a great measure it is the director's task to incorporate him fully into the ensemble. If a work assigns difficult and complex action to the extras or if very few rehearsals are scheduled for an average task, an assistant stage manager and perhaps a few singers of small roles are willing to put on costumes and serve as leaders for the large group of extras. All extras must realize that, though their part is mentioned last on the listing of characters, their wholehearted cooperation is needed for the success of the production.

REHEARSALS AND PERFORMANCE

THE PRELIMINARY WORK

Auditions

For all operatic groups which take their productions seriously, auditions are a necessity, because without them selecting and casting operas is done haphazardly. Civic and educational organizations, however, proceed in different ways. The first is primarily interested in finding choristers and aspirants for minor roles, except for those groups which are eager to cast as many parts as possible from available local talent. Most civic associations rely on guests for the leading roles, but colleges and conservatories consider participation of their students in productions indispensable to their program and therefore the appearance of guests remains an exception. It occurs, if not as a special attraction, chiefly when no suitable singer can be discovered among the students, graduates or even staff members. The casting of students and teachers together, incidentally, is quite a delicate matter for conductor and director who feel frustrated under these circumstances in correcting their colleagues in front of their students.

The audition procedure of a school is rather simple—it might better be called a try-out. Voice teachers know the capabilities and potentialities of their students very well and thus can easily give clear and definite information about voice and general attitude which will be of great help to the artistic leaders. The arrangement can be informal, perhaps with notice given only a week before the audition. Students, considered mature and ready, can be invited to sing in the auditorium or recital hall to show the teachers in charge of casting the quality and range of voices. The committee of civic associations may consist of the conductor, the stage director and, under favorable conditions, some experts from among the citizens such as voice teachers. These auditions must be conducted more thoroughly than those in a college, since the applicants are hardly known, or not at all, to the jury. Two arias or significant passages are a minimum that should be sung. If a candidate seems to be handicapped at the first hearing by stage fright or a cold, he should, by all means, be given a second chance.

It is very helpful to keep precise information on each applicant for further reference. These questions should be examined by the committee members:

1. What is the range and timbre of the voice?
2. Is the voice well trained?

3. For what type of roles is the applicant particularly suited?
4. How is his appearance and stage presence?
5. Is his musical talent satisfactory?
6. Is he dependable?
7. Is his health in good condition?
8. What is his experience?

There is a tendency to put too great an emphasis on the voice, while other points are neglected or only touched upon. It is as impossible to judge the potentialities of a singer by merely listening to his voice as it is to judge the dramatic abilities of an actor from his merely reading from a play. The applicant should be requested to act, not only to sing. Otherwise the risk of casting is twice as great. Some young singers who appear to be adequate at an audition are helpless as soon as they have to act. In educational institutions participation in courses and the opera workshop gives the teachers an opportunity to observe the students. Officers of civic groups, lacking this advantage, should make it a point to have the applicant act out an aria. They ought to realize that vocal and dramatic abilities can truly be judged only in a performance. Therefore they should expose beginners first in small roles before they entrust them with leading parts, and they should engage their guest singers on the basis of personal knowledge of their stage performance.

During the audition, committee members should make notes, especially about the applicant's voice. Range, handling of registers, breath control, purity of pitch, and clear rhythm are the essentials. Even though the singer's weak points thus observed may in the final conclusion not outweigh his strong ones, discovering them in time may save disappointment later on. Since ensemble singing is the main feature in many operas, it is advisable to have applicants sing a duet or even a trio in order to hear how the voices blend. Testing their aptitude in sight reading can be profitable, too. For the production of an opera with dialogue, or an operetta, the aspirant's competence in speech must also be determined. His stage deportment and acting talent in general are manifested when he presents an entire aria or scene. After the audition the committee members compare notes, and the last decision is made by the artistic director. The result is kept on file together with the address and availability (days, evenings or afternoons) of each singer. If possible a photograph should be included and also reviews of former artistic activities, items which can be valuable in rechecking an application.

It is better to separate the auditions for soloists and choristers. In all probability nearly everyone will apply for a solo part, although experience has shown that there are always singers who merely wish to join the chorus. Not that they think themselves inferior to others, but because they realize that they have not the time available for rehearsals as a role would warrant; sometimes they are also nervous, and hope to overcome this impediment by acting and singing with a group. In colleges, teachers in charge of voice classes and glee clubs know their students well enough to decide beforehand who can sing a solo part and who should join the chorus. The formation of the latter ought to be left almost entirely to the chorus master, who is a specialist in his field and is best qualified to select voices so that the various voice groups are well blended. This concerns the relationship between male and female voices and also the blending within each group (tenor-bass and soprano-alto).

Many organizations have more women than men in their chorus. The reason of course is that more women apply for membership, or that the existing glee club of a college has more "coed" members. If the difference is small in comparison to the number of choristers, it is irrelevant; but there have been cases of such a misproportion, as for instance ten men against twenty women, that the artistic effect of both sound and action was gravely impaired. Whenever feasible there should be an almost equal number of both voice groups; in a large chorus a few women more will not influence the timbre.

Selecting Operas

An audition is rarely arranged for the purpose of becoming acquainted with singers in general, but in order to find suitable singers for a special opera, or operas, which a civic group or college intends to prepare. First the particular work—or works—must be chosen, and this is a hard task. The requisite is that all those concerned with it must know the vocal requirements of a great number of operas in addition to the problems involved in their production such as acting, settings, costumes. Conductors and directors usually possess this knowledge, but it would be better if their collaborators could also acquire it. A few books provide the essential data but knowing these does not suffice to make decisions on intricate details. The description of the requirements is no substitute for studying the vocal score.

Opera groups concentrate on about forty operas from which they make their selection. These standard works are the best known and the most popular ones. The task is to choose among them the particular opera which can be produced at a given time. The possibilities will be quickly reduced if the questions listed below are carefully scrutinized:

1. Are suitable singers available?
2. Can the artistic and technical requirements be met by the orchestra, the chorus and the ballet?
3. Can the technical problems be solved with the available means?
4. Can the expenses of the production be carried?
5. Has the opera a satisfactory audience appeal?

These questions have to be examined from every angle before a decision can be reached. The first is the most significant one for without a good ensemble of singers, especially for the leading roles, the performance is doomed to failure. It is of the utmost importance indeed that the right type of voices be found; range and timbre must fit the part from every aspect. Once a young singer was chosen for a role only because his voice resembled that of a star who had sung it. This turned out to be a fallacy, in the first place because no two voices are alike and, secondly, the voice of a beginner and that of a seasoned singer should never be compared. Rehearsals and performances are such a terrific strain on a young singer that his voice must be mature enough to withstand the ordeal without ill after-effects. This point should be checked and rechecked conscientiously. A casting mistake in this respect can cause irreparable damage to the singer and the performance alike. It takes more than theoretical knowledge to select and to cast an opera; experience in listening to performances and to many singers is a substantial portion of the preliminary work.

Selecting and casting an opera are closely interrelated; the one cannot be considered without the other. Hence those responsible for the choice of an opera should be familiar with all operatic roles and their specific requirements as to range and timbre. In addition, files giving information on potential soloists should be explicit in describing the various types of voices. For instance, the term tenor is insufficient, being too general. A heavy tenor sings the Wagnerian roles like Siegmund, Siegfried, Tannhaeuser, and sometimes, Radames, Otello and Canio. Yet Verdi requires a higher range than the German composer. Thus Siegmund can easily be sung by a tenor whose lower and middle registers are strong, but whose high notes (b flat, b) are weak. To invite such a singer to take on Radames or Canio, merely because of his success as Siegmund, would be a fatal mistake. Then there is the lyric tenor, called also the Italian type, whose field embraces Rodolfo, Cavaradossi, Faust, Des Grieux, among others. A very light tenor voice will be entrusted with roles like Almaviva (*The Barber of Seville*), Hans (*The Bartered Bride*), and Pinkerton (*Madame Butterfly*). The *tenore buffo* sings Pedrillo (*The Abduction from the Seraglio*), Monostatos (*The Magic Flute*), Beppo (*I Pagliacci*) and Goro (*Madame Butterfly*); often he takes over parts that are called *tenore secondo*. Sometimes voices do not fit entirely into the enumerated categories; lyric-dramatic tenors can well be cast as Manrico or Radames, a light tenor as David in *The Mastersingers*, a role which can also be sung by the *tenor buffo*.

The baritone and bass parts are likewise to be subdivided. A Figaro in *The Barber of Seville* cannot vocally manage the same character in Mozart's *Figaro*; this is an obvious case, whereas it is not so easy to decide who could sing the Mozart role: *basso profundo*, *basso cantante*, and even *basso buffo* have performed it successfully. Here, the whole personality has to be taken into consideration; a rather stiff bass with little acting ability will be a failure, whereas that same singer can be a great success as the High Priest in Aida or as Sarastro in *The Magic Flute*. In a general way the voices can be organized in the following categories: heavy-dramatic, lyric-dramatic, lyric, light; high range and low range. If a voice fits the part of Germont (*La Traviata*), it is hardly suitable for Amonasro, or Escamillo, the latter being more dramatic than lyric, demanding a sonorous voice of dark timbre. Attention should be called to the fact that some minor characters in French and Italian operas are not definitely fixed as to their type even though they are written in the tenor clef. Conductor and director may choose a baritone or tenor depending on which one fits better into the ensemble as a whole.

What has been said about the men's voices is also valid for the women's. It is evident that a soprano with a voluminous voice is needed for Isolde and Bruenhilde. Leonore *(Fidelio)* is also the role of the heavy dramatic singer, and yet it has sometimes been presented by dramatic-lyric sopranos who would usually sing Sieglinde and Elizabeth, and also Leonore *(Il Trovatore),* Aida and Tosca. The pure lyric voice claims Madame Butterfly, Mimi, Manon and Elsa. The coloraturas fall into two groups: the dramatic coloratura with parts like the Queen of the Night and, occasionally, even Verdi's Leonore; and the light coloratura whose parts are Rosina, Zerlina *(Don Giovanni)* Filine *(Mignon),* Sophie *(Der Rosenkavalier),* and Musette. Among the sopranos too, there are voices as well as roles that cannot be classified. Here is a brief list of soprano characters which are best cast individually: Cherubino, Susanna, Elizabeth, Venus, Mimi, Marschallin, and Salome. Octavian *(Der Rosen-kavalier),* written for a mezzo-soprano, is often sung by a light dramatic soprano, primarily when her voice has a warm dark tone. Ortrud must sometimes be taken over by the dramatic soprano when the available mezzo cannot reach the sustained high notes particularly in act two. Kundry *(Parsifal)* is another dramatic mezzo part frequently cast with a soprano. Mignon, composed for a mezzo, is sometimes sung by a lyric soprano. Carmen, coveted by all singers, should preferably be given to the dramatic alto or mezzo. If a soprano takes on this role some passages must be transcribed since she cannot sustain the low register required in Bizet's score. This is no problem, for most vocal scores contain a transcription of these phrases. It is an exception nowadays to hear the role of Rosina sung as Rossini composed it, namely by an alto, because it is virtually impossible to discover a singer able to execute the original version; as a rule, a soprano coloratura sings Rosina. There are a few genuine alto roles, such as Orfeo, Erda, Amneris, Azucena, Marthe *(Faust),* Nancy *(Martha).* During the past decades some male characters, written for alto, have been performed by men; lately so, Siebel *(Faust)* and Orlofsky *(The Bat)* and even Orfeo. The almost unanimous opinion among connoisseurs and opera-goers in general, is that the change is all for the better dramatically and musically alike. As for some minor parts it is again up to the artistic director to decide whether a soprano, mezzo or alto is to be cast; this depending on the requirements in ensembles or the availability of singers.

At first sight Wagnerian operas seem to pose unsurmountable difficulties for the singers, particularly young ones. Yet a close examination will show that, in some of these works, the vocal difficulties are not greater than in a Verdi opera; they are only different. In cities in which the master of Bayreuth is a favorite, an opera group can therefore consider the production of *The Flying Dutchman, Lohengrin, The Valkyrie* or *Parsifal.* The latter, by the way, has become an annual event at Indiana University.

A task of foremost importance is the blending of the various voices into an ensemble. This is no intricate problem in *Tosca* and similar operas without involved ensemble scenes, but it takes a primary place over all problems in the works of Mozart and Verdi. The most demanding opera, as far as casting is concerned, is *Don Giovanni,* as its artistic success rests entirely on a perfectly attuned ensemble of eight voices. Whenever the engagement of one or several guests is planned, this problem must be weighed very carefully, for one dominating voice can throw the entire cast off balance.

As to the chorus, the choice of the opera depends more on the number than on the experience of its members. If the permanent chorus is small and the employment of additional members is not feasible, operas such as *Rigoletto, La Traviata, The Barber of Seville, Martha* have priority over *Faust, Carmen, Aida* and *Lohengrin*.

Another factor to be considered is the size of the stage and the settings. A few choristers in a spacious surroundings look lost and forlorn and, vice versa, on a small stage a large number cannot be artistically managed. Furthermore, it is advisable to begin operatic activities with an unpretentious rather than a demanding work. If a group intends to offer a series of operas during the winter season, particularly within a comparatively brief period, a wise choice is one or two works with sizable chorus scenes and the rest with only a few chorus scenes or none at all. This is expressly recommended for groups engaging soloists from out-of-town, since these companies rarely schedule many stage rehearsals. If the theatre has a stage of average size, a chorus of twelve men and twelve women is quite satisfactory for operas like *La Traviata*. But for a production of *Faust* twice this number is needed. Some conductors, and directors too, prefer a large chorus, even if not required in the score. The dramatic impact, vocally as well as pictorially, is infinitely stronger when numerous choristers are deployed in the ensemble scenes of *Fidelio, Carmen* and *Faust*. In this case, however, the usual number of forty or fifty musicians in the pit must be increased in the string body in order to keep the proper balance between chorus and orchestra.

Much thought is to be given to the orchestra. Even if a college or civic association can rely on a large, well-trained group, the lack of experience in accompanying singers should be considered, and so should the sometimes strange requirements of many modern composers. Therefore it is expedient to concentrate first on light operas like those by Rossini, Donizetti, Mozart, Flotow and Thomas. Among Verdi's works *La Traviata, Rigoletto* and *The Masked Ball* are not too complicated and demanding.

Stage director and designer should be consulted about the feasibility of meeting all technical requests. A small stage is in itself no obstacle as long as facilities, primarily the fly system, are adequate. But it is not always easy to define the term "adequate". A presumptuous director could have so many wishes for so simple an opera as *The Barber of Seville* that it might be well-nigh impossible to fulfill them on an excellently equipped stage; on the other hand, an experienced and reasonable director, supported by a versatile technician, can with ingenuity perform near-miracles. In small theatres most of the comic operas and operettas can be staged, and even more involved works, like *Martha, Mignon, Fidelio, The Tales of Hoffman, Hansel and Gretel, Tosca,* and so on. It must be remembered, however, that elaborate platforms, quick shifting of settings and complex lighting are frequently necessary. A resourceful director and designer can cover many defects of a poorly equipped stage, but not all of them. Closely related to the technical aspect is the question of financing the production. Expensive scenery, numerous costumes, properties and guest singers can raise the costs to prohibitive proportions.

In order to alleviate the financial burden, civic associations must cater to the public taste—in other words, offer the tried reliable masterpieces. And that is precisely what has heretofore happened. Lesser known and new works have had little chance for selection although many a precious musical drama may be among them. Civic groups can hardly afford to experiment with such ventures which might delight a few sophisticated aficionados, but keep the crowds away. A further obstacle to broadening the repertoire is the guest system prevalent among civic associations. Guests are willing to study any standard opera in their special field, but are naturally reluctant to accept a part in an unusual work that would entail the thankless task of memorizing it possibly for only a few performances. Although conditions at our educational institutions are more favorable to the presentation of a seldom heard opera, here again some students are aiming at a professional career which necessitates above all the study of the standard repertoire.

Civic associations planning an operatic season will of course give prime consideration to audience appeal in balancing the program. The repertoire of one season should not offer a whole series of comic or serious operas, of German, French or Italian works, but rather a variety of types, styles and periods. Surely, the outstanding operas of other countries must not be neglected: Russian, Czechoslovakian, perhaps Spanish, and indeed British and American. Even groups specializing in the production of operettas could at times insert a comic opera.

There is no need to compile a list of the best known operas; they are described in several useful anthologies. It seems opportune, however, to list some of the lesser known or neglected masterworks and also to name a few commendable short operas (one act and two act). It is a worthwhile task for institutions of higher learning and financially sound civic associations to expand the conventional repertoire by now and then producing some pieces otherwise rarely presented. Officers, conductors and directors of the various groups can arouse curiosity for unknown works through lectures in classes and clubs and over radio and television. Publicity managers and artistic directors can do a great deal in building up public interest. It is easier, of course, to revive a forgotten opera by a famous composer. And yet new ground can be broken too, if there is the good will and energy of all concerned. The greater the variety of

109

the operatic repertoire, the less the danger that the public will become weary of listening to the same works over and over again.

A superficial comparison of operas regularly offered and those found in a volume of history of opera shows the immense possibilities hitherto missed. Fortunately a few professional and educational groups select quite often from the "hidden" treasure of rarely performed works. Verdi indeed created more than the five or six operas commonly performed. His *La Forza del Destino, Don Carlo, Macbeth, Simone Boccanegra* and *Falstaff* had a renaissance at the Met and proved to be great attractions. Each of these works has so much beautiful music and enough dramatic impetus to fascinate an audience for which they are novelties. How often do we have the opportunity to see more than one work by Rossini, Donizetti, Massenet and Gounod—they did not compose just one opera as we are inclined to believe. The list grows if we scan the forgotten masters. Adam, Auber, Boildieu, Lortzing and Nicolai have written charming and entertaining light operas which are waiting to be "discovered". As for grand opera, Halévy and Meyerbeer have become mere names in books. Only recordings by former stars remind us that their operas were once an intrinsic part of the repertoire. The masters of the Baroque, Handel, Purcell and Gluck, fare somewhat better due to presentations in concerts. Gluck's admirable operas are still regularly seen in European opera houses where Handel also has a well deserved renaissance. All these masterpieces should have an honored place on American stages too.

From the broad province of short pieces, only *Cavalleria Rusticana, I Pagliacci*, three one-act operas by Puccini, and lately also the effective works by Menotti, are firmly established. Yet a brief survey of older works indicates that from the number of comic and dramatic operas in one or two acts a wide selection can be obtained. The early composers Purcell, Handel, Gluck, Haydn and Mozart and those of the 19th century Adam, Gounod, Flotow, Rossini and Offenbach have left us operas of this type which audiences can enjoy. Many contemporary short pieces receive only a single hearing; this is unfair to the composer as well as the audience, since only repeated productions can provide the familiarity necessary to appreciate them. As a rule, these operas require no elaborate settings, rarely a chorus and only a small orchestra. Educational groups cultivate this genre extensively as they provide marvelous material for studio and workshop performances and, particularly in a small college, for an evening combining two or three of them. Few civic groups choose this type but some might take cognizance and initiate productions of such operas, if not within their regular program, at least in performances arranged for schools or on special occasions.

During the past twenty years, fortunately, the almost forgotten and, more important, the contemporary works have been given greater consideration. The impetus originated in universities, music schools, and even a few professional companies. The Metropolitan Opera selects a new opera every few years—not often enough in the opinion of the avant-garde. If its score did not fulfill the

110

highest expectations, it is not poor either, since during recent seasons, the company has offered Samuel Barber's *Vanessa,* and Menotti's *The Last Savage* in addition to welcoming Alban Berg's *Wozzeck* in its repertoire. A wider attention to contemporary creations has been promised for the new Met at Lincoln Center which opened with Barber's *Antony and Cleopatra* followed by R. Strauss' *Die Frau ohne Schatten.*

A memorable example is the New York City Opera which has selected forty contemporary works, many of them premieres, since 1948. The good deeds of this company deserve special acknowledgment, since it does not merely add one new work each year, but sometimes several; in a few seasons the entire repertoire consisted of contemporary compositions which had never been heard in New York or in the United States, or were almost forgotten. Here are found not only famous names but a good many Americans who, in spite of great talent, were unable to place their creations. The most felicitous result of the courage shown by the New York City Opera is that its example persuaded others to emulate its enterprising spirit.

To list all new works which have been staged during the past decade takes more than a page; it is not even possible to name all the institutions and companies, ready to create a berth for contemporary works. Only a few significant examples can be enumerated. Among the professional and civic companies San Francisco displays a very progressive repertoire; during recent seasons Alban Berg, Carl Orff, Francis Poulenc, Dimitri Shostakovich and William Turner Walton were represented in addition to Benjamin Britten's *Midsummer Night's Dream.* Some universities go far beyond what could be expected of them and are pioneers for a modern program. The University of Illinois presents a praiseworthy combination of interesting old and modern operas; Indiana University, with the most elaborate organization of our universities, prepared *The Scarlet Letter* by Walter Kaufman and *The Darkened City* by Bernard Heiden. At Florida State University Carlisle Floyd was honored with the production of his three operas *Susannah, Slow Dusk* and *Wuthering Heights.* Northwestern University has selected demanding works by Poulenc, Sessions and Stravinsky. In addition to its extensive program of standard operas, the Julliard Opera Theatre produces at least one modern work every season. Among its recent selectons have been *Curtain Call* by Vittorio Giannini, *Elegy of Young Lovers* by Hans Werner Henze, *The Long Christmas Dinner* by Paul Hindesmith and *Katya Kabanova* by Leos Janacek. Los Angeles has two very ambitious institutions. At the University of California William Schuman's *The Mighty Casey* has been stated recently in addition to other rare works. And the University of Southern California decided to select a modern opera as one of its two annual productions; thus, *The Trial* by Gottfried von Einem, Benjamin Britten's *Peter Grimes* and *The Love of Danae* by Richard Strauss have been included in past years.

There remains some unfulfilled wishes: more opera groups of every kind should make the effort to project a more modern spirit. This does not mean

111

that they try to win the premiere of a work—it is just as essential that they select some excellent operas which were premiered by another company. It is even more important that earnest consideration is given to works which ten, twenty, or thirty years ago were produced successfully and then shelved. Who remembers *The Cradle Will Rock, Regina,* and particularly *Emperor Jones,* the first American opera which had an almost undisputed success at the Met. Our professional and several civic and educational groups are certainly able to acquaint their audiences with works, famed in Europe. Alban Berg's *Wozzeck* has been offered by three companies, yet his *Lulu* has been so far only at the Santa Fe Summer Opera Theater. As for Prokofiev, we are waiting to see more of his operas. *The Rise and Fall of Mahagonny* by Kurt Weill has been promised but not yet staged. The last work of Arnold Schoenberg, *Moses and Aaron,* was performed in Boston, but J. Pizetti's interesting *Murder in the Cathedral* became known only through reviews. Leos Janacek, the great Czechoslovakian composer, is still too much neglected. Ferruccio Busoni is just a name, although his operas, first of all his *Faust,* deserves to be heard and seen. This is also true of Ernest Krenek. One might ask whether we are sufficiently acquainted with Igor Stravinsky, as a composer of operas. The late Paul Hindemith is fully acknowledged as a renowned composer of symphonies, but his finest dramatic works, except for *News of the Day* at Santa Fe, have not yet reached our shores.

Casting

The most popular opera may be chosen, all technical difficulties may be solved, a fine orchestra, chorus and ballet may be assembled, and yet there will be no artistic success unless a group of good soloists appears in the performance. The cards, filled out during the auditions, are serving now as the source for the final selection of the singers. The artistic leaders have to weigh the potentialities, every pro and con of a singer. If two applicants are equally promising for a particular role, both can be cast, and the decision of who is to sing and who to be the understudy can be postponed until the coaching period or the first stage rehearsals make it apparent which one is better suited. Understudies are indispensable, for a slight indisposition can prevent a singer from going through with his task without endangering his voice. Members of the supporting cast can ordinarily continue to sing with a slight cold or inflammation of the vocal cords, but singers of demanding roles must be extremely careful. Organizations engaging guests do well trying to locate other singers who are available and capable of replacing a sick colleague on very short notice. The trouble is that cities are far apart and that most professionals live in New York, Chicago or Los Angeles. To be informed about an indisposition just 24 hours before the anticipated arrival of a guest can cause an emergency which has to be calculated in the planning of the performance.

Organizations relying on talent in or near their city ought to take heed that the right singers and understudies are on hand for the leading characters in the operas of their choice. In many cases, choristers, often good singers in their own right, are able and eager to study a minor role for an emergency. If possible, two complete casts should be selected from the start despite the disadvantages of an increased number of rehearsals implied in this system. In many cases, the understudies join the chorus and thus attend rehearsals anyway; consequently they can be asked to take over their solo parts on occasion. Otherwise it is expedient to have them practice separately with an assistant. Every understudy of an important role should also have the chance to sing with the orchestra. Colleges and conservatories know the immense value of double casting from an educational point of view. Provided enough trained students are available, it is the duty of the administration to offer them the experience of acting and singing a role in their special field. In order to rotate roles, assuring maximum opportunity for everyone, the singers of small parts could understudy the leading parts and vice versa, and choristers may understudy the bit parts.

THE REHEARSALS

Coaching

Whenever an opera is cast completely, or predominantly, with local talent, much thought must be given the early study of the roles so that all soloists have a chance to know their music and text at the time of the scheduled blocking rehearsals. The conductor, of course, supervises the coaching. As he may hold additional positions in the particular city or in others, it is necessary to engage a musical assistant who, after being duly informed by the conductor, takes charge of many practice sessions. The local singers are frequently voice teachers or members of choirs, and therefore musically reliable enough to be trusted with studying their roles by themselves. As soon as the parts are studied, if not memorized, the conductor must coach with each individual singer before working with the ensemble. The difficult ensemble scenes should not be taken up until every participant knows his notes and dynamics accurately.

During this period the conductor must impress upon the singer the necessity of memorizing his part in the most minute detail. The time value of every note and pause counts as much as the pitch; now it must be made clear to everyone that there is no "about" in a good performance. At first it will be hard on the beginner to take the matter of a quaver or demisemiquaver very seriously; he may be inclined to hold notes longer or shorter than required on the printed page. Relentlessly the coach must insist on the right value and pitch of every note. This concerns also the volume and each detail of dynamics. Singing a sort of *mezzoforte* throughout is as poor as singing *forte* where a *piano* is suggested. Only when all markings are observed to the conductor's satisfaction can true synchronization of stage and orchestra be achieved. Bruno Walter always considered coaching a kind of "educational activity—though it must not appear educational—the foundation of every constructive work in the theatre."

Good singers do not memorize mechanically but make every attempt to obtain an understanding of the emotional and intellectual facets of their roles and also of the entire opera. To build a foundation for this understanding, the conductor plays the work for the whole company. In addition the director can take some time to explain the plot and theme of the opera and, in particular, the intricate details of each character. Models of settings help greatly in clarifying many points. Advising the cast to read the original story or play on which the libretto is based can help too. Each soloist ought to examine the libretto carefully to detect details of the social and economic background of his character. The emotions of a character are better revealed in the music than in the libretto. Key, rhythm and instrumentations must be clearly felt and understood for such an analysis. All these tangibles and intangibles are decisive in the development of a role.

Early in his training the beginner should realize that in the end his individuality determines interpretation, expressed in his voice, appearance and characterization. A singer with a light voice and slim figure enacts his part unlike one with a heavier voice and body, and a vivacious person approaches his task very differently from one of an even temperament. Granting a singer some liberty in working out his part does not give him, however, the right to dictate to the conductor or director. An agreement can be reached about the length of a *fermata*, the strength of a *marcato*, or the executing of minor details of the stage business. Yet any such deviation is subject to the conductor's or director's approval lest these liberties mar the style of the performance. A certain freedom is permissible in arias and solo passages but in ensemble scenes, each singer is a member of the team, and all follow the artistic leaders.

Here are a few additional hints which have proved to be beneficial: whether a singer merely indicates or sings with full voice during the practice sessions he ought to be required to enunciate clearly and correctly every vowel and consonant. These sessions offer also the last chance to re-examine the libretto, particularly if it is translated from a foreign language. With the original text on hand corrections can be made; this is advisable in some cases because translators are not always fully acquainted with the capabilities of a singer; for instance the vowel "a" or "u" can be difficult in the high range. Some conductors and directors advise the singers to study and memorize the text before starting with the musical phase, a very good thought.

Coaching the choristers does not pose any new problems. The chorus master must of course thoroughly know the conductor's conception regarding tempo, volume, certain effects, and general interpretation. The conductor may want to take over one or more rehearsals with the chorus. He should not do so at an early stage in order to avoid the impression of interfering with the work of his collaborator. Whether women and men should first be called separately depends on the experience of the choristers and also on the difficulty of the score. But no matter whether the chorus master decides to rehearse with each group alone or with the male and female voices together he should first play all passages to

114

the entire group. Either he or the stage director may add a few words about the style and plot of the particular opera and about the part the chorus plays in it. Such information helps the choristers understand their actions more quickly and makes it easier for them to execute movements, handle properties, and to show the appropriate facial expression in the stage rehearsals later on.

The Rehearsal Schedule

The organization and scheduling of the rehearsals is mainly the director's responsibility. Naturally, the conductor's concern is with the orchestra rehearsals and the designer's is with the technical rehearsals. So the director has to see to it that everyone receives what he needs and that at the dress rehearsals, all phases of the production can be coordinated without unnecessary troubles. The amount of rehearsals, exclusive of coaching, depends on the following points:

1. Length of the opera
2. Difficulty of the musical score
3. Complexity of the stage business
4. Length and difficulty of the chorus scenes
5. Employment of understudies
6. Technical problems related to settings and lighting
7. Background and experience of the participants

The sum total of rehearsals is divided into these categories: preparatory work, acting, orchestra, technical and dress rehearsals. The first implies the coaching of singers, chorus, orchestra, and ballet; its work precedes the first scene rehearsal except for the orchestra whose preparation may coincide with acting rehearsals. This entire category is largely beyond the director's jurisdiction, since conductor, chorus master, coach and ballet master take care of these activities after all essentials have been discussed with the director. When the preliminary work should start and how much time it may take up cannot be defined in a few sentences. To state it briefly, the period allotted depends on the difficulties of the opera as well as the ability, experience and cooperation of the groups performing it. The coaching of the soloists should certainly begin at the earliest possible date; perfecting the dances can require much time too; chorus rehearsals should be so conducted that parts are completely memorized by the time the first scene rehearsal is scheduled. The orchestra begins practicing long before the performance, when it is part of an educational institution where rehearsals have to be spread over a long period; it will not be called together until the last week of rehearsals with soloists whenever the musicians are professionals.

If the stage where the opera is to be performed is not available for all rehearsals, a large hall of equal dimensions offers an adequate substitution, but for acoustical reasons at least one or two scene rehearsals with the whole ensemble should be arranged on the stage proper. This enables conductor and

115

director to examine every detail while the singers are using their full voices. Even if the conductor is present the director is in charge of all scene rehearsals, unless the conductor happens to be the artistic director as well, which would give him over-all authority. Every acting rehearsal must be attended by an accompanist (conductor, coach or chorus master), and so should technical rehearsals where scene shifting takes place during an interlude. As in the legitimate theatre there must be a stage manager who can function as the director's assistant; furthermore a prompter should always be seated on stage; prompting should not be left to the director, the manager, or the accompanist.

Acting rehearsals can be subdivided and taken approximately in the following order:

1. The blocking of the scenes with the soloists.
2. Scene rehearsals with the soloists.
3. The chorus and then ballet.
4. The training of the extras.
5. The coordination of all groups.

The sequence can be altered under given circumstances; it may be advisable to start with the choristers if their part is very important or when all or most of the soloists are guests who already know their roles. The ballet can be called in for the blocking with the chorus to acquaint its members with their exact positions on the stage; this method is also useful whenever the dancers participate in the action as extras. The supernumeraries are rarely asked to come until a few days before the dress rehearsal—sometimes on that very day—depending on the importance and difficulty of their part. In the interest of a perfect performance this group, too, ought to attend earlier rehearsals.

Practicing with settings and lights can follow scene rehearsals or alternate with those accompanied by the orchestra. Because of the complicated settings and light effects in most operas it is extremely hazardous to leave these technical rehearsals for the last few hours before the first dress rehearsal. A second technical run through may be arranged on the day of the performance itself. Operas like *The Magic Flute* depend in a great measure, on the smooth execution of lighting and scenic effects.

In scheduling scene rehearsals one should bear in mind that neither soloists nor choristers must waste their time. This requires separation of all solo scenes from those of the chorus. Arias, duets, and even ensembles ought to be practiced first. In some operas it is often irrelevant in what order the director rehearses these scenes. Out of consideration for the singers he can call in, for instance, Aida to rehearse her two arias; then Amneris can join her to practice the first scene of Act II. Any aria, duet or ensemble involving a great deal of movement and stage business needs special attention. But where the action develops more realistically, as in *Carmen* or *Tosca*, the soloists should be trained in the continuity of the score. And yet even in these operas it is possible to go through certain scenes with two or three singers at a time. (Micaela-Don José; Carmen-Don José; Tosca-Cavaradossi; Tosca-Scarpia); a method

116

otherwise mainly applicable to the classical type of opera divided into arias, duets and more complicated ensembles.

Chart indicating minimum number of stage and scene
rehearsals, each lasting from two to three hours
except for dress rehearsals which have no time limit.

		The Barber of Seville	The Magic Flute	Fidelio	Mignon	La Traviata	Aida	Carmen	The Mastersingers
Soloists	with piano	15	12	12	12	12	12	15	20
Chorus alone		---	1	1	1	1	2	3	3
Soloists, chorus, (ballet)		2	2	2	3	4	4	6	6
Orchestra (with acting)		1	1	1	1	1	2	2	3
Technical Rehearsal		1	2	1	1	1	2	2	1
Dress Rehearsal		2	2	2	2	2	2	2	3
Total:		21	20	19	20	21	24	30	36

The first dress rehearsal for *The Mastersingers*, a work which lasts four hours without the intermissions, may preferably be held in two parts; act one and two on the first day, the last act on the following.

The chart indicates that, under the consideration of all points previously listed, the first five works require about an equal number of rehearsals. At the first glance, *Aida* seems to be a very demanding grand opera, yet actually it does not need many stage rehearsals after the coaching sessions. *Carmen*, because of its complicated intricate action, requires more rehearsals. *The Mastersingers* problem is its sheer length. Wagner's *The Valkyrie* or *Siegfried*, can be produced with a few rehearsals if all, or most of, the solo roles are cast with guests; if singers who have never performed the leading parts are engaged the preparation of such a production requires much time.

No chart can be taken at its face value. Every director and his colleagues approach the problems involved from a slightly different angle, and therefore only approximate numbers can be inserted and these will vary from one organization to another. It is impossible to predict the exact time it will take two different groups to prepare *The Barber of Seville*, much less *Carmen*. If a leading character knows his role thoroughly and can easily adapt himself to a new ensemble, several rehearsals may be cut from the number given above. The chart has been worked out on the basis of a cast whose singers are not beginners; student singers require more attention, and in case understudies have to be trained, the total number will grow of course. If the conductor and director are perfectionists, as they ought to be, there is hardly a maximum of rehearsals. The limit is set when the capacity of the ensemble members has reached a certain point beyond which the artistic leaders are unable to develop them. Under ideal conditions, a one-act opera like *Gianni Schicchi* receives about forty scene and orchestra rehearsals; and a full length work may show a total of one hundred and more, which means that in a university between three and four months are devoted to a single production.

Annotating the Score

Before meeting the singers and choristers for the first time, the stage director must have worked out all details of the *mise en scène* in his score which should be interleaved to allow him more space for writing down his ideas about his approach to the production, settings, stage business and scenic effects. As a beginner, he should take the trouble of preparing his rehearsals in the most detailed manner; in later years, when he has gained experience, notes jotted down on the margin or any other available space may suffice. The more carefully the score has been worked through, the easier it is for the director to arrange his ensemble in every position and prepare it for every movement. During rehearsals changes may and should be made whenever his theories appear to be unworkable or whenever singers offer valuable suggestions.

The score must contain all eliminations and alterations as agreed upon with the conductor. The floor plan for each act or setting is to be inserted at the appropriate place. Pieces of furniture, all hand properties and costumes to be used in each act should likewise be marked on the page before that particular act and the light plot should be described; transitions, changes and special effects are marked wherever they are desired. If the score is not interleaved, sheets with the essential information about floor plans and so on should be pasted in. Simple stage business can be written directly above the notes; but for the grouping of choristers, extras and dancers, sheets pasted in the score are very helpful even for simple movements. Interleaved scores of operas and operettas requiring many properties and plenty of action, make everything clear and distinct at a glance. Whichever method is chosen by the director must include an exact description of every position, every significant gesture and facial expression, every use of property and certainly all movements like crosses, entrances and exits.

Before the director decides on any gesture or movement, on any use of properties or facial expressions, he must check the score first, then the libretto, because every business needs a basis in the music. A brief gesture will, in one situation, be synchronized with a chord; an extended one rather with a passage or melody. A turn and a move are subject to the same considerations.

Yet the director should never be pedantic; the neophyte can quickly fall into extremes asking for too many gestures and movements which disturb more than they underline; or he will overlook many opportunities leaving holes in the overall action. Further, it is essential to plan the action in direct contact with the character whose internal development is at least as indicative as his external behavior. Psychological considerations will help the planning. At any rate, every detail of the action should be marked in the score with a pencil to facilitate alterations called for during the rehearsals. Colored pencils, incidentally, make it easy to see at a glance what has to be done; a black pencil is good for stage business of the soloists, a blue one for that of the groups; red may serve all light cues and green all backstage cues such as gunshots, curtain, and so on.

Rehearsals with Soloists

In the staging of modern operas the director can hardly make a mistake if he adheres closely to the directives of the vocal score. A warning is necessary; the set-up of a score does not always make it possible to print the stage directions at the exact spot or passage where the composer and librettist wish to have them executed. Thus a careful examination of the music is the first step before a decision about the stage business is made. The operas of the 18th and early 19th centuries contain so few directives that the director is left to cull the action directly from his reading of the music. A thorough knowledge of the score, dramatic imagination and artistic taste are the prerequisites for working out every detail.

Although much can be learned by attending opera performances, the enthusiastic student must beware that he does not simply adopt sloppy conventional staging procedures of the standard works. The principle must be to avoid actions which do not advance the drama or are even detrimental to its style. Some significant examples will illustrate this principle. In a few productions of *I Pagliacci*, Canio used a handkerchief, a red one at that, to wipe his eyes at the end of act one, yet nothing in the score indicates such an ostentatious grieving which distorts the tragic mood. A scrutiny of the music and its style should prevent the pitfall of realistic business in the quartette of *Fidelio* for which Beethoven created a quiet meditative prelude. This mood has been spoiled by the barbarism of absurd actions which only detracted from the music, one of the most moving quartettes ever written. Another example of poor taste has been witnessed in *Carmen* when Micaela searches for Don José in a lonely gorge. Too often the prelude to Micaela's aria is abused by a guide who accompanies her; he gesticulates vividly until the young woman gives him some money whereupon he makes his exit. Neither the music nor common sense permit such inartistic insertions. A strange stage business has been added in act three of *Tannhaeuser* when a lonely pilgrim crosses the stage after all other pilgrims have left the stage. This very annoying effect—a rumor has it that it was introduced in

119

Bayreuth early in this century—purports to have Elizabeth mistake this man for Tannhaeuser returning from Rome and then, realizing her mistake, be so disturbed that she goes to the cross, kneels down and prays. An inexcusable solo scene has been given to the leading lady in the last act of *Manon*. Sometimes she has appeared alone, unescorted, although she is a prisoner and therefore must enter the stage with the group of all other prisoners. Manon may sit apart later on when the women are resting and the bribing occurs at the opposite side of the stage. Certain habits have been originated by some star many, many years ago and have been copied by generations of young singers and accepted by opera fans. Among those which are plausible and hence commendable is a trick, said to be invented by Enrico Caruso. While singing the *"Donna e mobile"* in *Rigoletto* the Duke plays with a deck of cards which he flips toward the ceiling with his last note.

Some stage directors are so absorbed in their work with a few soloists that they lose contact with the remaining parts of the opera and are consequently obliged to reblock these scenes later on when the choristers appear. They must never forget that the solo scenes are part of a larger unit and that the chorus and other groups have to be taken into consideration all the time. Therefore the interrelationship of all participants must be in the mind of the director who should explain to the soloists where the choristers will stand or move respectively. Conversely, in a practice session with the chorus alone the director must be aware of the soloists and their actions and must inform the choristers about the full blocking.

A clear artistic characterization is a must in the modern theatre. A superficial portrayal of a role expresses neither the music nor the text and ultimately leaves the spectators bored. Even secondary parts can be worked out with loving care. Thus two or more persons of equal rank or belonging to the same social class should not look and behave alike unless explicitly so requested. The two smugglers in *Carmen*, the courtiers in *Rigoletto* and the conspirators in *The Masked Ball* can and should be distinguished in looks and attitude. The three Genii in *The Magic Flute*, on the other hand, and the Pages in *Tannhaeuser* and *Lohengrin* belong to one type and they act accordingly. To treat the nine Valkyries in the Wagnerian music drama as individuals, integrating them at the same time into the ensemble as a whole, is indeed a feat, accomplished in very few productions.

The director must not only attend to the interpretation in general but has to work out every gesture, every step, the handling of properties, and the delivery of dialogue, an important element in some operas and in all operettas. A pertinent model is Wagner's precise description of the Dutchman's entrance in act two. It is so clearly written and composed that no error should occur. Every singer and director ought to study the dramatic recitative *"Die Frist ist um"* and then try to apply the lesson to arias and ensembles resembling it. In Traviata's recitative *"E strano"* for instance details of movement and gestures can be worked out during the brief orchestra bars and chords preceding the *andan-*

tino. Another more complicated and delicate task is the execution of Tatjana's letter scene in *Eugene Onegin.* The atmosphere depends chiefly on the sensitivity of the singer and her ability to project her passion across the footlights, but a few hints from the director, accurately followed, will help convey the inner tension of this exciting piece. Good material for practicing is found also in the entrances of Manon, Carmen and Tamino. Early in his studies the singer should become accustomed to create the mood of passages by relying on vocal and facial expression rather than on superficial gestures and movements. The prayers of Desdemona and Elizabeth, the dream in *Manon,* Traviata's sad arietta, *"Addio",* and Tamino's aria, *"Dies Bildnis",* are scenes where slight, only indicated gestures suffice for a good characterization if the general attitude and musical interpretation are in keeping with the atmosphere.

Singing in a sitting position apparently imposes some difficulties. There the stage director must know how to help the handicapped singer who should not be permitted to sit on the edge of the chair, to stretch one foot to one side or almost behind the chair. To avoid such awkward positions, higher chairs should be used giving the singer the opportunity to sit like a normal human being and, at the same time, obtain his needed breath support. Operas of the Baroque and Rococo periods are an exception, for costumes and customs of that time allow the performer to sit on an edge. Since the furniture of that period is comparatively low, it is possible, furthermore, to place a cushion on a chair or sofa without violating the style of the scenery. Today singers must be able to proceed in any position. Madame Jeritza did not mind singing *"Vissi d'arte"* lying on the floor; many other Toscas have copied this effective position which is now accepted as the correct one in performance of this scene. Ariadne in the Strauss opera is expected to sing long and difficult passages stretched out on the floor; Rodolfo, Des Grieux, Kundry, Salomé, Tosca and other characters sing sitting, or lying on couches or on the floor. The director can sometimes alleviate an awkward position either by building a ramp on which the singer can lie, or by giving his feet support through a border nailed at the end of the ramp or couch. Even walking can call for special attention by the director. Walking is a characteristic symptom; steps moreover must be taken in keeping with the music. To walk properly ought to be practiced above all by women who play the parts of men like Cherubino, Siebel or Octavian. Women choristers appear frequently in trousers as in *La Bohème* (the urchins) and in *The Mastersingers* (the apprentices); often, as an expedient, female members of the chorus represent real men. Therefore, women must learn to walk fittingly.

Hand properties or adequate substitutes should be used in rehearsals as early as feasible, since it takes time to handle them with ease, as it does also to get accustomed to platforms, stairs and ramps. Civic associations have, as a rule, difficulties in obtaining a stage as often as is desirable; and those devices might not be ready soon enough. Conditions are much better in educational institutions with theatre buildings of their own. There, most of the time,

121

the rehearsals can be scheduled on the stage proper with platforms and properties on hand. The singers adjust themselves without much trouble to walking on stairs, ramps and different levels if they can practice with them regularly. But being exposed to these paraphernalia for the first time at a dress rehearsal can make the singers quite nervous indeed; as a result they either concentrate on singing or on acting and thus give an uneven performance. The early use of properties facilitates the development of the characterization. Writing a letter in a play often takes careful timing; the same action in an opera such as *Tosca* or *Eugene Onegin*, however, is far more intricate, for the singing, technically as well as musically, leaves no leeway for beginning and ending the letter nor for the rhythm of writing it. Therefore intensive practicing is needed to perfect the execution. Swords and other weapons are so frequently employed that it is profitable to spend sufficient time on using them during rehearsals. If the fighting in the first act of *Otello* or the killing in the last acts of *Rigoletto* and *Carmen* look awkward, the production suffers. All these cases have to be rehearsed in accord with two principles: the action must be synchronized with the music and must be executed dramatically and naturally. A very delicate task is the playing of a harp or guitar as requested in *Mignon*, *Faust*, *Tannhaeuser* and *The Mastersingers*. The singer should practice the finger technique when he memorizes a role, yet it is the director's responsibility to watch for errors which can slip in during rehearsals when the performer concentrates on his singing.

Rehearsals with the Groups

The staging of chorus scenes brings to the fore the problem only few play directors are prepared to meet, namely the handling of crowds. In their productions they may occasionally have had some extras, or even many, but in opera, scenes with chorus and other groups are the rule. The director must adapt himself to the requirements of the particular opera and to the number of available choristers; in addition, it is often necessary to incorporate dancers and extras into the action. Coordinating these various groups with the soloists, fusing them into a whole, is technically as well as artistically a difficult assignment.

Only too often the choristers are placed as though a concert were being presented, not a lyric drama; sopranos and altos take the front right and left, or stand directly behind the soloists, while tenors and basses arrange themselves neatly behind the women. The prime aim, however, must remain to integrate the chorus, that is, to make them a real part of the production so that they lose the anonymity they occupy in the program. Careless arrangements, entrances, exits and movements are disturbing. And yet the most accurate performance of these details alone is of little value so long as the director neglects to have the chorus really participate in the action. Productions with first class soloists have been spoiled by a poorly directed chorus. Beware of the straight line and the semi-circle in the arrangement of groups! The opera director, mindful of this warning, can be spared many esthetic blunders. There are a few exceptions to this basic rule such as the array of soldiers, priests and a similar body and the directing of certain scenes in operettas, above all, dance numbers. Even then, the director could try to create variety, to keep soloists as well as choristers off center, and to arrange them in the more effective diagonal and triangular positions.

Soloists have no special privilege in the downstage area; the choristers, too, have a right to use it. There are so many possibilities for natural and dramatic groupings that tradition, scorned by outstanding directors, should be abolished altogether. Although a soloist is musically their leader and often speaks for the chorus, he should not be treated as their superior on stage unless he actually is (say an officer leading soldiers). Such a wrong approach becomes ludicrous when the soloist addresses the choristers standing behind him. If this procedure is, moreover, accompanied by a lack of characterization and of interest in the action, the performance turns into a caricature. It takes accurate training by the chorus master and assiduous practicing with the director on stage to give chorus scenes their full theatrical impact. Naturally the better prepared the director is before meeting the chorus, the better he can project his ideas and materialize his dramatic vision, which, of course, must at all times be in harmony with the music.

In his desire to bring the chorus scenes to their highest artistic accomplishment the stage director, not too well-versed in the operatic field, will discover a great handicap. He cannot place and move choristers at will; he must consider their proper voice groups. He may disregard contact of the various voice units only within such limits as will enable the conductor to give them cues. In some operas a mob scene can be so arranged that couples are standing or walking around; then sopranos and tenors, altos and basses can be kept together. In realistic scenes, however, as in acts one and four of *Carmen*, act two of *La Bohème*, acts one and three of *La Traviata*, and acts one and four of *Manon*, the various groups can mingle when there is time between cues for such action; but as soon as a difficult passage comes up, the voice units should have contact, if only a rather loose one.

As a rule, people should not be arranged in clusters and tight groups. The old principle not to stand too close together should be heeded; thirty choristers, in groups of two and three, create the impression of a crowd, thus enhancing the scenic effect, while at the same time, the choristers are thus in a better position to see the conductor. Although "realistic" scenes benefit most from such an arrangement, any tight grouping should also be avoided in scenes of a "stylized" character. The larger the chorus, the more it is mandatory to place its members so that contact with the conductor can be maintained in difficult ensembles.

Soldiers, courtiers, priests and nuns must often look and act like a single unit. This type is necessary in *The Magic Flute*, *Aida*, *Parsifal* and the two *Iphigenias* (Aulis and Tauris). The opposite, often a realistic, treatment is needed in *Carmen*, *La Bohème*, *La Traviata*, *Manon*, *Louise* and similar works. Several operas embrace scenes of both categories: for example in *Il Trovatore*, the nuns enter in a procession whereas the soldiers and gypsies move much more freely. In *Lohengrin* most of the chorus scenes allow, even require, a strictly non-realistic arrangement, yet before the arrival of the swan the excitement rises to such a height that the knights break rank acting almost individually.

Whatever the conditions, the chorus master can be of great help in the preparation of the mass scenes, if he places his members according to the dramatic requirements. This may best be done in the last practice sessions when the musical part is memorized. Thus each chorister will learn early that opera means not merely singing, but singing under sometimes trying circumstances.

For the treatment of stylized scenes the director can learn a great deal from modern ballet. In staging an opera by Handel or Gluck he will closely collaborate with the ballet master, and usually he will be wise to accept the latter's suggestion for the arrangement of chorus and dance scenes. This form of opera can even be directed by a ballet master in case his taste and experience are so well-developed that he refrains from transforming soloists into dancers. In Handel's *Julio Cesare* or Gluck's *Orfeo* the spectator should not be able to distinguish between chorus and ballet members; both groups ought to move in the same manner and be arranged in harmony with the baroque style of the music. The rhythm of their movements must approach the dance form.

A gratifying task is in store for the director when individualization of the chorus is recommended. To accomplish this he will not simply talk to sopranos, altos, tenors and basses, but will give them names. In *Carmen* men and women should imagine themselves as being Spanish people in act one, and smugglers later on. Director and choristers must cooperate to achieve a personal touch. In *La Traviata* or *La Bohème* French names of the nobility or common people respectively can be chosen to give the story a true atmosphere. The first act of *Carmen* and the second of *La Bohème* offer the widest opportunity for working out realistic details of characterization; extras should be included in this game. Everyone should feel part of the drama: rich and poor people, vendors, beggars, policemen, soldiers, workmen, factory girls, monks, and many other characters can be introduced without overloading the action. Children too can be employed to great advantage, and certainly not only in the scenes in which they participate according to the score. The director's task is to create commotion that does not interfere with the singing; this means that whenever the interest is focused on a musical passage, the groups' acting must not detract from it. Sometimes he may have small groups or individuals walking across the stage or standing in a corner. But, for instance, the duets between Micaela and Don José and Carmen and Don José must in no way be disturbed; a beggar can sit in the background, a policeman stand at a corner, and, at some place, a soldier can walk around the guardhouse. Tricks to animate the stage should never be used to the point of spoiling the music; this danger exists and some directors have succumbed to the temptation.

124

Overdoing hurts a production artistically, but overlooking an opportunity, or bungling it, is just as ruinous. The choristers should not be timid when a sense of urgency is required, nor disinterested when the situation demands active attention. In the great finale of *La Traviata* the chorus grows really angry at Alfredo; this tense mood must be expressed not only through tempo and volume of voice, but also by the attitude and behavior of every individual. When Rigoletto implores the courtiers to help him their facial expression must show their reaction, that is, their lack of sympathy, which is all the more important as the choristers do not sing during Rigoletto's aria. In the beginning the director has some trouble in loosening up singers. Although he will certainly succeed after some practicing, the choristers are sometimes slow in executing his wishes; this puts him in a real dilemma. If there is danger that the available rehearsals do not suffice to train beginners in carrying out the right gestures, it is better to let them stand still and have the appropriate facial expression and significant poise indicate the mood than to have a scene spoiled through vague or false actions.

An enormous amount of work is required for the preparation of *Aida, Lohengrin, Tannhaeuser* and *The Mastersingers*, four operas with many difficult and long chorus scenes. But every group will take pride in performing these operas well. Ensembles with orchestra and *a cappella*, sequences with the chorus subdivided, and scenes in which stage business is demanding, make adequate experience imperative before the presentation of these works can be undertaken. A large chorus, well-trained, can earn laurels of its own in the production of such masterpieces.

At this point attention is called to the fact that in a comparatively small chorus the men, when outnumbered, might have to make more effort than is good for their voices. In such a situation the conductor should restrain the women's group; this however may be detrimental to the vigorous choral passages. An unpleasant condition arises in operas when men and women are supposed to move in pairs most of the time, but there are too many women! Here male extras may help out.

In *Cavalleria Rusticana* one chorus is on stage while another sings in the church; the latter need not be large but must be strong if it is to balance the first one. *The Flying Dutchman* suffers artistically if an average chorus is split into two parts for act three, when Norwegian sailors sing on stage while another group of men is needed for the Dutchman's crew. A complicated set-up appears in the famous finale of *Aida*, act two. A full chorus is necessary for the Egyptian people, a separate group of tenors and basses for the priests, and a third chorus for the prisoners, consisting of sopranos, altos and basses. The prisoners can be few in number since, as a rule, they are placed favorably near the footlights, but the priests must be fully cast and so must the Egyptians. An experienced conductor can eliminate some of the subdivisions but he must always be mindful of the vocal balance. Act one of *Carmen* is difficult to stage unless a double chorus of men is available. In a small company the few men dress first as soldiers and then change to citizens for the entrance of the leading lady or they come on stage as citizens already for the opening scene. Either

125

solution causes awkward staging.

Observing habits and customs of various countries and periods is indispensable for a good performance. Institutions of higher learning have accomplished much in this regard; their teachers can spend more time in elaborating on many details. Civic organizations' are customarily hard pressed for time and yet they too have sometimes succeeded very well in working out the complicated stage business in many operas. It takes, for instance, not only a thorough understanding of Wagner's score, but of medieval court etiquette as well to execute properly the entrance of the guests in the second act of *Tannhaeuser*. The composer-librettist is very clear in his objectives leaving scarcely a chance for misinterpretation; a study of old paintings and special books provides additional information. Thus the staging should proceed as follows. Before the first chorus cue is given most of the princes and knights with their wives, sons and daughters have entered the hall. Men and women are seated separately, in different rows of women in front and men in the rear, or on different sides, even on different levels, that is, the women on a kind of balcony. Each group of guests is led to the Landgrave by two pages. Everything is executed in keeping with the medieval court ceremonial. While the chorus begins to sing other members of the nobility arrive and join the singing as soon as they have taken their places; the employment of extras is recommended to permit movement during the final passages of the chorus. At the proper bar the minnesingers appear, singly or in pairs, followed by their pages. Tannhaeuser should not, as is sometimes done, enter alone after a pause; this is not in accord with Wagner's music or directions. The singer's pages stand behind their masters; those of the Landgrave should not sit at the foot of the platform of the throne but stand behind it. The subsequent singing contest is at times poorly treated by directors who fail to perceive the dramatic contrasts created by Wagner. There are many opportunities for arresting groupings and effects, primarily after Tannhaeuser's confession.

La Traviata, often mistreated, can be quite interesting and spirited under good direction. There is the entrance of Violetta's friends in act one. Here, effective variety can be achieved if the director and the choristers follow the advice to create individual characters. The chorus scene in the third act resembles the first so strongly that entirely different settings and groupings have to be found for it. For this reason it is sometimes staged in a garden instead of in a hall. The ladies and gentlemen of *La Traviata* become common people, though individuals, in *Cavalleria Rusticana* and *I Pagliacci*. A particular atmosphere surrounds *The Bartered Bride*. A great deal depends on the ballet master's ability to arrange Bohemian dances; yet the chorus too can contribute much to the right mood. Each act offers splendid opportunities for singing and acting. The most enjoyable scene is perhaps the circus in the last act; its score is quite extended, and thus a company possessed of means can present a "real show". If the ballet group is small, however, the director should suggest having that part of the circus scene trimmed.

Handling of properties and acting on platforms are as important for the chorus and other groups as for the soloists. The advice given previously is valid here. Weapons should be used as soon as possible. If spears, swords and shields are not available, substitutes will do; better a cane and a piece of cardboard than nothing. Choristers and extras should be able to handle their properties well before the dress rehearsals lest they provoke sneers for wrong motions in the performance. Long spears, in particular, as required in *Il Trovatore* and *Lohengrin*, take careful practicing to prevent their bearers from being caught in a flat or, even worse, from hurting someone. Rehearsing early on platforms, ramps and stairs is of threefold advantage: it helps the groups to become acquainted with complicated movements, it clarifies the director's blocking, and it gives the conductor a better opportunity to supervise the entire ensemble.

Although the singer is expected to know the fundamentals of manipulating hand properties, and how to move in period costumes, he still has to be taught many specific matters during rehearsals. The young soloist, chorister or extra who is not trained sufficiently must have instruction to boot, in carrying a costume on stage, and in handling any kind of property. Falling, dying, jumping, fencing, fighting, drinking are common occurrences in opera. Experienced, and all the more inexperienced, singers must learn to perform these acts true to the character and to the incident involved. Choristers and extras participate in drinking and fighting scenes; hence they must be able to use glasses, cups, bottles and pitchers of different periods. Daggers, knives, swords, pistols and guns are employed not only by soloists but by groups of choristers and extras as well. For military affairs it is expedient to call on members of the well-trained National Guard or of the American Legion to collaborate in the training. The changing of a guard or a procession is much more effective when properly executed. Sometimes the advice of officers, historians, folklore experts, pastors or rabbis may be sought concerning particular ceremonies and customs.

Lyric and also dramatic scenes, written for children, are part of several operas. The best known appearance of children occurs in *Carmen* where in act one urchins habitually draw much attention and applause. Special passages for young voices are included moreover in *Otello, La Bohème, Hansel and Gretel*, and in the rarely performed *Boris Godunov* and *La Gioconda*. Not forgotten should be the use of children's voices in act one of *Tosca* and in the temple scenes of *Parsifal*. Conductors and directors sometimes like to invite children to participate in these works if there is a well-trained chorus available in the city. Emphasis is laid on "well-trained", for these operas abound in technical difficulties, involved in the precise delivery of rhythm and pitch. Yet it has been proved with success that gifted youngsters though inexperienced can be properly trained under a good leadership within a brief period of time to execute the musical and acting phases with ease. If the children know the score, their uninhibited naturalness adds spice to the action. As their voices are often weak, a fairly large group should be selected. To strengthen

127

them conductors prefer to have a few women of the chorus join their passages. Exceptionally gifted children were very good when they took on solo roles which are usually cast with young women. It looks indeed more natural if boys of about twelve years sing the pages in *Lohengrin* and *Tannhaeuser* and also the Genii in *The Magic Flute*.

Coordination of Soloists and Groups

When soloists, choristers, dancers and perhaps extras practice together for the first time, the stage director must coordinate the actions of these groups which have previously rehearsed separately. Theoretically he has done that by telling the chorus where the soloists move and the soloists where the choristers stand. Nevertheless difficulties can arise, since each group might insist on certain prerogatives. A singer's feelings may be hurt because a chorister "intruded" into his acting area, whereas the chorister thought he was in his proper place. Misunderstandings of this nature may result from errors on the part of either one, the director or from any member of the ensemble. It is not possible to arrange every detail of the action as though the stage were divided into small squares that become the property of one person. No one should have any privilege. Personal vanity must be forgotten. Neither a soloist nor a chorister has any special right to stand in front. The director decides for purely artistic reasons who stands and moves where.

In operas like *The Marriage of Figaro* and *The Abduction from the Seraglio* or *Tosca*, chorus and soloists have only loose contact; their actions and reactions are not closely interwoven; participation of the choral groups is at a minimum. Perhaps the most involved task is presented in *Carmen* and *La Bohème*. All performers, soloists, choristers, extras, children and even dancers mingle freely in what may look like a pell-mell, but must be a well-organized turmoil. Harmonious functioning of all groups is equally important in most operettas, where close contact exists not only in dancing numbers but in ensembles as well. The director determines the degree to which the distinction between the groups can be erased. Yet he needs the full cooperation of all concerned, specifically of guests who sometimes are inclined to perform in their accustomed manner of standing in front. It is essential that all the people on stage, soloists and extras alike, understand that everyone is needed to perfect a production. Whoever spoils the coordination, picturization, and timing impairs the success of the performance.

ORCHESTRA REHEARSALS

Preparation

The practice with the orchestra proceeds in four stages:

1. Orchestra alone
2. Orchestra with soloists (and chorus) without acting
3. The same with acting on stage
4. Dress Rehearsals

No conscientious musical director can be satisfied with one orchestra rehearsal, a so-called run-through. To engage an orchestra just for the dress rehearsal is frivolous and can cause a catastrophe in the performance. At any rate, such a decision creates mental and physical agonies for both the participants and the listeners. Professional musicians cost money, but it is money well spent if they are given the opportunity to play the score first without soloists. Thus prepared everyone attends to his task better when acting is added, and the final rehearsals can proceed without these nerve-racking tensions which interfere with artistic achievements.

To have the orchestra material checked before the first orchestra rehearsal is an imperative task for the conductor. Otherwise much precious time is lost, not to mention that the mood of the musicians will be badly affected. The more thoroughly the conductor knows the intricate instrumentation, the better can he correct technical mistakes and also organize the entire musical picture. During all the rehearsals he must be aware of:

1. The artistic interpretation
2. the metric course and dynamics
3. the melodic line
4. flaws and errors committed by musicians and singers.

To accomplish this the score should be nearly memorized; details will then further impress themselves upon his mind, until, in the end, he will watch them almost automatically.

Memorizing the orchestra score, however, does not mean conducting by memory. In concerts it has often been demonstrated that this can be done, but in operatic productions only a few conductors have had the courage to close the score. The reason is obvious; the conductor of a concert, should his memory fail him, can rely on his musicians who have their parts on the desks. In opera he can also trust the orchestra in the pit in most cases, but not the soloists and choristers on the stage who depend upon him for cues. If, in a tense moment, he forgets for one second whether the next cue comes on two or three he is lost and so is the ensemble. To conduct from memory the popular operas of the 18th and early 19th centuries is no bravura accomplishment, but to go through the performance of modern operas, relying on memory alone, is almost reckless. Conductors have directed the overtures of many an opera without glancing at the score; but they refer to it as soon as singing begins. A renowned conductor settled the matter with these words: "Why should I run into a situation in which I waste my energy by trying to remember whether the next cue is to be given to the French horn or the trumpet, to one singer or another when one look at the score tells me clearly what I have to do."

The full, not the vocal score should serve in orchestra rehearsals and in performances, except for some old and little known operas and most operettas the orchestra scores of which are not available. If the conductor cannot secure the orchestra score he must study all instrumental parts and annotate his vocal score. Using the latter in performances of a standard opera is a sign of incompetence. There are two kinds of orchestra scores, the original, ordinarily quite a tome, and the modern pocket edition. The beginner may find it advisable to become acquainted with the pocket edition while studying an opera. But when he actually conducts he can more distinctly read the picture in the large edition. The pocket edition naturally has a rather small print and consequently the text can scarcely be deciphered at all; although the general set-up is clear, single instruments cannot be read at a glance. Hence only he who is experienced and thoroughly conversant with the music should choose the pocket edition for orchestra rehearsals and performances.

Accurate annotation of the orchestra score is part of the preliminary work. The extent to which the conductor will mark his score depends on his knowledge and experience. The beginner will certainly annotate more as an aid in recalling the cues. But the student should remember that "he must have the score in his head, not his head in the score." Every important cue for instruments, soloists and choristers should be marked; also the beat, and rhythm in the beginning and any change thereafter. Every *crescendo* or *decrescendo* as well as any sudden *fortissimo*, *sforzato*, or *pianissimo* must be noticeable at a glimpse. Pauses for the entire orchestra in recitatives should be counted and indicated. Frequently conductors take colored pencils for these markings, especially red or blue ones for very important matters. It is also advisable to fasten together with clips pages that are omitted and to indicate the cut itself clearly with a *Vi-de*. In case the conductor himself gives the curtain cues and directs, through his assistant, stage band or chorus backstage he should mark this in his score. The conductor who has meticulously studied his orchestra score will be relaxed when he leads his musicians and singers. He who fumbles around looking for cues, unsure of beat and rhythm, is of no help to the ensemble; on the contrary, he wastes precious time and energy, for without unnecessary interruptions, rehearsals can be conducted more smoothly.

Attendance at some of the scene rehearsals gives the conductor the opportunity to acquaint himself with the singers' positions. He can then practice his technique at home in front of an imaginary orchestra and stage. Watching stage rehearsals may also inspire him to improve the musical execution of a transition, a change in the length of a hold and similar details. Furthermore, his doubts could be confirmed regarding some high notes of a young singer, who may not be able to sustain them in action on stage. By transposing an aria the con-

ductor can relieve the strain on a voice. A request for transition is occasionally made by an indisposed singer even on the evening of a performance. In
that case, however, the conductor would be wiser to risk a singer's bad note
since it is dangerous to let an inexperienced orchestra transpose at sight. Yet,
to be prepared for any eventuality, the conductor may practice with his musicians transposing the especially exposed arias. The famous *stretta* of Manrico
in *Il Trovatore* is one of those which are sometimes presented in a lower key.
The high C at the end, incidentally, is not printed in the score but is sung by
tradition.

It would be ideal if all orchestra rehearsals could be held in the pit, but this
is not feasible as the auditorium serves various groups and purposes and as it
is too expensive to rent it. Therefore the practicing begins in a hall; in this
case the conductor should insist on an arrangement that comes close to that in
the pit. When the soloists and possibly the choristers join the orchestra they
ought to stand behind it and not in front of it. And it may be better for all concerned to have a platform for the singers on which they can sit or stand. After
the rehearsals with the orchestra and the singers, certainly all musical elements ought to be in good shape. As soon as the orchestra is in the pit and the
ensemble acts on the stage, it should no longer be necessary to interrupt the
rehearsal for minor musical details. One dress rehearsal must sometimes
suffice if the rent is high, musicians too expensive, or the leading roles are
sung by guests. However, it must be clear that two dress rehearsals are an absolute necessity for a good production; a third should be planned if understudies
are used. At the point of the rehearsal schedule, there should be no experimenting with scenic effects. Dress rehearsals are supposed to run smoothly and to
leave the overall impression of good preparation work in all phases. Particularly the second dress rehearsal must resemble the performance proper and not
serve for the working out of details. Those in charge should be aware that
nervousness and weariness of all participants must be avoided by all means.

Seating Arrangement

As previously mentioned, the seating arrangement in the pit is different
from that on the concert platform. Only a few musicians are in front of the conductor while the majority is seated to his right and left. This collocation requires the conductor to turn, more than in concerts, to both sides; the players
likewise must adjust themselves to the new order. On the concert platform the
flutist can hear not only his colleagues of the woodwind section but also, without much trouble, the string instruments in front and the brass group behind
him. In the pit he is in close contact with his own group of woodwind players,
he may also hear others, depending on the prevailing arrangement, but he has
difficulty in listening to the instruments farther off, particularly those at the
opposite side. Members of an operatic orchestra must therefore be blessed with

very sensitive ears. Under these conditions the conductor becomes the intermediary and guide, explaining orchestration and relationship of the various sections.

Some conductors still prefer the traditional collocation,—first violins on the left, second on the right, and violoncellos in front. On the left are also the woodwinds and French horns, on the right violas, brass sections and percussion instruments. Depending on the available space, double basses are arranged behind the cellos or on the right or left of them. About forty years ago a different set-up became widely accepted, all string players being placed in front and to the left of the conductor, with the wind and percussion instruments located on the right side. This arrangement is of some advantage to the conductor in giving cues. The listener will hardly notice the difference if the pit is comparatively deep. But if the players are seated only a foot or two below the floor of the auditorium, the acoustical impression is somewhat distorted. People sitting on either side of and near the pit receive an overdose of instruments on their side, or in other words too much of the string or the wind section, respectively.

In a fairly deep pit, reaching below the apron, the volume of instruments like double basses, trumpets and trombones placed there will be toned down somewhat. Should, however, the pit be on a level with, or only a foot or two lower than, the auditorium floor, the double basses, with their long necks extending over the footlights, must not be in front of the conductor; they ought to be set up to the far left.

The "mystic gulf," as planned by Richard Wagner for Bayreuth, was adopted only by a few opera houses. In this pit, that is both deep and wide, most of the instrumental groups are placed under the apron of the stage and under a hood that covers the front of the orchestra. Almost each section is located on a different level, with the violins on the highest, right and left from the conductor. The woodwinds, French horns and harps are seated in the center of the pit which is open. The brass and percussion sections, and double basses are at the bottom under the apron. As a result of this arrangement all groups are well-blended before the sound reaches the audience. The acoustical effect is excellent for the Wagnerian music dramas and other works demanding huge masses of instruments; it is less favorable for lightly orchestrated scores.

In this country very few auditoriums and theatres have been built with an understanding of what operatic productions require. Consequently the pit is usually unsatisfactory. It is too small to seat fifty or more players; ordinarily about thirty or forty can play unimpeded. Our auditoriums are generally so wide that the space right and left of the pit can sometimes be used.

It is of the utmost importance that every musician has enough elbow-room for playing his instrument. Ten square feet are needed for a violinist, a flutist and those with similar instruments. The harpist needs twice as much space as the above-mentioned musicians. Fifty or more square feet should be saved for the percussion instruments. All desks, which should be of solid construction, must be arranged so that each player can see the conductor without having to turn his head. The pit should be so wide that three desks with six musicians can be placed between stage and audience. And for acoustical reasons, floor and walls ought to be of wood and not of concrete. It is likewise important that musicians can read their parts easily. Lamps should well illuminate the desk in front without spilling light that could affect other musicians. Special bulbs of a soft bluish light minimizing reflexion from the white sheets are used now and then. Sometimes it is possible to obtain orchestra parts with notes printed in white on black paper. These devices cut down the spilling of light on the stage.

In the center of the pit close to the audience, the conductor's platform occupies a dominating position. Twenty square feet suffice for this platform in case the conductor uses a normal stand. Twice as much is needed, if a small piano or a harpsichord is placed on it. The arrangement of lights on the conductor's stand is a very essential matter. Three lamps, one at the top and one on each side of the desk, will throw enough light on the orchestra score and on the conductor himself. The platform should be raised at least one foot above the floor of the pit so that the conductor can see everyone in the pit and on the stage and, vice versa, that all people in the pit and on the stage can see him.

This raises the question whether it is better for the conductor to stand or to be seated. If the pit is deep or the conductor is somewhat short of stature, he will prefer to stand, so that the singers on the stage can see him all the time. On the other hand, if the pit is rather shallow or the conductor is a tall man, he will better sit, out of consideration for the spectators seated behind him. He will likewise sit rather than stand in front of a comparatively small orchestra of thirty to forty members. Apart from these factors of expediency, his decision will be in keeping with his personal attitude. Some conductors feel hampered and get even tired, when conducting in a sitting position with their arms perpetually held up. Psychologically the conductor who stands gives the illusion of greater dominance over orchestra, ensemble, and, perhaps the audience too.

A small opera organization may at times have difficulty in finding musicians for all instruments. In such an emergency an organ is an appropriate substitute, primarily for some wind instruments. A piano, besides replacing the harp or harpsichord, can help fortify the volume in choral passages. Notes and passages to be played on the piano or organ respectively must be designated by the conductor after a careful examination of the orchestra score. This arrangement is not "a consummation devoutly to be wished," but in the beginning such a makeshift might be better than no production at all. There are moreover many old operas such as *Bastien and Bastienne* and a score of other French, German and Italian pieces of the 18th and 19th centuries which can be presented very well with a small number of musicians. A good string section and a few wind instruments suffice. For purposes of education these operas offer excellent material; artistically they introduce a welcome interruption of the conventional fare. Modern composers, too, have written works for an orchestra of only thirty or less players. Even Richard Strauss, who requires so many musicians in his best known operas, composed *Ariadne on Naxos* for an orchestra of about thirty-five musicians.

In an opera, as in a concert, string and wind sections must be well-balanced. If the latter group, complete with full brasses, is too strong the string instruments will be overpowered. The conductor can, of course, hold the winds back but not to such a degree that a few strings can successfully combat an entire brass division. A well-balanced and sonorous orchestra can be attained by following a pattern like this:

CHART

	Violin I	Violin II	Viola	Violoncello	D. Bass	Flute (Piccolo)	Oboe (E.H.)	Bassoon (C.B.)	Bassoon	F. Horn	Trumpet	Trombone	Tuba	Wagn. Tubes	Percussion	Harp	Total
Marriage of Figaro	6	4	4	3	2	2	2 (1)	2 (1)	2 (1)	2	2				1		32
Il Trovatore	8 (6)	6 (4)	4 (3)	3	3 (2)	2	2 (1)	2	2 (1)	4 (2)	2	3 (1)	1 (0)		2 (1)	1	45
Faust	8 (6)	6 (4)	4 (3)	4 (3)	3 (2)	2	2 (1)	2	2 (1)	4 (2)	2	3 (1)	1 (0)		2 (1)	1	46
La Bohème	8 (6)	6	4	3	3	3 (2)	3 (1)	3 (2)	2 (1)	4 (2)	3 (2)	3 (1)	1 (0)		3 (2)	1	50
The Mastersingers	8	6	4	4	3	3	2	2	2	4	3	3	1		2	1	48
Siegfried	10 (8)	8 (6)	6 (4)	6 (4)	4 (3)	3 (2)	4 (2)	3 (2)	3 (2)	4	4 (3)	4 (3)	1	4 (0)	2	2 (1)	68
The Mikado	6 (4)	4 (3)	4 (2)	3 (2)	2 (1)	2 (1)	2 (1)	2 (1)	2 (1)	2 (1)	2 (1)	3 (0)			1		35

(The numbers in parenthesis are meant as an alternative in case some instruments have to be eliminated.)

There are many questions that cannot be answered in a chart. Thus it is difficult to list the precise number of musicians necessary to handle all percussion instruments. Moreover, modern composers require sometimes a piano, a celesta or saxophones. In *Faust, Il Trovatore*, and *The Mastersingers* for example, an organ backstage is needed. Not all auditoriums and opera houses are equipped with an organ. Then a portable organ must be rented which of course does not always give a satisfactory volume and sound. Furthermore, possible demands for a stage band have to be considered. Small civic and educational groups may prefer to have the particular passages played in the pit or by a few musicians who will leave the pit to play backstage, such as can be arranged in acts two and four of *Carmen*. This solution is hardly workable in *The Mastersingers*, *Aida* and *Der Rosenkavalier*, operas for which a separate group of musicians must be available on stage or backstage respectively.

As the chart indicates, it is feasible to dispense with some instruments occasionally. Thus in *Il Trovatore* the second oboe and other instruments may be omitted without great harm, if not enough good musicians can be found. However, this is only recommended in an emergency. Adaptations of this kind are sometimes available through the service of a renting agency. They are particularly helpful to small groups which plan to produce an opera by Puccini, Wagner and other modern composers. Instead of the original three and more wind instruments only two may be used. The orchestral sound as a whole is not palpably affected; moreover, these eliminations represent some financial savings.

No maximum number is given for the string section. In a large auditorium more strings than the number listed should be employed, notably if the musicians are young and perhaps unable to produce a full sound. As educational institutions often have too many wind players, it is not a poor practice to double the wood wind section; these additional instrumentalists should however only join in ensemble and chorus scenes. A good many organizations have trouble finding the minimum number of string players. In that case they are advised not to select operas which are very demanding in this section, to be specific, those which show the violins and the other string instruments in subdivisions. This pertains for instance to *La Traviata* and *The Valkyrie*. In a simplified version these pieces do not sound as they should.

A final hint: Always have a solid foundation of strings! Eliminate wind instruments, first of all in the brass section, if your strings are weak!

The Actual Conducting

For all his concentration on detecting and correcting errors and flaws, the conductor must never lose the great line of his conception. Corrections must not be pedantic; to be sure, every deviation from pitch or rhythm must be amended, yet this is not his ultimate goal. His aim is a euphonious ensemble well-blended into the symphonic web of tone. Only a performance that is impeccable in all technical aspects can also be artistically perfect.

Whether or not he should practice first with the string section is a question which the conductor decides upon weighing the technical difficulties of a given opera and the skill of his musicians. The difference between a concert and a stage performance should be pointed out at the first run-through of a score. Since the singers do not attend the first rehearsals, the conductor can somehow hum certain important passages of the singers, especially in a *recitativo accompagnato*. This is the best procedure to acquaint the musicians with the cues they have to watch on the stage. As has been stated, the material has to be checked beforehand; now the musicians must ascertain that all markings of dynamics and special effects are correct. From the first hour of practicing everyone in the pit must be conscious of the singers and accordingly must often modify the volume demanded by the composer. The utmost care must be taken that the voices are not drowned out by the waves of the full orchestra. The complaints about too strong a volume of an orchestra are legion, while there have been seldom any about too soft a tone. Again it must be emphasized that, except for some climactic moments and passages, a *forte* is not a *fortissimo*, rather a fortissimo should be played only forte in an operatic production. To cut a brief chord accurately should be a superfluous hint, but listening to several orchestras makes it advisable to insert this fundamental requirement. The orchestra has to get accustomed to the fact that a conductor may cue the singers with his left hand while giving signs to the musicians with his right. The conducting of a dramatic recitative and a *cadenza* have to be clarified early. The players ought to be fully informed about the conductor's habits. A baton should be used not just for the last rehearsal and the performance, but all the time since the conductor's technique should not vary.

Orchestra rehearsals, whether in a hall or in a theatre, belong to the conductor even when singers and choristers act. The director must not interrupt or interfere beyond the necessary orders for beginning, entrances of singers, and changing the settings. Whenever he wants to talk to a singer he must wait until the conductor stops the ensemble for a correction. The conductor, on the other hand, must abstain from any interference in the field of acting. The statement "I cannot conduct this scene as it is staged" should not be heard, since it reveals the conductor's inability to give clear cues or the fact that his ensemble is musically ill-prepared. Expert directors know very well what can be expected of singers and what may and should be done to render a production dramatically interesting. This refers mainly to fight scenes and comic sequences in which acting is very prominent. The conductor who insists that everyone face him should remember Toscanini's attitude. He made it clear that he preferred dramatic action to having singers stand around and stare at him. This freedom of action, however, must not degenerate into musical anarchy. In a well-prepared performance, singers and conductor have an agreement about important cues. The stage director can always arrange positions so that singers see the baton out of the corner of their eyes while facing another character on stage. Sometimes the singers can take care of themselves, by holding hands, one of them marking the rhythm, as for instance in a *cadenza*. In a recitative or a lightly orchestrated passage the conductor should not even object to singers turning fully away from him.

The amount of cues to be given depends on the difficulty of the piece, the ability and experience of singers and musicians, plus the number and intensity of rehearsals. And yet, even in the best prepared performances, errors may

136

occur. The conductor must incessantly be on the alert to correct any mistake. Through exhaustive rehearsals singers and musicians alike become accustomed to watching the conductor's eyes and baton: his left hand should be used for additional cues and the correction of errors such as singing off key or starting too soon or too late. If a singer missed a cue he should not make up for it by increasing the tempo, which could throw the whole ensemble off balance; instead he ought to wait for the next cue. When he is off key the conductor's index finger of his left hand tries to correct this mishap. Whenever singers or choristers pause for a while the conductor prepares the next cue by having them look at him beforehand. In conducting subdivided beats (binary, ternary) the subdivisions must remain so clearly cut that they do not overrun the main beat.

Platforms serving as acting areas should be set up for the orchestra rehearsal for reasons of acoustics and of preventing disintegration of the stage director's blocking when everyone tries to see the conductor. No change of positions should ever have to be made in the dress rehearsal, for then the director has to supervise numerous other items. In the orchestra rehearsal the singers should also have at least their essential hand properties, such as a harp or guitar, the pretended playing of which they have to synchronize at that time. Whenever the sound of a property is part of the musical pattern as the hammering in the second act of *The Mastersingers* or the first scene of act two in *Il Trovatore*, it must be practiced in every rehearsal.

Blending the individual voices with the other singers and the chorus is a major task, left to the last rehearsals. The acoustics in a theatre are very different from those in a practice hall, the acoustics in a crowded house differ from those in an empty one. Hence the conductor and the director should be conversant with the acoustical conditions of the particular auditorium. The conductor may give his baton to an assistant and move around in the house, as some competent conductors do in new surroundings, with a new singer in the cast or a new opera. In this way, he obtains an impression of the performance as it is offered to the audience, an undivided unit. Of course, all members of the ensemble must sing with their full voices when the conductor is checking the acoustics.

Particular problems arise in open air theatres with large stages. The distance from the singers to the conductor and on to the last rows of the amphitheatre is so great that the voices cannot be heard without amplifiers. Microphones and loudspeakers however, while removing part of the difficulty, bring out in turn a new one of their own. These devices moreover do not prevent a breeze, let alone a strong wind, from upsetting the tonal balance, if not silencing voices altogether. Aside from space and wind, a sudden drop in temperature or a change in humidity can cause unfortunate results. A change through a rush of cold and above all damp air can throw the string instruments out of tune and affect, as well, the singers' voices.

Stage Band and Backstage Chorus

As if the conductor had not enough to worry about with singers, choristers and musicians, he has to supervise two more groups, stage band and chorus offstage, both vital elements in many operas. Frequently an assistant does the actual conducting, yet the accurate coordination is the conductor's responsibility. There is comparatively smooth sailing when the band is on the stage proper as is the case in the impressive finale of act two of *Aida* and the first finale of *Don Giovanni*. For want of instrumentalists the music can be played in the pit with extras on stage simulating the playing. This strategem may be profitably applied also in scenes where the band has to walk while playing. Of course, if the stage band is experienced enough to be entrusted with this difficult task it should by all means play the music itself. In *La Bohème*, for one, the effect of the military band actually playing while marching across the stage is incomparably stronger. And this holds equally true of the second act of *Otello* when Desdemona enters accompanied by a group of peasants—one of the most delicate operatic scences as regards synchronization of orchestra, singers, chorus and stage band. Here, a workable solution is to let the band play backstage and to have extras feign the playing of instruments while they come along with the chorus.

Sometimes a composer writes a passage for instruments on the stage, but it is seldom presented in this fashion. Often a singer "plays" an instrument as part of the action; Manrico *(Il Trovatore)* blows his horn, Siegfried the shawn (oboe in orchestra) and horn, and the shepherd in *Tannhaeuser* also blows the shawn. The soloist simply simulates while a musician plays these passages, preferably back stage, not in the pit. Should he be in the pit, however, then the character ought to stand at least on the side of the stage where the corresponding sound comes from the orchestra. In *Lohengrin* and *Aida* brass players in costume playing their passages on stage are very impressive indeed.

The dance music in the last scene of *The Masked Ball* sounds better coming from backstage, but it can be played in the pit without ill effect. In act three of *Der Rosenkavalier* the backstage band is so characteristic for the atmosphere that it cannot be omitted. In *The Three Penny Opera* by Brecht and Weill the orchestra, actually a band, was seated in the original production upstage center on a platform behind the acting area.

There are some chorus passages backstage, accompanied by organ, others by a small band, and some sung *a capella*, as in *Il Trovatore, Cavalleria Rusticana, Carmen, Tannhaeuser* and *Tosca*. The women in the first act of *Madame Butterfly* begin singing offstage but after a few measures, enter the scene; in the following act, another tune is sung behind the setting. In *The Mastersingers*, act one, the choristers are visible to the audience but in some productions with their backs to the audience. A great portion of the difficult swan chorus at Lohengrin's arrival in act one of *Lohengrin* is executed by the chorus facing the wing, which causes the same dilemma as singing backstage.

The wedding chorus (women) in that opera begins and ends backstage, while the men join the singing on stage. In act three of *The Flying Dutchman* a double chorus is required, the Norwegian sailors on land, and the Dutchman's crew on the ship. The latter can appear on board or may sing off stage.

The execution of an *a capella* choral sequence is fairly simple; it is entirely in the hands of the chorus master. But coordinating pit and chorus or band backstage takes good ears, technical skill, and quite an amount of knowledge. Both conductors, in the pit and on the stage, must have more than a mere agreement about tempo, beat and volume; they must keep in close contact during these scenes to achieve synchronization. Direct contact can be obtained by way of a little hole in a flat, behind which the assistant stands on a chair or ladder to conduct the chorus and/or the band. He can thus watch the conductor before the cue and control the coordination during the passages he has to conduct. This method requires the assistant to memorize the music for he has no opportunity to follow the score when watching the conductor through the hole. In some professional opera houses a tactometer is used. This is a keyboard with four buttons to the left side of the conductor's desk; he taps them in accordance with the rhythms of the passage, giving the first beat or more depending on the tempo of the piece. The assistant on stage sees numbers (1-4) flashing up on a stand in front of him. This device can be installed at certain key points around the stage or made portable. But many conductors have complained that the electric tactometer is not foolproof, for the time between pushing the buttons and the reaction and its transformation into action again leaves an interval for discrepancies in rhythm. And chances for a difference naturally increase with the distance between band or chorus and the pit. To synchronize orchestra and music backstage the beat of the chorus master (assistant conductor) must of necessity anticipate that of the conductor in the pit. In the temple scenes of *Parsifal* an exceptionally complicated task is to harmonize the orchestra with the bells, the voices of the chorus and the soloist, seemingly coming from the cupola of the hall. More than one assistant is needed for these assignments.

Another device, consisting of microphone and earphone, affords accurate timing whenever close contact between pit and backstage is vital. With a listening post, a microphone, installed in the orchestra pit, the backstage assistant can easily follow the music with his earphone. Of course this method needs an experienced man as the visual cue is missing. A modification of this procedure was successfully employed in a production of Menotti's *The Old Maid and the Thief*. The orchestra was placed behind the setting, and microphones installed in the footlights enabled the conductor through his earphone to synchronize the soloists and instrumentalists. Television has given us the best system of coordinating backstage singing with the conductor in the pit. A camera trained on the conductor with a microphone picking up the orchestra and a monitor plus a loudspeaker backstage make it easily possible for the assistant conductor to hear the music and see the conductor. This monitor system was probably installed for the first time in 1956 in the reopened opera house in Vienna; it has been adopted by other opera houses.

An assistant conductor is not always needed, for a soloist who has to sing a brief passage backstage can take an earphone and thus cue himself. This solution is feasible among others in the last act of *Rigoletto* when the Duke repeats his song backstage, in the first act of *La Traviata* for Alfredo, and in the first scene of *The Bat* (Fledermaus) for Alfred. There is also a possibility of using a microphone offstage for a singer; a loudspeaker, installed on the stage or in the pit, will carry his voice into the audience. This trick is especially effective for a ghost-like or supernatural sound, as is desired for instance, for the Commendatore and also for the trombones in the cemetery scene in *Don Giovanni*, for Mephistopheles in the church scene of *Faust* and for Fafner in *Siegfried*. It can also be employed for choral tunes like that of the crew on the Dutchman's ship and in the last scene of *Don Giovanni*. The dramatic impact is determined to a large extent by the engineer's ability to select the right place for the microphone and loudspeaker and to regulate the tone volume.

The placing of a band or chorus backstage is contingent on both the size of the stage and the dramatic situation. A chorus supposedly singing in the rear of the setting should not sound as if the voices came from the wing. Echos of a strange nature create such impressions at times. Experiments will tell where the chorus should be located. The question is more complicated when the music fades in or out, indicating a group drawing nearer or leaving the scene. Starting and ending the vocal passage with a soft sound is of course necessary, but the best result is attained when the choristers really approach the stage from rather far away and then disappear on the opposite side. If the stage is not wide enough or no corridor available, the choristers should face the side wall (or back wall) of the stage at the beginning. After crossing the setting, they again turn their backs to the stage.

Significant scenes in this respect are the pilgrim chorus in *Tannhaeuser* and the brief Bacchanal in the last act of *La Traviata*. These various assignments demand of the chorus master a peculiar sort of agility; he must be able to conduct standing on a chair or ladder, moving in front of his group, or walking backward. Since every vibration counts, he must not only know his score thoroughly, but possess reliable pitch and rhythm as well. On first thought, all these matters seem to be almost irrelevant and inconsequential. But practical experience will demonstrate to the aspiring conductor that only consideration of everything will lead to a performance of a high artistic standard.

TECHNICAL PROBLEMS

Acoustical Aspects

Stage director, designer and conductor should learn the fundamentals of acoustics and their application on the stage. A misconception seems to exist

140

about the influence of certain material surrounding the singer on the volume and quality of his voice. Fears have been expressed on occasion that settings consisting of drapes swallow the tone. Some singers, in addition, are opposed to performing in front of a cyclorama or in any area which in their opinion is too far upstage. They complain about being unable to hear themselves in certain locations. In fact, some settings support the singer and there are others which impair his voice.

It is certainly easy to sing in a rather small auditorium which is acoustically well-devised. A shallow box setting likewise is favorable to the projection of the voice. But the average auditorium is large and so is the average stage. Consequently acoustical problems exist, the nature of which is known. Within a few years any disturbing factor can probably be eliminated. An echo in a theatre or auditorium, for example, can be removed by hanging draperies in doors, over windows, by covering, or better yet, padding walls. At times there is an echo in the empty house which disappears when the hall is filled with people. Chairs covered with soft material also have a mellowing effect. Simple remedies like these should be tried before the recommendation of microphones and loudspeakers is advanced. A loudspeaker system is no remedy for poor conditions, certainly not in a small auditorium. Yet even in a large hall it should only be employed after consultation with an expert. This applies also to open air theatres. Whenever microphones are installed, the singers should not stand too close to them; the most favorable position for picking up and blending voices is between six and ten feet away.

A solid surface projects sound forward. Therefore an interior setting made of plywood and covered by a ceiling represents the ideal solution, comparable to the resonance box of an instrument. Unfortunately not many companies can afford to spend money on scenery made of plywood. The traditional setting of painted canvas strung across wooden frames offers approximately the same amount of support to the voice. For acoustical reasons it is better to have a ceiling over the box setting.

Open wings are the rule rather than the exception in operatic productions. When, in the course of action, singers turn toward the wings, certain difficulties arise which basically correspond with the measurements of stage and auditorium. Engineers understand generally how to eliminate echo and distortion and how to achieve adequate vibration and reverberation. If acoustical conditions in the auditorium itself are known to be good, no particular trouble should arise from the stage. The singer can face the wing confidently or even turn his back to the audience without fear that the volume of his voice will be restricted to any noticeable degree. He has to realize, though, that he must increase his volume and in addition watch his enunciation very carefully.

In front of a cyclorama, especially of the dome type, precaution is necessary. Depending on its shape (radius of curvature) it can cause what is commonly called a dead spot—even two dead spots. If a singer stands at such a spot, his voice possibly sounds dull, or an echo is noticeable. This happens whether the singer faces the audience or turns toward the cyclorama. Such hazards must be discovered through calculation or experimentation. The stage director and the designer are then in a position to plan the settings accordingly by placing a pillar, column or tree at such a spot or between it and the cyclorama. Furthermore, the action can be so blocked that the singers are kept away from standing near such a hazardous spot.

Curtains, draperies and carpets absorb or at least reduce sound. We know that heavy material like velour can dull any voice if a singer stands directly in front of it. But at a distance of a few feet the volume or brilliance of his tone will not be affected. In such settings singers act instinctively in the center of the stage near the curtain line. To some extent they are right and should therefore not be asked to sing too near or against the absorbing material. Although an ordinary ground cloth (floor covering) of canvas is most suitable, rugs, even heavy ones, are not bad for the voice as long as the singer stands erect and projects his tone straight forward or slightly upward.

Singers sometimes insist on presenting delicate and difficult passages close to the curtain line because they erroneously believe that this area is acoustically the most favorable. The fact is, however, that the best space is usually several feet (6-10) behind the proscenium frame and tormentor. In general we may say that the artist should not be asked to sing such passages upstage unless the dramatic situation necessitates this. Lohengrin, for example, to address the swan stands rather far away from the footlights and turns his back to the audience and the conductor as well. In *The Magic Flute*, the Queen of the Night appears and sings on a platform upstage in act one. There is no good reason for permitting Des Grieux in act two of *Manon*, Violetta in act one of *Traviata*, and many other characters to move downstage for their arias. But each case must always be examined in conjunction with the orchestration and the dramatic situation.

Special Effects

Librettists and composers call for gun shots, thunder and noise of various origin. Thus sound effects backstage are an important part of the action. In one work a pistol is fired, in another a big gun. Sometimes the extras or choristers have to "rebel", or the impression of the insurgent mob is created in the orchestra; in these cases there is no need for additional noise behind the scene. The greatest complication is involved in effects like fire, smoke, rain, snow, fog, lightning, and thunder—or moon, stars, rainbow, and even sun. It takes more than ingenuity to solve these problems. Here the director needs the advice of the designer, the technical director and/or the master electrician. Close cooperation must be obtained to find an artistic and practical solution.

The first step is to cull all effects from the score, to evaluate their significance, to determine the time duration allotted to them by the composer, and to find the proper place on the stage for their execution. Whatever the solution, the synchronization with the music is the predominant factor. In one opera it may suffice to indicate lightning with a borderlight; in another a grandiose thunder-storm must be created. A fire may be a simple wood fire in an open hearth, or a real conflagration; in either case the indication is more effective and artistic than a "realistic" imitation of a fire. The glow of every fire should be whitish, perhaps yellowish, rather than reddish. Under certain circumstances slight or heavy smoke rises from a fire. A suitable device to simulate smoke is a fog machine, because it is easy to handle and its mist does not harm the voices. If smoke bombs are used, their possible effect on the singers' throats must be examined.

Many phenomena such as stars, lightning, moon, and rainbow can be made visible to the audience by means of projection. The intensity of the light source (lamp) to be used depends on the size of the stage, the distance from the lens to the scrim, and the measurements of the desired projected picture. Slides for simple effects can be made by the technical director or the electrician. A blackened slide upon which merely the shape of a waning, waxing, or full moon is left uncovered, is very effective when projected on dark drapes, on a back-drop or on a cyclorama. The same procedure can be employed for flashes of lightning. A piece of thin metal with very small holes helps in projecting stars; the moon may be projected in similar fashion. But stars and moon and sun can also be produced "real", notably for comic effects.

To create an impressive effect which includes a wide and high scrim or the cyclorama is not an easy task. The projection of a dream castle, a street or a landscape requires more than a simple magic lantern. For such complicated ideas a slide projector with special, rather expensive lenses and other attach-ments is needed. A designer can transfer his sketch directly on a small glass plate; special paint (textile lacquer) is suitable for this work. The thickness of the applied paint and the choice of colors has to be determined experimentally. As material for the slides hardened glass can be recommended along with mica and plexiglass. Most designers now prefer to have color photos made of their sketches. In that case the photographing has to be done rather early because firms developing color photos are not available in many cities. A bluish back-drop for the projection should be avoided, lest many colors appear blurred or washed out. The best surface is provided by a white muslin scrim (which must be transparent if the projector is used from upstage). A first class slide projector creates a picture of 30-35' by 20-25' from twenty feet away. For a very large scrim or cyclorama two projectors may be necessary. In the latter case the two pictures have to be designed and projected with utmost care so that the dividing line is almost unnoticeable. Projection can be thrown also on black drapes if the design shows merely lines. Thus the outline of a window, a door or even an entire hall can be created.

If the purchase (or rent) of regular slide projectors is regarded as too ex-pensive, another device is quite useful. This is the Linnebach projector, known since the twenties and described in several books on lighting. A drawback is that its projected pictures are not very sharp. As its images are rather unreal,

143

this instrument is most suitable for the creation of fantastic pictures. Its advantage is that it is cheap and easy to operate. A final warning: have two sets of slides, as glass plates can be broken; moreover, the lamp of a slide projector is very strong and the heat can cause breakage. The heat can also cause the painted colors to run even if a ventilator is attached to the projector.

Of prime influence is the position of the projector. It may be set on a well-anchored catwalk behind the proscenium arch. Great care must be taken that the beam does not touch any teaser, and that actors keep some feet away from screen or backdrop. Director and designer must consider these matters when they plan the settings. In case there is no solid catwalk, or none at all, a high platform can be erected in the left or right wing; the second wing may be preferred where the stage is rather deep or the desired pictorial effect comparatively small. A distance of only a few yards is required for the projection of stars and similar, small effects. Under certain conditions, the projector can be placed on the floor behind a transparent scrim; this is not advisable if the auditorium has a balcony as the spectators sitting there are able to notice the light source. Wherever the projector is installed, the picture on the scrim or cyclorama is distorted. This does not matter much if the style of the production allows an exaggerated fantastic impression. But if a more natural image is desired, the distortion must be reduced to a minimum. The designer can take the angle of the beam into consideration when drawing his sketches; or the photographer must shoot the designs at an angle. To obtain the best solution a mathematician should be consulted.

The potential use of microphones and loudspeakers has been touched upon. These modern devices, which have been improved almost to perfection, can be applied also to fortify such variegated sounds as bells, chimes, wind, thunder, and waves. Depending on preference and conditions, recordings or live sound respectively can be selected and amplified. Live sound is often preferable as it is difficult to find a recording of sounds that match the pitch necessary in a given opera. This concerns bells and chimes. As to wind, thunder and waves, acceptable recordings are hard to discover. Most colleges possess excellent means to tape many sounds, and civic groups can have this done in a professional studio. If the artistic leaders are not completely satisfied with the results they should experiment with amplifying the live sound of bells or chimes. A similar treatment will do for the sound of wind, thunder, or waves. Quite simple devices which are described in almost every book on stage craft can be used, and properly placed microphones and loudspeakers bring better results than recordings. The same solution works if a concert organ is not available and a portable organ must be rented. Conductors and directors may try similar experiments with a weak backstage chorus or band. A loudspeaker system, delicately handled, can considerably improve these defects.

Additional technical problems are dealt with in Appendix III.

144

DRESS REHEARSALS

During the first dress rehearsal all artistic and technical elements are co-ordinated. If platforms and most of the properties were made available in advance, little trouble should arise when the settings, lighting, properties and costumes are added. Yet if the singers and choristers confront the entire technical apparatus without sufficient preparation, considerable nervousness can affect the stage business, let alone the singing. One final rehearsal is too great a strain, primarily on the leading characters. In the first dress, while adjusting their stage deportment to settings and costumes, the singers may use *sotto voce* to husband their voices. They will be ready to give their all in the second dress rehearsal which should essentially be equal to a performance. Whenever guest artists are engaged for all or the most important solo parts, one dress rehearsal must sometimes suffice. But a second is indispensable if local singers serve as understudies. The guests have, in most cases, sung their roles previously. Nevertheless they should not arrive just to participate in the dress rehearsal but ought to be in town available for at least three days, if feasible a week, prior to opening night. A superficial understanding with the conductor is not sufficient to achieve even a reliable performance. Every guest should welcome the opportunity to become well-acquainted with the entire cast, the settings and the blocking. Conductors and directors try to accommodate renowned singers in every possible way but they must never let the integrity of the ensemble be disrupted.

The first dress rehearsal offers the best time to check every factor, as the director, the designer and the conductor can observe for the first time the results of their combined efforts. These three men are by now aware of potential flaws in the singing, the acting, and the scenic effects which may need special attention. Director and designer are free to make notes during acts, but the conductor is handicapped. Until he is thoroughly seasoned he should have an assistant sitting behind him to write down critical remarks. In operas with dialogues or recitatives which are accompanied by an assistant, the conductor can make notes for himself during those scenes. Both the stage and the musical director are cautioned to check all pertinent questions during the first dress rehearsal and re-check them during the second. This check and re-check should include not only obvious errors committed on stage and in the pit but numerous "little things" which cannot truly be evaluated in earlier rehearsals. Musically it is essential to assure that in all places of the auditorium the words can be clearly understood in recitatives, in dialogue scenes, and in soft passages, and that no scenic effect or business distracts from the singing of a delicate melody. Not until this time does the balance of orchestra and ensemble receive its final polish. The stage director and his collaborators will of course examine the settings, the lighting, the costumes and the make-up from every angle. This work begins on stage with testing the safety of all stairs and platforms, the proper functioning of all doors, etc., and goes on during the rehearsals to check in several locations of the auditorium whether the actions are clear and impressive and whether all scenic effects are executed as planned. From the house the orchestra lights must be checked too, as they can interfere with the light effects on stage as well as irritate spectators sitting in the first rows. Now is the last chance to take corrective measures.

Careful planning, intensive work, and full cooperation of all participants are the prerequisites for satisfactory dress rehearsals. In educational institutions organizing a production causes no excessive demands, but conditions are quite different in many civic associations which rarely have a theatre of their own or, anyway, the premission to use the building whenever and as long as they need it. Their preparatory efforts must therefore be greater in order to reach their goal, since they practice in another hall, have to bring in settings, costumes, properties and possibly lighting instruments from a number of places or from out of town. Any negligence—it may be just an oversight—can lead to unwarranted delays and defects. If everyone has attended to his duties, there is no reason why the dress rehearsals should not begin on time. Unless, because of an emergency, not all chorus members are in costume or made up, a property is lost or whatever else may happen, the curtain should open precisely at the hour set. Much depends on the technical director, but the conductor as well as the stage director can see to it that everything is ready.

Conductor and director should not interrupt the final rehearsals. Only a breakdown of the musical ensemble, of the technical setup or of the action gives them the excuse to stop the performers. Every unwarranted interruption is a waste of energy and time with the probable loss of money for overtime pay. Such interruptions interfere with the unfolding of the drama and thwart the inspiration of the artists. Minor errors can be corrected by the perpetrators themselves. The last rehearsal, at any rate, should give the impression of a real performance, where invited guests may function as a stimulus to the artists giving the performers the feel of an audience by way of laughs, applause or any other response. Wholesome criticism can come from friends of the organization who, sitting in different rows and corners, may comment on visibility, audibility and the like.

The stage manager takes over and is fully responsible for the running of the dress rehearsals. By now he must have an accurate prompt book containing all cues for curtains, entrances and scenic effects. Operas in which the chorus plays a significant part require simultaneous attention to so many details that the director may want to give the manager an assistant. The chorus master is, to a great extent, responsible for his group; yet he or another musical assistant can also take care of cues for the electrician and crew. Still, the stage manager is in need of a call boy, unless an adequate intercom system is installed.

During dress rehearsals singers and other participants like to see from the house scenes in which they do not participate. It is the call boy's task to have everyone on stage when wanted for an entrance. In these rehearsals, as in a performance, there should be no disturbance backstage, nobody present who

146

does not belong there. And the musicians in the pit should concentrate on their task and refrain from standing up to watch the events on stage!

By this time also the prompter's place must have been designated. A few opera houses have a special box built in the center of the footlights. It is a good solution because, from there, the prompter can be easily heard by the singers and he can even give them some cues. Sometimes a prompter's box can be installed in the pit, but this arrangement looks so clumsy that most groups prefer to have the prompting done from the wings. Depending on the size of the stage— and most auditoriums have rather wide stages—it is useful to have two prompters, one in each wing behind the tormentor.

The stage director informs the conductor when everything is ready; he then takes his seat in the auditorium, where he can see the entire stage, unhampered by anyone sitting or moving in front of him, and yet not too far from the pit, so that he can communicate with the conductor if necessary. A covered light, enabling him to jot down notes should be installed on his special desk, and an intercom phone, providing contact with the stage manager and electrician ought to be available for corrections that have to be made at once. Otherwise an assistant or call boy will have to carry messages backstage. In a well-organized theatre the director should not be obliged to run errands himself. In the auditorium the director's collaborators will also be seated: designer, technical director, ballent master and wardrobe mistress, each prepared to make notes.

Intermissions are utilized to discuss errors and modifications with the singers and others. Choristers, dancers and extras should be dealt with first so that these large groups may leave the stage which can then be taken over by the technical director. If possible the director gives his criticism to the soloists in the green room. There after talking to the musicians in the pit, the conductor will join.

No incisive alteration should be made at this time. Any changes in singing, dancing or settings must have been arranged at an earlier stage. Yet attention to many details can help improve the performance. *In singing:* retarding, accelerating, giving more volume, holding a *fermata* longer or cutting it short, balancing voices within the ensemble and the like. *In acting:* clearer distinction in forming groups, more accurate execution of movements, little gestures and turns instead of standing motionless. *In technical matters:* changing light cues, smooth transition, shifting furniture that interferes with the action, alterations on costumes and in the make-up, adding or eliminating properties. It is imperative, however, that every detail thus varied must be rehearsed either during intermissions or in a separate rehearsal on the following day. But, to repeat, no essential alterations must take place at this late date lest the performers become nervous and confused.

It is a wise custom to have an intervening day between the two dress rehearsals. On this "free" day a few hours can be spent practicing weak scenes. Another day of rest between the last dress and opening night is a boon to the

147

singers of major roles. Young singers in particular feel the strain of performing an exacting part with full voice. Whether or not a call for a brief rehearsal is advisable before the first performance depends on circumstances. Perhaps the conductor wants to go once more over some difficult passages. Perhaps scenic effects should be practiced to make sure that a quick shifting of scenery or intricate lighting transitions will run smoothly. Civic groups will consider this advice a rather expensive proposition, yet it is money well spent for the sake of a consummate production.

An artisitic venture is not merely the result of inspiration but to a high degree of hard work. And this work is based not on improvisation but on "know-how".

THE PERFORMANCE

During the three or four hours of the performance, the public becomes the sole judge of the achievements of the entire company, these few hours being the climax of all the preceding study and effort. It is then only wise and timely to set the patrons in a pleasant mood. Providing the right atmosphere for the enjoyment of a production is the task of the house manager and his helpers. The following hints are well known, but sometimes neglected; therefore it is advisable to enumerate them here. It begins at the door, in fact at nearby parking places. Arrangements should be made for easy parking and a convenient path to the theatre, well-lighted. Whoever is in charge of the box office must be friendly and business-like. In the lobby there should be, if possible, two windows or counters, one for the general ticket sale and another for reservations. Ushers, properly instructed, must know how to guide the patrons to their seats. It is also the responsibility of the house manager to have the theatre aired beforehand; he should keep it comparatively cool, because a large crowd will raise the temperature within an hour. The main curtain should not be closed until the time when the spectators are admitted. But check city ordinances which sometimes order the closing of the asbestos at certain hours. At any rate, everything should be done to have the same temperature on stage and in the auditorium so that no disagreeable draft disturbs the singers as well as the audience. The bell system, too, belongs in the domain of the house manager. He has to inform the stage manager when to ring the bells before the performance and at the end of an intermission. If bells are not available, the house and stage manager should arrange for flashing of lights in lobby and lounge. A gong is another suitable device if it can be heard throughout the theatre.

Long before the overture begins, the musicians can be seen in the pit unless it is rather deep. But they should not be heard tuning their instruments which should be done before they enter the pit. The concertmaster and other first desk players supervise the tuning which should be done about fifteen minutes before curtain time. It is indeed imperative to re-check the pitch in the pit, but this can be done pianissimo. When the house lights are dimmed and the conductor enters the pit, no sound should be heard. In professional opera houses it is customary for all musicians to appear dressed in tails, tuxedos, or, in a few cases in dark suits. There is a twofold reason for this habit. To begin with, uniformity is desirable and impressive and the dark colors do not reflect light on the setting. As soon as the performance has started, the ushers should not permit anyone to enter the house until after the overture or even after the first act. If act one is too long, spectators may be allowed to stand and sit down in the rear or wherever they do not disturb others.

Behind the curtain, where everybody's nerves are on edge, conductor and director must keep calm and self-controlled. The players may make mistakes in the performance but the conductor must at all times be in a position to set these errors right again. The stage director too should exercise a soothing influence upon cast and crew. All the toil of preparation can come to naught if the leaders show infectious nervousness. The conductor naturally is not immune against the high tensions surrounding him but he must not be caught in it to such an extent that he gives wrong cues or commits other major errors. General excitement may cause him to retard or to hasten a tempo a little, yet he has to control himself since his responsibility in the performance is greater than that of anyone else. On stage, the manager is in charge although the director remains responsible for whatever happens. Supported by the crew heads, perhaps also by an assistant and a coach for some difficult musical cues, the stage manager runs the entire production. The director's place is in the auditorium, in the green room, or wherever he wants to be, but not on stage unless an emergency requires his presence.

Some groups still arrange for a pep talk to be given a few minutes before curtain time, as it used to be done in play productions of many high schools, colleges and community theatres. This outdated custom has no place in a professional or any high class production. Conductors and directors like to say a few encouraging words to individuals. This is of course recommendable; it may soothe frayed nerves and give comfort and inspiration. On the other hand, criticism of any sort must be avoided. It is unwise moreover to give new instructions shortly before the opera begins. Such last minute directions will hardly be observed anyway in the excitement of the performance. All the participants should be protected from diversions. Thus every group should make it a rule to forbid well-wishing outsiders to appear backstage or in the corridors leading to the dressing rooms before the performance and during the hectic intermission periods. Friends and relatives may come backstage after the final curtain.

Applause after arias and great ensembles is an accepted custom with many operatic theatres. Therefore singers are to be informed during rehearsals when to expect special applause. Some educational institutions disapprove of this habit, contrary to most civic companies, who consider it essential to the atmosphere and a welcome token of the patrons' appreciation. To stimulate applause, a claque is sometimes placed at strategic points in the theatre. The experience in legitimate opera houses has been that the audience becomes quite wary of this group and refuses to join in the acclamation. Opinions about the usefulness of the claque system are divided, but agreement on the importance of taking a curtain bow after acts and above all, at the end, is general. The director plans this business which is to be supervised by the stage manager. The procedure should be so rehearsed that no valuable time in the evening is lost. A good procedure is to have the leading singers take a bow in front of the curtain after each act or even subdivision of an act, as for instance, in *Il Trovatore*. On the other hand, in *The Magic Flute* interrupting the many scenes will adversely affect the performance. A musical interlude naturally excludes acknowledgement of applause. Minor characters join in the curtain call for a particular act. It is customary, furthermore, for all soloists and the conductor to appear before the curtain after the first great finale, such as after act two of *Aida* and *Marriage of Figaro*, act three of *Martha* and *Otello*, the first act of *Madame Butterfly* and *Don Giovanni*, as well as at the end of the opera. The stage director, and sometimes the designer and the choreographer, may join the group on both occasions, or at least at the end of the performance.

From a technical viewpoint the last rehearsal ought to be as finished as can humanly be expected. And yet, should such a felicitous condition ever occur, there is still something missing that will make its appearance only during the evening of the performance itself; it is the excitement and elation that grips the whole ensemble and lifts them out of their everyday life. We may call it sensation of accomplishment, sense of responsibility, or plain stage fright. Often it is a combination of all three. Every participant is affected by the presence of an audience. The beginner has the opportunity of being heard and seen, and his ability to interpret a master piece is appraised. For a civic group or an educational institution the performance means a triumphant reward for weeks and months of hard work. In the professional theatre success or failure of a single production may perhaps decide the fate of the entire company.

COSI FAN TUTTE
By Mozart

San Francisco Opera
Settings by George Jenkins
Photo by Thomas L. Colangelo

TURANDOT
By Puccini

Houston Grand Opera
Settings by Peter Wolf
Conducted by Walter Herbert

151

SUSANNAH
By Carlisle Floyd

New York City Opera
Photo by Fred Fehl

LA BOHEME
By Puccini

Santa Fé Opera

THE LOVE OF DANAE
By Richard Strauss

University of Southern California
Musical and Stage Direction
by Walter Ducloux

DIDO AND AENEAS
By Purcell

University of Illinois
Conducted by Ludwig Zirner

153

INFIDELITY FOILED
By Haydn

University of California, Los Angeles
Adapted and conducted by Jan Popper

THE LONG CHRISTMAS DINNER
By Paul Hindemith

Juilliard School of Music
Conducted by the composer
Directed by Christopher West

154

THE BEGGAR'S OPERA
By John Gay

Asolo Comedy Festival of the
Florida State University
Conducted by Richard Collins

THE RAKE'S PROGRESS
By Stravinsky

Northwestern University
Conducted by Thor Johnson
Staged by Robert Gay

TSAR AND CARPENTER
By Lortzing

Louisiana State University
Musical and Stage Direction
by Peter Paul Fuchs

CARRY NATION
By Douglas Moore

The University of Kansas
Staged by Lewin Goff
Conducted by Bob Baustian
Settings by James Hawes

156

PEER GYNT
By Werner Egk

University of Hartford
Settings and Staging by Elemer Nagy
Conducted by Moshe Paranov
Photo by Jack Gomez

THE MERRY WIVES OF WINDSOR
By Otto Nicolai

University of Mississippi
Leland Fox, Director of
the Opera Theatre

157

THE ORGANIZATION BEHIND
THE PRODUCTION

The Producing Group

While a special production staff may be assigned to each production, a permanent board should head the organization regardless of whether one production is planned or several. This is the practice of professional companies and should also be made the principle of all civic and educational groups.

Thorough planning of all business affairs even for one performance is as mandatory as organizing the artistic and technical preparations. Relying on improvisation and makeshift arrangements causes intolerable conditions in a musical production. A drama can be staged with a rather small cast and crew in a little theatre, but not an opera with its many participants, complicated technical requirements, large auditorium and consequently with a far greater risk. If a series of productions is intended during a season, much thought and time has to be devoted to the establishment of a permanent organization.

Many an operatic enterprise has sprung up almost over night through the energy and initiative of one person or a handful of enthusiasts. They often officiate automatically as constituents of the governing board until a growing membership expresses its confidence in them or decides on a change. Glee clubs, music-study clubs or simply a group of young singers under the leadership of their teacher have been the originators of opera associations. From such a core the first impetus may come. After months, perhaps years of propaganda, the time grows ripe for founding an opera company. This has happened in colleges and with civic groups alike. Anyone anxious to start operatic productions ought to bear in mind that they are not meant for a selected group but for the public-at-large.

Membership, the basis of the whole organization, ought to be as wide and all-embracing as can be. Nothing will be more harmful than the obvious predominance of one individual or a small clique. There are few civic companies which can afford to rely on their reputation or on their faithful friends for a crowded house, hence on a guaranteed income. In order to arouse greater interest among music lovers and to draw them more closely to the association, it may be a good idea to make every purchaser of a season ticket a voting member. Certain matters of general policy will be submitted to the decision of the entire membership such as the election of the governing board. A cautious inquiry can also be made into the preference of members concerning the choice of operas and cast, although these artistic questions should, normally, be left to the discretion of the artistic director and the board of directors. Under no circumstances must the members feel that they are merely participating in another social club. At every meeting emphasis is to be put on cultural aims. To this end, lectures on operatic subjects, concerts, and unpretentious performances of scenes, acts or short operas could be made part of such meetings.

If a membership is very large and thus seems to be difficult to manage, efforts could be directed toward building up an affiliated club or a guild, explicitly organized as a nucleus of a working group in collaboration with the producing company. The best example of this type is given by the Metropolitan Opera Guild which has been emulated in other cities. Institutions of higher learning can make use of existing clubs or form a new guild to promote interest in musical productions. Dramatic and music clubs, already active in various phases of the theatre, could combine their efforts to advance the producing of opera. They will not only attract singers and musicians, but technicians and managers as well. These groups can also take a vigorous part in publicity campaigns.

A few points will be clarified for the initiators of an opera association. Little indeed can be achieved without a widespread interest in opera. It can be taken for granted, however, that today in every sizable city and on every large campus there are people idealistic enough to give time and, in civic companies, some money to further the arts. The extent of interest can quickly be determined in talks with well-informed leaders of the community. A handful of persons and a small sinking fund for expenses like printing and mailing of circulars are enough to begin with. If the first reaction is satisfying, not to say enthusiastic, the next steps may be taken. The sponsors must be thoroughly acquainted with the auditorium they plan to use for their productions. Preliminary talks have to be conducted with the people or officials who are in charge of this auditorium to discover a basis for a possible contract or at least a tentative agreement. The questions to be frankly discussed are: under which conditions can the civic auditorium be rented? or the auditorium in a college, a high school? or one that belongs to a service club? Are the facilities such as stage, pit, house, light equipment, dressing rooms satisfactory? Is one of these factors inadequate?

The most urgent decision is to engage the artistic leaders at an early date, as they will carry a heavy responsibility. A contract is usually made with a conductor who receives the title musical director, artistic director or general manager. It is far less common to engage also a stage director at once. The best conditions are created if both the conductor and the director are engaged at the same time and one of them is made the artistic director. The two leaders will discuss with·the board of directors or the governing board the basic question of whether to rely mostly on guest singers or mostly on local talent. Before productions can be scheduled, all financial, technical and artistic problems should be aired and an agreement found which should be binding on all concerned. In colleges and music schools where all participants are staff members and students except for the rare situation when guest singers are invited, a decision concerning these matters can be rather easily reached. To assemble a governing board is simple for an educational institution with its closely knit and uniform staff. Even in a large university where the artistic leaders may be drawn from available staff members of various departments the task is not complicated. In spite of a certain potential academic jealousy, cooperation will be good in most cases. A special committee can be appointed by the dean of the school of music, fine arts or liberal arts respectively. The scope of the plans and the size of the institution will determine the number of committee members. The conductor or the director of theatre may serve as chairman unless the dean himself intends to supervise the operatic activities. Staff members of all the divisions concerned join in formulating the fundamental policy. Among them may be the head of the voice division, head of the orchestra, the designer, the costumer; perhaps a graduate student or two could be asked to attend the meetings. In a civic association the president or the board of directors appoints the members of the various standing committees who have to take over the many duties in the preparation of a production. The constitution of an organization should contain clear statements regarding the responsibilities of the board of directors and all committees.

At times it is to the advantage of a civic association to make the artistic director or business manager a member of the governing body. As a matter of fact, conductor, director and manager could well belong to the executive committee, for their advice is being sought anyway. Some groups invite them to attend meetings where they report on past events and on plans for the future. Under such procedure the three do not participate in the voting on the final decision. Usually the advice of these experts will be heeded. Only on rare occasions will the governing body disregard their recommendations. Not to do so means a vote of no-confidence, of course, and often leads to resignations when essential matters are involved. The artistic leaders should be spared the burden of too many managerial duties, implied in a large association, unless one of them is also the general manager. When the conductor and the director reside in that city, as they should, they can supervise the entire preparatory work.

All officers of an opera association ought to read the memoirs of Giulio Gatti-Casazza, successful general manager of the Met for many years, and take his advice. Naturally he discusses the professional theatre, but his viewpoint pertains to the semi-professional and educational company as well. The noted impresario sharply criticizes "dilettantes and inexperienced persons" whom he blames for many failures of operatic companies. He stresses the importance of experience for anyone who wishes to direct an operatic group. In his opinion, the director must be, above all, artistically minded and practical as well. He summarizes his views in this counsel: "A theatrical organization should be founded on order, sound management, discipline and variety of productions and the best possible quality of spectacles and artists."

The Production Staff

Every organization is eager to engage artistic leaders who are gifted, experienced and reliable enough to be entrusted with the preparation and execution of the production. It will furthermore try to find a team of leaders who are anxious to collaborate for years and to assemble a harmonious staff whose cooperation is based on mutual understanding. Changing leaders every season, if not for each production, brings confusion and delays a progress so much desired. To be sure, guests may be called in on occasion, for they stimulate new ideas and add momentum to the entire group. They should, however, be an exception.

Obviously three divisions grow out of the production work; music, stage and management. Whether the head of the third, the business manager, should be a member of the production staff or of a permanent board is to be decided by each association on its own merit. Strictly speaking, conductor and director head the producing staff. Their duties and responsibilities have been defined in earlier pages. Also the various groups involved in rehearsals and performances have been discussed. The following chart gives a picture of the relationship of the diverse leaders and groups, based upon the assumption that an artistic director is charged with final authority.

I *Conductor*	*Artistic Director*	II *Stage Director*
Chorus Master		Assistant Stage Director
Assistant Conductor	III	Designer
Coach		Stage Manager
Orchestra		Prompter
	Soloists	Technical Director
	Choristers	Stage Crew
	Ballet Master	Electricians
	Dancers	Property Mistress
	Stage Band	Extras

This chart shows in column I the range of the conductor's authority; in column II, the director's authority over all matters connected with staging. Only the components in the third column are really subject to a dual authority, their work embracing music as well as drama. In order to forestall endless disputes and friction between leaders, a danger inherent in the dualistic system, it is advisable to make either conductor or stage director the artistic director. Sometimes business managers show a remarkable capacity for leadership in an

162

artistic enterprise. Yet whoever is to be considered for this position must be trained and experienced in all three spheres: music, stage and management. He must know enough of each one of these to form judgment and to be able to make decisions on a variety of issues.

In smaller groups, which have no artistic director, the president of the company may decide to act as mediator in the event of a controversy between conductor and director. In an educational institution this would be the task of the dean, the director of theatre, or whoever is the chairman of the production staff. A single head, whether his title is general manager or artistic director, could raise the standard of the production considerably, provided this person has persuasive ability, artistic taste, and a good deal of energy and tact. His spirit and ideas will permeate the company as a whole and put the stamp of his personality upon all performances.

Lacking a permanent paid office staff and stage crew a civic company relies on a host of volunteers to relieve the leaders of many chores, such as keeping files of choristers and extras, collecting properties, checking costumes and the like. Special committees, selected by the president or governing board, can be of invaluable assistance in all these matters. In an educational institution student assistants usually attend to these tasks, but in civic groups voluntary helpers must be found among the members willing to spend many hours of work that, for all its great value to the artistic and technical perfection of the final performance, is barely noted in the performance itself. It is best to incorporate the volunteers into the production staff whether or not they are members of any standing committee. The number of persons or committees in demand depends on the requirements of the particular opera. Their task is less the work itself than the supervision of it.

One will understand the need for a vast host of volunteer helpers if he takes note of the multitude of people taking part in an operatic performance. Participants in a single production involve:

Soloists	3 - 30	Stage Crew	6 - 30
Choristers	0 - 150	Electrician	1 - 6
Dancers	0 - 40	Property Crew	1 - 3
Extras	0 - 50	Costume Crew	1 - 8
Musicians	20 - 80	Make-Up Crew	1 - 8

The list of participants, which does not include the office staff, ushers, the technicians in the several workshops and the maintenance crew, is considered for a wide range of productions. Obviously two rather simple one-act pieces of the 18th century demand a far less complicated organization than difficult works like *Aida* or *Boris Godunov*. Most operas and operettas fall into the medium range.

163

Financial Aspects

At the head of the staff supervising and executing management is the business manager. His duties embrace roughly the setting up of a budget, publicity, ticket sale, supervision of all expenses, the house management and the accounting after the performances. In addition, he may function as a clearing house for all committees.

Some associations give these duties to a vice-president or treasurer; others prefer to engage a specialist when the extended range of the work makes it advisable. If he has no paid assistant, the business manager also has to rely largely on volunteers. He works in close contact with the conductor and director regarding rehearsal facilities, publicity, and the like, and has to be consulted about all expense items such as salaries, costumes, settings, properties and scores. Regardless of whether or not the business manager is a member of the governing body, it is clear that his responsibility reaches across many departments.

Generally speaking, the manager's work encompasses the same tasks as in any theatrical organization, but the broader scope of operatic productions makes it more exacting. The large number of participants and the complex technical requirements cause high expenses and thus involve a great financial risk. Consequently the manager is obliged to use all his ingenuity to attract a large audience whose tickets will cover the expenses, or at least a good percentage of them.

A play can be financed with little money under favorable circumstances, as for instance, a non-royalty classic drama, staged without scenery and in modern dress. This is not possible in opera. Therefore it is extremely important to plan carefully and to control the financial end of the whole organization. No matter what the purpose of a company, whether it presents an operetta for entertainment and amusement or a music drama for enlightenment, whether the producing staff consists of beginners or semi-professionals, the business department must be managed with great efficiency.

Granted, too complicated a budget can, at first glance, frighten the less aggressive members of a civic group; it should not however intimidate the authorities of an educational institution. They can discount many factors, for they must merely be concerned with production expenses proper, such as settings, costumes, scores and properties, the remainder being manipulated through the general budget of the school or department. Expenditures of a civic association do not lend themselves as readily to an itemized account, because they largely depend on the type of the producing company. For the sake of clarity, however, all possibilities are here enumerated.

Office Personnel.

Artistic director or general manager
Assistant business manager
Secretary
Publicity manager
Artistic secretary

Box-office manager
Librarian
House Manager
Comptroller
Receptionist

Other Permanent Expenses.

Building engineer
Carpenter
Electrician
Property Mistress
Janitor
Workmen's compensation
Rental of building
Amortization
Maintenance
Insurance of theatre
Liability insurance
Depreciation
Electricity

Gas
Water
Telephone
Postage
Telegraph
Furniture
Typewriter
Office supply
Publicity campaign
Entertainment of guests
Traveling
Miscellaneous

In the cost of the production itself nearly every detail is of importance, whether it concerns a civic or an educational group. The latter relies chiefly on work done by its regular staff members and students (thus reducing its costs) except for some colleges which call in guest singers, directors or conductors. In many respects the educational institution has an advantage over community associations. Settings can be built and costumes made in its own shops. Union stage hands and union musicians are seldom needed. Our best civic companies, on the other hand, trying to achieve an excellent standard, have naturally the highest budget. They must rent scenery and costumes or have them made to order; as opposed to the majority of colleges, they do not own an auditorium; instead they have to pay rental, usually a small amount if the hall is city owned, but quite a considerable sum if conditions require the lease of a legimate theatre. In most cases instrumentalists and stage hands are unionized; only under certain circumstances (when promoting a new enterprise) can amateurs and professionals join forces. As soloists, associations often engage well-known singers whose fees can be considerable. Beginners are employed for small parts, seldom for leading roles. There are few civic groups who rely solely on volunteers.

165

In general, the personnel of a production comprises:

Conductor	Designer	Extras
Assistant conductor	Costumer	Stage hands
Chorus master	Ballet master (mistress)	Electricians
Coach	Technical director	Property mistress
Stage director	Singers	Wardrobe crew
Assistant stage director	Instrumentalists	Make-up crew
Stage manager	Choristers	Ushers
Prompter	Dancers	

The salaries of some, such as conductor, chorus master, director and designer may fall either under permanent personnel or under production expenses depending on the extent of the company's aims. Material costs, incurred in a production, consist of:

Auditorium rental	Scores and parts
Settings	Royalty
Costumes	Posters
Furniture	Mailers, brochures
Hand properties	Office supplies
Portable switchboard	Programs
Spotlights	Advertisement
Sound effects	Tickets
TV monitor	Complimentary tickets
Make-up material	Photographs
Transportation	Miscellaneous

A few items listed above seem negligible in importance, yet a manager must evaluate every detail in its relation to the whole budget. Even complimentary tickets for critics, participants, and honored guests should be counted, since in an otherwise sold-out house, they represent a reduced income, ergo indirectly an expense. In the budget as many specified items as possible should be enumerated instead of lumping together all minor matters under miscellaneous. The latter heading ought to be strictly left for emergencies such as breakage of rented properties and similar accidents.

The rather high expense of operatic productions necessitates a very conscientious analysis of all financial resources and possibilities. There are everywhere people of means, willing to donate a lump sum to guarantee the budget against loss. To these is added a list of potential patrons paying more than the price asked for a season ticket. Then there are the pillars of the undertaking, the regular subscribers. Finally, the large group of opera-goers who purchase tickets for one or another performance. It is a worthwhile task to find out the names of the last category and to persuade them to become regular purchasers of season tickets. A most valuable clientele is found among the students of high schools and colleges. This group of course ought to receive tickets at a considerably reduced price, as it is essential to interest the young generation whose members may turn into steadfast patrons later on. The manager can get some income by selling advertisements in programs, perhaps also in an annual brochure. Moreover, concessions for selling librettos and drinks should be considered, to increase the revenues. The possibility of obtaining some material such as lumber, canvas, paint, wiring, and so on, free or at a nominal cost should not be overlooked, for every dollar saved is a gain. Several groups have had good luck with special dinners and balls they arranged to improve their finances. The printing and selling of an operatic calendar interspersed with articles and pictures may bring in a nice surplus. In some cities firms with thousands of employees became interested in the civic opera association; they ordered a large block of tickets which were sold at price or below. Radio and television stations can be of tremendous importance through free publicity by giving time and space to special programs. FM stations in particular can support a forthcoming production by playing the recording of the opera or of guest singers who appear in the performance. Much has been written about the tremendous part played by newspapers in pushing a civic venture; thus it is unnecessary to point out here their potential contributions.

Balancing the Budget

It is an old adage that you can figure out your expenses but you can only guess your receipts. This certainly holds true of the theatre where it is virtually impossible to make even an approximate estimate of the revenue which is nevertheless an inevitable factor in setting up the budget. On the other hand, opera being a big affair for a modest civic or educational group, expenses must be very carefully weighed against potential receipts. The capacity of the house, the price of tickets, and the appeal of the production are instrumental in drawing up a tentative budget. There is quite a difference in having the receipts based on a house with a capacity of 800, 1500 or 3,000 seats. A small house means at once limited receipts. The ticket price is of course related not only to the standard of the production itself, but also the economic status of the prospective audience.

Guest singers whose names are good for publicity purposes have a certain drawing power; yet they also push the expenses into the upper bracket. A well-known opera or composer warrants greater attraction than the works of unknown composers. If a good house is assured by way of subscriptions, a lesser known opera is of little danger to the budget. Few compoanies, however, are so fortunate as to be able to rely on the sale of season tickets alone. Attendance at each performance must be sought. As Verdi put it when suggesting a careful scrutiny of the receipts at the box office, a theatre is meant to be full and not empty. Yet not even he was able to find a foolproof method for filling the house all the time.

Some pure artists loathe to have the term "business" mentioned, but it is unavoidable to consider the financial phase of a venture. In setting up the budget, both the possible expenses and receipts have to be brought into relation. Expenses can be itemized fairly accurately, and a thoughtful manager will make every effort to hold the budget. Revenues too can be figured out, to some degree at least. The first rule is not to rely on a sold-out house. Ordinarily the expenses are based on no more than seventy-five percent of its capacity. In fact, prudent people prefer a smaller percentage.

Experience has taught to weigh the following points in selecting works, in choosing performance dates and in devising the budget:

> The state of business in general
> The state of theatre business in particular
> The strength of local tradition
> The strength of local opera fans
> The possibility of competing events
> The artistic leadership
> The drawing power of name singers
> The drawing power of a given opera
> The potential effect of publicity within and outside the city

The value of each factor may vary for each group and the importance of each factor does not always follow the order of the listing above. The enumerated points need no further elaboration except for one which deserves special attention, namely publicity. The main difficulty lies less in arousing the fundamental interest than in overcoming a certain lethargy in the face of obstacles. A vigorous propaganda campaign is one thing; it is quite another to push the sale of tickets that should accompany or follow it, and must be pursued with even greater intensity. Cards and letters must be written, models and photographs exhibited, lectures given at all conceivable clubs, tickets sold by telephone or in a house-to-house canvass, as it were. The ticket committee especially should have energetic representatives of every interested club and group in town—every music club, service club, women's literary and drama society, and so on. If ever any group should be entertained and specifically indoctrinated and given a special field or list for sales at the same time—this is it. The chairman of the tickets sales committee holds a strategic position. He, or often she, must be an enthusiast, an aggressive and dynamic person, well known and respected—a real salesman.

Mistakes in the choice of an opera or its production are bound to occur. It is impossible to satisfy every wish and taste all the time. The concern of the management is rather to give everybody something. It is quite a challenge to reconcile the grumblers, to keep the faithful happy, and to win new friends. What this amounts to is that a program ought to please lovers of grand opera and those of light opera, admirers of classical works and friends of modern ones, aficionados of beautiful singing as well as partisans of experimental staging. To be sure, all this cannot be done with two or three productions in a single season, but it can be accomplished within two seasons.

It is important to obtain early as close an estimate as can be procured for every item of the expenses. The department heads (conductor, director, designer) must submit to the business manager precise wishes and an approximate amount for expenses. The conductor must give the number of musicians and of orchestra rehearsals needed; the director the number of extras, dancers and the amount of properties to be used. The designer in consultation with the director must clarify his ideas about settings, costumes and furniture in exact figures of material and money.

Sometimes associations have, to their dismay, discovered after a production how much money they could have saved through more careful planning. Savings can indeed be effected without any harm to the quality of the performance, provided the departmental heads recognize what is essential and what is not and act accordingly. Often cheaper material can be substituted for the more expensive. Well-organized rehearsals, primarily the last ones, can reduce the costs in overtime for stage hands and musicians which can amount to several hundred dollars. A conductor can forego a few musicians, a director can eliminate some costumes, and other savings may be attempted. If a guest singer is considered, it may pay to search for one who happens to be in the vicinity at the time of the planned performance before engaging somebody from the far end of the country. Lastly, the price for rented settings and costumes should be weighed against the costs for having them made in town. At first glance it seems rather expensive to have everything executed to order, yet in the long run, it might turn out to be cheaper. Rash decisions should be avoided, for they lead to expensive errors.

A survey of operatic activities demonstrates that it is well nigh impossible to balance a budget without financial support of some sort, be it a grant, a subsidy or an endowment. The receipts of the majority of groups cover close to two-thirds of their expenses, eighty percent and more in several instances, mainly in universities and music schools which, as described, proceed under conditions much more favorable than those in civic groups. In addition to the Metropolitan Opera whose unique position suggests a separate treatment there are three companies which, because of their longer seasons and their numerous well-paid singers and other participants, work with a budget of seven digits. The expenses of the opera companies in San Francisco and Chicago reached $2,000,000 in 1966, as did those of the New York City Opera. Several civic associations, presenting four productions within a brief season or spread throughout the fall and winter, spend $200,000.00 and more. Yet there are also companies which manage their productions with half this amount. And there are many whose aim is not to rely on name singers but to engage local or young singers; these groups are in a position to keep their budget between $20,000 and $30,000. Lastly, a few groups announced that their expenses for two productions did not exceed $3,000. The conclusion may be drawn that the minimum for a satisfactory, if modest, production is about $1,500, the average runs to $20,000, and the maximum spent by very large companies comes to $40,000, and even $80,000 for a single production which of course is performed several times. To make a comparison is inadvisable since the budget depends on the aspirations of each group.

A scrutiny of educational institutions also shows tremendous differences of financial organization. The reader will keep in mind that in these budgets several items which play a large part for civic companies do not appear in the expenses of music schools and colleges which, in most cases, are unconcerned about the salaries of staff members and musicians, and have not much trouble in paying for settings, costumes and properties. Some colleges report that the sale of tickets almost pays for their operatic performances; this is true first of all of small and middle sized institutions which try to manage everything with a budget of roughly $1,000 and less for a production. As an average, the opera workshops or opera theatres rely on a budget from $5,000 up with which to cover two or three productions, each being performed twice or three times. A few institutions stage four, even six operatic events annually. The maximum in the budgetary phase reaches beyond the $100,000 mark, but this amount is available in the extremely rare cases of schools which should be called professional. The comparatively low budgets of colleges and music schools are of course based on their overall lower expenses for many items. Colleges show that it is possible to prepare a one-act piece with less than $500 and a full-length work with about $1,000. The average production in this group costs between two and three thousand dollars; the maximum expense comes close to $10,000.

Indeed the educational groups are anxious to balance their expenses and receipts. An administration of a university or music school can or will seldom sign a blank check for the operatic productions. More often than not, these groups incur a deficit, at least theoretically. The difference between expenses and receipts is covered in several ways: the institution grants a special fund from the general budget of the institution; a dean has the possibility of making up the difference; a small amount is donated from the student activity fund; a patron of a college pays for special expenses such as a guest singer; or an opera guild or donors collect a sinking fund. In general the production expenses are shown in the budget of the music or theatre department or come from both.

It is worth having a close look at the financial conditions of the Met, not because other groups face the same extreme problems at present, but because the problems the Met must solve every year may come to the fore if and when other companies grow to the point that they will be able to expand their productions to a season of several months. The basic material is easily available to anyone willing to write to the general manager of the Met for the annual Statement of Operations and the financial statements. From *Opera News* and some New York newspapers further informative data can be culled. All these sources refute the belief that operatic activities of a high standard can and will pay for themselves. For many years the Met would have shown a deficit had it not found other means to bridge the difference between expenses and receipts. As a matter of fact, without financial support from many people and several organizations the Met would have had to close its doors long ago.

It cost the Met more than $9,000,000 to cover all expenses for the 1964-65 season which offered close to 200 performances in New York and an additional two score on the road. Of this amount about $7,000,000 were received through the sale of season and individual tickets, radio and television fees, and some incidentals. The gap between these receipts and the total expenses was made up by contributions of several kinds: Metropolitan Opera Guild, Metropolitan Opera National Council, special gifts for new productions, subscribers' supplementary payments, and other fund-raising activities which resulted in a total subsidy of about $1,500,000. Thus a merely negligible deficit was left. Particularly note-worthy is the fact that many patrons volunteered to pay more for their season tickets than they were expected to and thus they contributed more than $286,000; in addition, a series of fund-raising events brought the amazing sum of more than $320,000. The data naturally change from year to year; in a few cases the budget has even shown a slight plus.

The Met cannot complain about poor attendance. Many of its performances are sold out or nearly so. Almost ninety percent of all seats are in the hands of season ticket holders during the first season in the new Met. Superficially such a splendid attendance record does not leave the impression that the manage-ment has any financial worries, but a glance at the budget tells a different story. Unless every effort is constantly made to have sold-out houses, the very exist-ence of the Met is imperiled in spite of the generous contributions. This tight situation is, rightly or wrongly, the main reason for its hesitancy to experi-ment with contemporary operas.

As if the Met had not enough work on its hands, it added educational ventures of great impact. For many years it arranged special performances for students of the metropolitan area to acquaint the younger generation with the master works. Even more important are its opera studio and national touring company which were developed during recent years. In this endeavor about thirty schol-arship singers are trained in the art of opera, and these young professionals have then the opportunity to perform in the schools of New York and far beyond the Hudson River. Early in 1967 the Met's management dissolved the touring company because of extremely high operation expenses.

Endowment of Operatic Activities

An examination of budgets of civic and educational opera groups testifies that nearly each one is, in one way or another, subsidized to cover an antic-ipated or incurred deficit. By now this state of affairs is tacitly accepted, if not officially. Yet a change in the attitude of people is noticeable. No one doubts that opera has become an enterprise of national significance which needs and deserves financial support.

It is no longer restricted to New York and a few large cities but reaches into many smaller towns and campuses. By granting a charter to ANTA (The American National Theatre and Academy) Congress laid the groundwork for a

National Theatre. In this organization representatives of various theatrical groups, professional, civic, educational, and also individuals interested in theatre arts meet to help evolve and support, with advice and money, expansion of the American theatre. Since the means available to this clearing house are still very limited, the crux of the question remains indeed where the necessary sums can be secured to conduct or manage any theatre whether of either drama or opera. There are three possibilities—private endowment, government subsidy, or a combination of the two with a sinking fund derived from both private and public money.

The situation at institutions of higher learning is clear. It has already been mentioned that all permanent expenses, such as for staff, office work, building and so forth, are taken care of in the general budget of the school. In addition, some schools provide generous sums for the opportunity for their students to work and appear in or merely to see and enjoy operas. Since a good number of universities are financed by states and cities, we may rightly maintain that public means are used as subsidies of operatic productions. Since contributions to private colleges and music schools are tax deductible, these too belong to some degree in the same category.

The three possibilities to help finance operatic activities are of deep concern to the hundreds of civic companies. Hitherto, mainly private endowment has been adopted. Opera lovers apparently have been quite willing to contribute small or large amounts in support of good productions. When a call came to assist the Met in buying its house or in creating a special fund for the company, thousands upon thousands sent their dollars from all over the country. But these contributions, together with the revenue from broadcasts and television programs, were still not large enough to provide a solid foundation. The overhead will be far greater at the Met's new theatre at Lincoln Center, because it will be very costly to run and maintain the most modern technical apparatus and to acquire a series of new settings.

The burden of providing a sound financial basis to secure a modicum of continuity has become so heavy that the sponsorship by individuals and small organizations is hardly sufficient any longer. New resources have to be tapped. Fortunately the wealthiest foundations have shown a deep concern for the development of the performing arts, opera included. Both the Ford and Rockefeller Foundations have blazed the trail; they have stimulated interest in the lyric theatre by giving substantial sums to a number of deserving companies. Their support has been invaluable to composers, singers and entire groups. Many corporations followed suit; in some cases they contribute directly to the fund drive of an opera association; in others they sign generously for a community drive from which several artistic ventures benefit. We may well experience that in the future there will be a trend toward combining the efforts of individuals, clubs, guilds and large corporations.

The second solution, public ownership and subsidy, either municipal, state or federal, is the accepted norm in most European countries and in some of the

Americas. In the United States many people, anxious to see opera grow, raise objections to public subsidies on the ground that these would encourage undesirable political influence. This can happen, but it is not a necessary result. On every level of our administrative system there are committees whose members are not nominated strictly because of political affiliation. Libraries, parks, health services, city management and the like have proved that undue political influence can be eliminated considerably. And there exist already a few theatres owned or, at least, subsidized by a public agency.

The connotation of public subsidy as being synonymous with government interference in free enterprise is apparently the chief culprit in holding back much support. It cannot be denied that this danger exists, for unscrupulous officials have misused their position to exert direct or indirect influence. As so often, felicitous conditions depend on the fair judgment of those who grant and those who administer the subsidy. Political interference in artistic matters is intolerable. But so is economic or personal interference exercised by individuals or heads of clubs and corporations. People who are afraid of undesirable influence should look in two directions, namely to the government agencies and the private sponsors and firms. Good as well as obnoxious examples can be submitted for either solution. In the end it is the individual leader of an opera company and his relationship with those supporting it who will determine the policy and the spirit of the opera group.

The British Government, impervious to any sort of financial aid to art before the last war, sponsored theatrical enterprises during the emergency under the auspices of Winston Churchill and, after the war, consolidated its new policy through the establishment of the British Arts Council. Parliament approves the necessary sums, but the Council is above and beyond politics, operating on the foundation principle. Its main purpose is to support art in every field and in different ways. Thus some opera companies obtain a subsidy while others receive a remission of ticket taxes, "a guaranty against loss". Today Royal Covent Garden is no longer a private enterprise, since this celebrated house now belongs to the Crown which through the Council contributed £750,000 for the season 1963-64. Smaller amounts are given to the popular Sadler's Wells Company and the festivals in Glyndebourne and Edinburgh.

The success of the British Arts Council has been noted in the United States. Various associations concerned with promoting and supporting the arts have tried to interest legislators, congressmen, governors and the Federal Government. The first breakthrough came with the initiation of the New York State Council on the Arts which, since 1961, has given support to professional companies in the state of New York, among them the New York City Opera to tour to other cities, and to local groups to help them overcome some obstacles or to stage a demanding work which otherwise would have remained unknown. Under the auspices of the Council a study was made of all opera companies existing in New York State. The result was the foundation of a league which serves as a kind of clearing house for all groups. The Council discovered that with comparatively little money much good could be achieved. In 1963 only $166,800 was spent on operatic activities. A few of the principles underlying the Council's work are of particular value: local organizations bear the lion's share of the expenses; tickets must be kept at as low a price as is feasible to make it possible for most people to attend these performances. The aim is to create a receptive atmosphere for all the arts and to enable people in all cities of the state to see and hear productions of high quality. Those who are interested in promoting the basic ideas of the New York Council in other states should not hesitate to obtain its booklets and reports. Yet none should expect to be handed a blueprint as to how to approach this task in another state, for the New York Council bluntly declines to set forth an overall plan, because "each state has its particular artistic identity." In several states, furthermore, an arts council is already operating or at least under consideration and there is hope that, within a few years, others will be added, all of them to become a contributing factor to the furthering of deserving opera groups.

A mixed organization, endowed by private and public means, represents the third category. It too has been tried with good success, mainly in Switzerland and Germany. Theatres of this type have a basic idea in common, which is to merge private and public interests in the promotion of ART. Yet these theatres developed according to conditions peculiar to a given city. In some cities a group of individuals joined with city administrations to establish a sinking fund large enough to build and/or operate a theatre. A holding company was organized, with shares given each individual and the city. If private citizens keep more than fifty percent they also hold the majority in the governing body and, thus, become dominant in the management. In another case, the theatre built by the city is controlled by a combined body of private citizens and officials. These arrangements, however, still leave the question of who is to pay for any deficit. A straight endowment would probably not be quite satisfactory unless the sum was rather high. It may be easier to find the means for an annual subsidy. If a building owned by the city is given free of charge for rent, upkeep, repairs, cleaning, and utilities, this gift practically equals a subsidy of thousands of dollars in cash. A contract like this prevailed in many European theatres until cities, or states assumed full responsibility for the budget.

The collaboration of private and public interests is well known in the United States. Many cities have built an auditorium and/or a theatre which is leased to civic groups at a nominal fee, which indeed resembles a subsidy for these groups. School boards are willing and often anxious to contribute a lump sum to an opera association in return for special student performances. Counties and cities are inclined to vote a subsidy for an orchestra which plays also in the pit for opera performances. In order to raise the necessary money for such a subsidy a special tax has been introduced in a few cases—for example in San Francisco. During recent years city councils and state legislators have been approached with several ideas of special taxes with which to support artistic ventures. A wider acceptance of such plans has probably to wait until the per-

174

forming arts have gained much broader recognition among the population than they hitherto have.

Slowly but surely this is happening today. The awareness of theatre as an ˺ ⸴actor in our culture has spread so widely that Congress took notice of ˹˺ In the late forties a resolution was submitted and sponsored by ⸴tor Elbert D. Thomas and the then Representative Jacob ˹l theatre and a national opera and ballet." The ⸴ginning that the recommended support would ⸴ortunity to expand and thus to build a more ⸴llowing fifteen years, the original idea was re- ⸴ now entitled the National Art and Cultural De- ⸴ the energetic chairmanship of Senator Javits and ⸴son, Jr., the National Council on the Arts Act was ⸴ A rather small amount was granted for its operation ⸴ot all the bill's sponsors had desired, but there is at ⸴Congress will, in the years to come, be more favorably ⸴nd a broader definition of the Great Society.

⸴agreed to appropriate $15.5 millions for an arts center ⸴which after the assassination of President Kennedy, was ⸴F. Kennedy Center for the Performing Arts. In this en- ⸴government joined private circles interested in planning the ⸴and its manifold activities. The amount granted by Congress ⸴amount collected by citizens and organizations. In several ⸴sembles the plan and basic organization of the Lincoln Center ⸴in a far less elaborate manner.

⸴ional Council on the Arts, thanks to its approval by Congress, will ⸴erve as adviser to federal agencies and as a clearing house for ⸴ups in the country at large and their diverse aims. Without in- ⸴the privileges of others, the members of this Council can be of ⸴It would be an immense boon for the leaders and their co-workers ⸴ous art centers, specifically of those in the planning stage—there could ⸴ about one hundred in the near future—to have a place where they could meet to exchange views, to strengthen their ideas, and so improve their plans. In serving as a clearing house the Council in Washington can contribute much to each group and to culture in general. The Council's members can be instrumental in creating an atmosphere favorable to the arts, through lectures in many cities and articles in periodicals and newspapers. If Congress should grant more money later on, they will be in a position to expand their activities. A worthwhile task will be the improvement of our relations with foreign countries. During the past decade private companies have performed plays and also *Porgy and Bess* in Europe with some financial backing by the Department of State, yet these ventures were rather haphazardly planned and lacked a clear policy in Washington. Several other tours to foreign countries never materialized for want of the necessary financial support. If we intend, and we should, to

175

send operatic productions abroad, we must insist that only the best are seen and heard. The Council can certainly serve as headquarters for the preparation of these international travels. So much has been said and written about the necessity to improve our image in foreign countries, so often distorted by Hollywood and Madison Avenue, that it is almost superfluous to state it again. But it cannot be emphasized too strongly how important it is to show the world our highest cultural accomplishments.

The direct and indirect involvement of public agencies, federal, state, county and city, is a fact. The question is therefore not whether this condition can be reversed but rather what can best be done with it. Every friend of opera should examine the present situation and its possibilities in the future. Both the artistic and managerial problems should be analyzed and a solution recommended which ought to be related above all to the local level, then to cultural affairs within the state and neighboring states, and lastly to national conditions. Art begins with the individual who meets others of his spiritual and intellectual kin. Art cannot be organized from the top down to the local level. In spite of the high regard due Congress and the Federal Government for their interest in the performing arts, cultural development remains fundamentally a city-wide problem. Those in Washington who are deeply concerned about culture are fully aware of the implications their plans could project. Like the responsible persons in the New York Council, they wish to leave everything, or almost everything, to individual groups in the country. There is no plan to force ideas on reluctant people in the fifty states. The prospect for a healthy development of opera is promising if individuals as well as city and state governments do their part in developing and keeping conditions propitious for the lyric theatre. If local authorities fail to discharge their responsibility, it may happen that disappointed opera-lovers will cry for outside help. Obviously the National Council would listen and offer its own remedy. By default cities may experience that what should have been their business will be realized by outsiders. Therefore people in each city and their officials should cooperate to the fullest to create a reliable artistic and financial basis for their operatic endeavor. Moreover, they ought to associate with groups in cities of their neighborhood and near-by states.

An opera league on the national level may be profitable for all concerned. Aims of this kind have been advanced. The National Association for Opera (N.A.O.) appeals primarily to civic companies but it has also many members in the educational field. Colleges and universities assemble mostly in the Musical Theatre Project of the American Educational Theatre Association (A.E.T.A.). The American National Theatre and Academy (ANTA) too shows much interest in the lyric theatre. Who knows, one day the National Council for the Arts may become a kind of holding company for all these groups and their interests! At least, it does not hurt to dream about miracles.

176

A SUMMING UP AND AN OUTLOOK

A survey, even a partial one, of conditions in the field of American opera brings to the fore numerous positive achievements, but also a series of imperfections and some weaknesses. In general, the condition is good and highly promising. It is as good as can be expected after so short a period of time devoted to developing the exacting art of opera. Within the brief span of a generation the number of operatic groups has grown at such an extraordinary rate that it is impossible to keep track of all newcomers. A most welcome factor is that opera is performed by children who have their own companies, by students in high schools and to a larger extent in colleges, universities and conservatories. Civic companies have been organized in a few hundred of our cities. In large and smaller cities corporations have also formed groups which regularly stage light or grand operas. A special branch of the Armed Services has undertaken the production of musical works in camps at home as well as overseas. This multitude and variety of activities is one of the strongest elements. Giving credit first to all these groups, many of which are amateur, does not mean underrating the top achievements, particularly those of the few companies which are able to conduct a season of several months or weeks. Yet the small number of companies of the highest rank represents also a weakness of the system, for we cannot really brag about our great achievements until, in a vast country like ours, we possess perhaps ten times as many good opera houses open for a season of many weeks.

Our lyric theatre is very sound in the field of singers who do not have to fear competition from other countries. The troublesome condition is that the limited professional operatic activities in our country do not offer sufficient opportunities for the multitude of talented singers, many of whom go to Europe to gain experience and make a living. Our singers find themselves caught in a vicious circle. It is not only the lack of opportunities that thwarts the full development of their talent, but it is difficult, nay almost impossible, for them to secure an engagement in a provincial city without having been acknowledged in New York. On the other hand, it is equally complicated to obtain a chance in the metropolis without previous experience with smaller companies. The painful consequence of this condition is that few singers receive an adequate income from their operatic work and thus try to make a living in radio, television, concerts and as teachers.

The many productions are not always of the high standard they ought to have. The reasons are complex: one is a dire need of experienced outstanding conductors and directors to improve the staging and musical phase. Yet some of the imperfection is caused by the prevailing system which requires preparation of a performance with an insufficient number of rehearsals. The emphasis on engaging name singers who are not available for an extended period of rehearsing is part of this problem.

Only in New York is it possible for an opera lover to enjoy the masterpieces during the major part of the year. In all other cities, operatic performances can be attended in a limited way, for a few weeks or a few times during the year. A special word of praise is due the many institutions of higher learning in small cities which enable people to see and hear opera. Thus they offer a unique chance to opera-lovers who would otherwise be unable to give their lives this precious enrichment. It is particularly noteworthy that several colleges and music schools have on their staff excellent conductors and directors who have done much in training their students for a professional career.

Complaints about inadequate facilities can be heard from many groups. The criticism is directed against the lack of space backstage and of technical equipment, against' the imperfect orchestra pit, and also unsatisfactory rehearsal halls. The improvement of operatic activities indeed includes the building of satisfactory auditoriums or the rebuilding of existing theatres where gifted artists can work with a minimum of handicaps.

The purely commercial approach of some groups is as harmful as is that of others who with the exaggerated enthusiasm of amateurs believe that their grand ideas can replace knowledge and experience. Just as harmful is the blind imitation of tradition which only stymies the imagination and progress. Recognizing weaknesses is the first step toward improvement; the next is to seek better ways and to devote more time and effort to artistic experimentation.

Our repertoire is too limited. Instead of repeating again and again the standard works, unknown operas of the old masters should more often be selected and those of contemporary composers added. Every effort must be made to keep audiences interested. If they do not receive occasionally new stimuli, they may some day get tired of attending the works they know too well. Particularly we ought to concentrate on staging contemporary works. Except for several splendid musicals, there is not a single full-length American opera which has obtained more than a respectful acceptance.

Since operatic activities are recognized as an essential artistic manifestation, they should not be forced to struggle along without a reliable financial foundation. Although conditions have improved during recent years, the argument between art and money is frequently still won by the business manager. The present means of endowment are insufficient to guarantee a proper artistic development.

The aim of many citizens, thoroughly acquainted with the prevailing conditions, is indeed to create a basis which is sound from an artistic and managerial viewpoint. All over the country people are becoming aware of the fact that the performing arts are part of our culture—like schools, colleges, libraries, orchestras and museums—and thus deserve a subsidy. Cities and states are taking steps to help this art form, but this is merely a beginning. Congress and public agencies are discussing methods of how to back the performing arts and have voted financial support for this purpose in a search for the most effective procedure to accelerate the growth of a movement that will bring first-class performances to many cities. It may be the task of our generation to channel the necessary means in such a manner that talent, energy and money will not be wasted. A good start has been made and more must be done. Emphasis must be on deeds planned and executed in each city, and in each case the question has to be solved whether the operatic program can be supported by private means, by public means or by mixed management.

If the current interest in opera remains and, let us assume, grows, it should be possible to consolidate the gains and to think of expansion. More productions may be planned under favorable conditions. The final aim of course should be a regular season of several weeks or longer. To broaden the appeal, companies should examine the possibility of performing also in near-by smaller cities. Longer seasons are a prerequisite for perfecting the entire program. With the growing trend toward summer performances, certainly a few possibilities to present operas in open air theatres or air-conditioned auditoriums will be detected.

To what degree colleges and music schools are in a position to expand their operatic activities cannot be stated conclusively. A few large universities and conservatories already offer a degree in opera with an impressive program of teaching and producing. There remain the hundreds of additional institutions which perform operas but do not include specific training in the art. It is doubtful that under these circumstances many good artists can be developed, for the presentation, despite sometimes excellent leadership, has necessarily an air of improvisation. Perhaps many of the colleges will consider the introduction of special courses for those interested in operatic productions. Singers should be asked to enroll in a course on acting, perhaps in another on pantomime. Such requirements should be a minimum, and those who disagree ought to remember when play production was an extra-curricular activity which seldom rose above dilettantism and compare these days with the present situation in many universities where for the most part those who take courses in theatre arts also participate in the productions.

An urgent recommendation concerns a greater effort in training students who choose a professional career as singers, conductors or directors. Toward this end various suggestions can be made, each having merits. Round table conferences and workshops are often held in connection with annual meetings of the national associations specializing in opera. Their advantage is the little time they require, a day or a few days into which much material is telescoped. Their disadvantage is of course the inherent superficiality of such events which do not permit thorough discussion or demonstration. Workshops, lasting several weeks, have a better chance to succeed in their purpose, but again the question is how much can be achieved with people who lack the fundamental knowledge that can only be acquired through prolonged study, observation and experience. The

179

question must then be pondered how to devise a degree plan which provides enough opportunity for the student to acquire an adequate repertoire. This brings us to the crux of the whole matter; how many works can the department of a university or music school produce within a year? A student majoring in opera has theoretically the possibility to build a repertoire within his four years of professional training (two years at the undergraduate level and two more years as a master candidate). To give this project practical form two ways are here suggested. An institution organizes a resident company which includes experienced as well as beginning singers, the latter to be designated as apprentices. Such a group, which would be more or less independent of the regular academic program, would be in a position to prepare a sufficiently large number of works every season which could be presented in near-by cities in addition to the campus. The second possibility implies collaboration with a civic opera association. This presupposes that the educational opera theatre is strong enough to offer a tempting proposition. If a workable agreement can be reached, the civic association will thus add some very gifted participants and the students can gain the most valuable experience.

Those who strive to give operatic art the honored place it deserves, and the opportunity to forge ahead, must look forward, not backward. The repertoire must above all reflect the 20th century, not the past. But we cannot build a new repertoire without experimenting with new operas. Love and admiration for the old masters must not prejudice us to the point of shunning everything that has been composed later. Our contemporary, particularly American, composers have a right to be heard. What is mandatory for the repertoire, is also mandatory for the productions. Settings should not reflect the taste of the 19th century but the present. In the all important phase of acting, the meaningless superficiality of yesteryear should be completely thrown out and a modern psychological concept introduced. We are no longer receptive to the swashbuckling or sentimental types of the melodramas and the early movies, but we want to see singers act and react like human beings and their characterization must be believable and impressive. And indeed we expect that the musical style of a given work permeates the entire production. Finally, means should be collected to build opera houses and auditoriums equipped with the technical facilities needed to stage outstanding productions.

Though the stress is to be on the local level and its cultural background, civic and educational groups should collaborate with other groups more than at present. State, regional and national organizations will be salutary for the development of operatic art and the propagation of opera as an essential part of our culture. If a common basis and a common aim can be found, it should not be difficult for all concerned to collaborate in this spirit for the best of all and everyone.

The talent is at hand, waiting to be called upon. The organizing ability of this nation is immense, as is its financial foundation, upon which the management of all theatres must be based. The first goal must be to pay attention and to give opportunity to genuine aspirations and to make the productions easily accessible to all who love opera.

The past generation has seen the rapid growth of opera in the United States. The day seems to be near indeed when this art form will be the peer of the other performing arts, and moreover our operatic activities will equal those in other countries.

APPENDICES

I

GLOSSARY

Included in this glossary are the terms often found in books and in reviews. Many of the definitions are based on the excellent *Harvard Dictionary of Music* by Willi Apel.

Ballad Opera

was a popular type of entertainment in England during the 18th century. The music was seldom original, mostly adapted or borrowed. Gay's *Beggar's Opera*, music arranged by J. Pepusch, is an excellent example. The modern version by Bertholt Brecht and Kurt Weill is a revival of this type.

Classicism

represents a school of strict form, clarity and emotional balance. According to some scholars all composers after J.S. Bach belong to this school, up to and including L. van Beethoven. Other authors confine the term to the prominent representatives of the Viennese classics—Haydn, Mozart and Beethoven. The term "neo-classicism" is applied to some compositions by Hindemith and Stravinsky.

Comic Opera

a dramatic work, based on a light libretto, with musical numbers often interconnected by dialogue. It usually consists of sentimental as well as farcical elements. The Italian type is called *opera buffa*, its French pendant, *opera comique*.

Comedy with Music
also **Musical Comedy**

is precisely what the title indicates, a light farcical play with songs, dances, even an overture and entre-act music. Originally this category needed no chorus or ballet, and only a small orchestra.

Dramma per Musica

a term used for the early Italian opera, particularly of serious character. *Lyric drama* means the same with reference to English opera.

Expressionism

is the opposite of classicism, though form cannot entirely be dispensed with in music. Emphasis is put on rhythm and peculiar, often dissonant harmonies, rather cacophonies. The first traces are found in *Salomé* and *Electra* by Richard Strauss. Arnold Schoenberg was the protagonist of this movement.

Grand Opera

is frequently applied to all serious operas that are composed throughout. In particular it refers to the French type of the mid-nineteenth century, such as *Les Huguenots* by Meyerbeer, *Là Juive* by Halévy and *William Tell* by Rossini.

Impressionism

had its origin in the dislike of composers for the heavy Wagnerian pathos, the sentimentality of some romanticists and, in addition, for Beethoven's dynamics. Even Wagner's own *Tristan and Isolde* contains passages of this style, the outstanding composer of which was Claude Debussy *(Pelléas and Mélisande)*.

Intermezzo

was a brief opera inserted between acts of a drama or opera, serving as interruption. An outstanding model is *La Serva Padrona* which originally was just an intermezzo. In his *Ariadne on Naxos*, Richard Strauss makes telling use of this early type.

Incidental Music

is really an integrated part of a play. Some dramas are heavily interspersed with music, the majority however uses very little. Demanding scores were written by Beethoven for *Egmont*, Weber for *Preciosa*, Mendelssohn for *Midsummer Night's Dream*, Grieg for *Peer Gynt* and Bizet for *L'Arlésienne*.

Light Opera	another term for *Operetta* or *Comic Opera*.
Lyric Theatre	also *Lyric Drama*, sometimes used for opera or operatic art.
Melodrama	is literally dialogue accompanied by music. The second scene of act two of *Fidelio* offers an instructive example.
Mise en scène	a term, borrowed from the French theatre, which indicates the style of the production or sometimes refers merely to scenery and costumes. Literally it means staging.
Musical Comedy	see *Comedy with Music*
Musikdrama	also *Music Drama*, refers to the Wagnerian type of opera, in particular to his later works. Wrongly this term is also applied to *Serious Opera* and *Grand Opera* in general.
Neo-Classicism	see *Classicism*
Opera	denotes a drama, tragic or comic, partly or completely sung to the accompaniment of an orchestra. Generally it means any type of this art form as against the spoken drama. The term, *opera in musica*, is also used in this sense, referring to the Italian form. As of late, lecturers and writers sometimes substitute *lyric theatre*, *poetic theatre*, *music theatre*, *romantic theatre*, *lyric drama*, and *musical drama*.
Opera Buffa	see *Comic Opera*
Opéra Comique	see also *Comic Opera*, a French style derived from *vaudeville*. It resembles somewhat the *ballad opera*. During the 19th century librettists used it for political satire.
Opera Giacosa	is a playful work. Mozart used this term for his *Don Giovanni*.

Operetta	its literal translation is little opera. The word was introduced late in the 18th century to indicate a short opera. Through the success of Gilbert and Sullivan in England, Offenbach in France and J. Strauss in Austria, it won an independent place for itself. Its librettos are light and simple, less so the scores as a rule. Dancing gained in importance, in separate scenes, as well as in combination with songs and ensembles. Also called *Light Opera*.
Pasticcio	is pastry in its original sense. It signifies a kind of light opera or operetta to which several composers contributed one or several numbers each.
Recitative	is a vocal style intended to preserve as much as possible the natural flow of the spoken word. Notes are mostly short, little inflection being used. It is employed in the Italian style of opera in contrast to the lyric composition of arias and ensembles. *Secco recitativo* is accompanied on the harpsichord or, today, on the piano; *recitativo accompagnato* or *stromentato*, by the full orchestra.
Revue	grew out of the French *opera comique*. Closely related to the modern operetta. When the plot is conceived on a rather small scope, it resembles more a comedy with music. The librettist prefers to deal with present-day problems in a satirical vein.
Romanticism	is an antithesis to classicism. It can be traced back to the late compositions of Beethoven. Weber and Berlioz were its leaders in the field of opera, while Wagner became its climax. Tchaikovsky, R. Strauss and others are late comers of this style; they are also called *neo-romanticists*.

188

Semi-classical	is a journalistic word to indicate a musical piece not quite good enough to be called "classical". It is not used by serious writers.
Show	in its colloquialism is any kind of theatrical production, including film and television. In a narrower sense it refers to the spectacle on the stage, i.e. visual matters such as settings and costumes.
Singspiel	this German art-form has two sources, a serious and a comic one. Its operas are not composed throughout, but contain dialogue scenes. Outstanding among them are *The Abduction from the Seraglio, Fidelio* and *Der Freischuetz.*
Stagione	the Italian term for season, indicates a series of operatic productions presented by a company remaining in one city for a shorter or longer period of time. Occasionally *stagione* is also applied to the company itself that visits various cities.
Stylization	refers to settings, costumes and/or acting that is not treated realistically.
Vaudeville	meant in France of the 19th century a comedy interspersed with popular songs. Originally it was just one song. Today it includes a variety of pieces, skits, songs, dances, even acrobatic numbers. It rarely has a coherent book.
Verismo, also **Verism**	applies to operas such as *Cavalleria Rusticana, Louise, et al.* The protagonists of these operas are everyday people instead of princes or heroes. This style corresponds to realism in drama and novel. But opera can never be realistic like the other arts because music excludes realism or naturalism in their proper sense.

189

II

DRAMATIC EFFECTS

The following scenes may serve for practicing dramatic effects suggested by the situation rather than required in the score.

SCREAMING:

Tosca	Cavaradossi, in act two off stage, when being tortured. Tosca's outcry on discovering that Cavaradossi is dead.
I Pagliacci	Nedda's scream at the end of the opera when being menaced by Canio with his knife.
Carmen	Don José, act four, when Carmen throws the ring at his feet.
Cavalleria Rusticana	Santuzza at the end of her duet with Turridu.
Rigoletto	When in the last scene Rigoletto discovers that his daughter has been killed he must express extreme pain.

LAUGHING:

La Bohème	Musetta's laugh at the end of the second and third act.
I Pagliacci	Nedda making fun of Tonio in the first act. Tonio in the second act.
Mignon	Filine's coquettish laughing in act one.
Hansel and Gretel	The Witch laughs repeatedly.

190

WEEPING:

I Pagliacci

Canio may weep after his great aria "*Ridi Pagliacci*."

Cavalleria Rusticana

Santuzza, when telling the mother of her faithless lover her tragic story.

Tosca

When she realizes in act three that Cavaradossi has been shot.

La Bohème

Rodolfo cries softly when he learns that Mimi has died.

MOANING:

Otello

Act four, last scene.

La Traviata

Alfredo at the end of the opera.

Madame Butterfly

Susuki in act two and three.

DISGUISED VOICE:

Hansel and Gretel

The Witch, particularly if played by a tenor.

La Bohème

Marcello during the dancing in act four.

Gianni Schicchi

The leading character when he pretends to be Buoso.

SPEAKING-MELODRAMA:

Fidelio

Leonore and Rocco in the first scene of act two.

Macbeth

Lady Macbeth reading a letter in act one.

Tosca

Tosca has to speak a sentence after she kills Scarpia.

Cavalleria Rusticana

Santuzza yells at her lover Turridu.

La Traviata

The dying leading lady reading a letter.

III

STAGING PROBLEMS

Numerous technical problems were touched upon previously. An additional series selected from the standard repertoire is discussed on the following pages. For each problem, which often carries an artistic implication, a solution is suggested, in some cases more than one. Before examples from specific operas are offered a few problems common to several works are briefly delineated to avoid repetitious statements later on.

Animals.

Several librettoes ask for, or at least indicate, the appearance of live animals. If well-behaved and well-integrated, animals can add a fine flavor to the action. But caution must be taken as animals, particularly horses and dogs, can develop stage fright and then endanger settings, properties or performers. The director who wants to use them should invite their owner or trainer to dress in costume and to accompany them on stage. If this is not feasible, a veterinarian could give the animal a tranquilizer. Watch that the horses' shoes are muffled by wrapping cloth around them! Stuffed birds are indeed more useful than live ones! In general, in case of doubt the four-legged participants should be eliminated.

Glowing Effects.

Fireflies become visible, phials and bowls light up in some operas. As to fireflies, a few tiny bulbs are mounted on thin wires and connected with a battery. A switch at the handle gives the stage manager and his assistant the means of making the flies visible for brief moments. Two or three sets, employed sparingly in different wings, create a thoroughly satisfactory illusion. A similar method is used for creating transparent phials. Small bulbs are placed inside the phials and connected with wires to batteries carried in the pockets of the costume. In groups of three to five they are very effective. The glowing punch bowl or chalice requires a good-sized lamp and battery with a switch installed in the properties. No wire should lead to an off-stage switch lest someone trip over it!

Gunshots.

The first law is that a character who fires a pistol or gun must never aim directly at the other character but rather above his head or to his left or right.

The second is that the stage manager should be ready in the wing with a pistol to fire in an emergency, for it can happen that a gun does not go off. The third is that the blanks to be used in the evening be checked beforehand as some are too strong for safe handling in a performance. If a cannon shot is to be heard, a good method is to shoot a pistol into an empty barrel placed far away from the acting area.

Smoke, Mist.

A spirit is conjured, or the "earth" opens to swallow a bad man. It would be good to have a trapdoor available for sudden appearances and disappearances, but only a few stages possess this contraption and thus another solution must be found. The electrician can put, on a small square piece of asbestos close to the wing, a bit of gun powder or other chemical material that will produce a flame and smoke. Wires connect a fuse wire through the material with a switch off stage. On cue the switch is closed, and the resulting flame and smoke permits the singer who has been waiting in the wing to make his entrance. The same procedure can be applied if the effect of a flame bursting from a "rock" is desirable. In a few scenes a mist rising and hiding the upstage area is indicated. A fog machine is a suitable device. Any chemical used for creating smoke or mist must be thoroughly checked lest the singers' throats be irritated!

Thunderstorms.

Thunder and lightning play an important role in several operas. The force of a thunder is indeed related to the particular orchestra passages. Timpani tuned to fit the given key will be satisfactory for a small classic orchestra. A drum too can serve well in such instances. For a real crash however these instruments are not enough. A shot into an empty barrel should precede the roll of the drum or timpani. A sharp piercing sound can be obtained with a large piece of metal suspended by wires from a solid stand—it is hit with a drumstick. Lastly, iron balls rolled across the backstage floor also achieve a striking impact. In some scenes, a wind machine may be added to heighten the storm effect. Lightning can be executed in various ways. By means of a projector flashes can be thrown on the backdrop or cyclorama. In other cases, a flood-light will serve to brighten the stage for a split second; a better method is the use of a carbon arc (spotlight) or a series of low watt bulbs as for instance in a borderlight. Good planning is advisable to avoid throwing light on a scrim or certain areas which should be kept dark. In every case it is essential to read the score carefully in order to find the instrument that describes the lightning, often the piccolo flute. The stage manager must watch that the lightning coincides precisely with the musical phrase. Synchronization is also necessary for executing the thunder that follows the flash.

Beethoven: *Fidelio*

In the second scene of act one, when the prisoners are led into the courtyard, the grills of their cells must be opened extremely carefully to make them appear very heavy; or the prisoners might come through a trapdoor from underneath the grounds, as it were. In act two, Leonore brandishes a small pistol which she had hidden inside her jacket. Spectators rightly complain that in some productions this pistol has been manipulated in a wrong manner—the leading lady did not cock it. Fidelio is dressed in the costume of the 17th centruy, more recently, also in that of the 18th. Either period requires the old type of pistol with cocking action. In the next scene Pizarro, when arrested, ought to give his sword to the officer of the guard. In both acts guards march on stage; the soldiers, carrying halberds or muskets depending on the period chosen for the staging, should realize that marching and other military actions must be executed with precision.

Bizet: *Carmen*

We may presume that Spanish soldiers of the 19th century were rather informal. Nevertheless, the changing of the guards must be performed with a certain discipline, no matter whether the chosen procedure is historically correct or not. During the opening scene, a mule or donkey can cross the stage, either loaded with bundles or with a peasant or monk riding it. This is one of the few scenes in which it is not dangerous to bring an animal on stage. Toward the end of act one, Carmen tries to stab a girl with a knife. Since she has the opportunity to turn her back to the audience at that moment, no particular precaution is necessary. In the last act, however, Don José should use a trick dagger to kill Carmen; this is a dagger whose blade disappears inside the handle when it hits an obstacle. Otherwise accidents may occur despite all the care the tenor may take in turning the blade away from the victim. As a matter of fact, some Carmens have been injured in this scene.

In act two and three, many of the smugglers should carry pistols or daggers; a few guns may be added. These properties are more or less a part of the costume. Remendado and Dancairo, however, brandish their pistols to menace Zuniga. The scene since it is slightly comical can be enacted informally. More care is required for the duel sequence between Don José and Zuniga. Swords are worn by the two characters in act two; thus their brief but vehement fight must fit this type of arms. In the subsequent act Don José fires a shot at Escamillo who enters a moment later. In the same scene Escamillo and Don José draw their daggers; although it is fairly dark on the stage, the fight has to be thoroughly planned and timed, since the two men are close to the curtain line. Both men wrap a kind of short blanket around their left hand and arm while holding the dagger in the right. Lunge and parry, attack and defense follow rapidly in order to create tension. For act two, Carmen, her two girl friends and possibly a few dancers ought to be well-acquainted with playing the castanets. They must practice with them under expert supervision—and indeed not wait until the last rehearsals.

The technical director has to watch a problem in act three, where the choristers, the soloists and a group of extras descend from a high platform to the stage floor. This platform and the stairs leading to the lower level must be wide enough for the numerous characters to climb down within the time duration set by the music. Since the stage is dark or semi-dark, the edges of the platforms and steps should be protected by strips or borders to prevent falling or tripping.

Donizetti: *Don Pasquale*

This comic opera may be compared with a soufflé, and in order to make it a success on stage both the singing and the acting must be perfect. A small theatre will be a better frame for its staging. If the auditorium and the stage are large, the designer should narrow down the acting area as suggested in a previous chapter and have a low platform a few feet from the curtain line across the entire stage. Arias and other scenes too may be played downstage whereas the entire acting area serves for ensembles. The director and the designer must decide on how many settings to devise for this farcical gem. Of course Norina needs a separate room in act one. The other scenes can be played in one setting, though in act three this has to be more elaborate. It is advisable to mount a special decor for the last act which needs a suitable niche build for the love duet and appropriate space for the dance-like movements of the chorus.

Flotow: *Martha*

In act two the four leading characters use spinning wheels. Martha and Nancy are fortunate in being allowed to bungle the job, but Lionel and Plunkett must be able to show the two girls how to do it. Spinning itself is not an easy task for our generation, let alone spinning synchronized with music, and therefore it must be well practiced. In the following act, the chorus women, dressed in hunting costumes, enter with spears in their hands. In some productions, more fittingly, they carry riding crops which are less awkward to handle.

Gluck: *Orfeo*

In act one and three Amor appears. If the director intends to have him come on stage, his position must be separate from the other characters and therefore on a platform upstage. A blackout before his arrival is desirable unless he can quickly appear. On the other hand, if the director believes that a god's voice is just as dramatic he uses a beam of light to indicate Amor who sings backstage or in the pit, whichever location is accoustically more favorable. The most demanding scene occurs in act two when Orfeo, standing high above the chorus and ballet, enters Hades. The staircase which he slowly descends is far upstage; the steps must be wide to permit several dancers to storm upwards against him and then to retreat when his singing soothes their fury. Orfeo, incidentally, should practice the playing of his harp. The dramatic impact of the entire scene depends to the uttermost on a perfect treatment of the light plot and the movement of the dancers.

Gounod: *Faust*

Swords are drawn in two scenes. In act one, the male choristers hold up the handle of their swords forming a cross to drive the Devil away. To perform this stage business in the allotted time takes careful rehearsing with the weapons. In act three Faust fights a brief but fierce duel with Valentine. The action has to be timed to the score, particularly the hitting of Valentine. Shortly before this duel Mephistopheles plays a serenade on his guitar. This instrument must be prepared to break easily (yet not too easily) when Valentine hits it with his sword.

Other problems, like the appearance of Mephistopheles and Marguerite, and the latter's ascension in the last act, can be solved in various ways. Faust conjures the Devil in the opening scene—naturally the appearance should come as a surprise to the audience. A few minutes later Mephistopheles shows Faust an image of Marguerite. Projection on drapes or a dark backdrop will best produce it. If drapes cover the upstage area they can be opened to present the character herself. The last scene of the opera features the ascension of the saved girl. In olden times the spectators could actually see Marguerite rise from the stage floor toward the border (by way of a flying device). Today, the opera either ends with the backstage chorus "*Sauvée*", whereby part of the final music is omitted, or a projection shows, as it were, the saving of the young girl's soul: the prison is darkened, the backdrop raised and on a screen, cyclorama, or a black backdrop an aureole is projected, or sunbeams are shown breaking through clouds.

Humperdinck: *Hansel and Gretel*

Every dramatized fairy-tale requires many technical tricks, and this favorite of audiences the world over is no exception. Director and designer must first decide whether they can manage to stage this opera without intermission, which would mean that the settings would have to be shifted during two interludes. This concise form increases the dramatic intensity, but requires thoughtful planning, designing and organizing. In addition, it can only be presented on stages with good technical equipment.

On a wide stage the interior setting of act one can easily be built in the center with bushes and trees of act two visible to the right and left. Almost the entire setting of the next act can stand ready behind the little room. When, in the forest, afternoon turns into evening and night, a series of effects is demanded by the libretto. First fireflies. Then the evening "mist"—it should not

196

appear until darkness sets in on the upstage area. Thereafter a gauze net may be lowered from the flies; it should be heavier in the middle and upwards so that the audience does not see how the backdrop is lifted and some trees are removed. On a deep stage the Jacob's ladder will stand in readiness; otherwise the minutes between lowering and raising of the gauze must be used for the necessary shifting.

At the beginning of the last act the upstage area is concealed again by "mist". After its disappearance the lights go up on the house of the witch, the cage, the oven and the fence. The little house should really look as though made of ginger-bread; Hansel and Gretel even break off bits from it. The dramatic highlight of the explosion can be exalted by having the house collapse at the very end—it must be built accordingly. Two wires connected with hooks attached to the flats will turn the trick. The oven certainly must fall apart; since it stands near the wing, or almost in it, this can easily be arranged. Fire and steam should pour from the oven; colored bulbs will serve for the fire and steam may be piped in from the central heating system. But a few stage hands, sitting and smoking in or behind the oven, are just as effective and how they enjoy doing this! During a musical interlude the witch flies off on a broom. On a stage with a high grid there is no trouble in performing this feat. Without such a system the flying can be contrived with the aid of wires, rings and hooks. The property man has a dummy fastened to a broom; both are connected with wires to a batten or just to rings in the ceiling. The dummy is held in the wing, until the wires are pulled from the opposite side, making the figure fly across the stage toward the ceiling. For the landing the procedure is reversed. Lightning (switching on and off a border or spotlight) can accompany this sequence. The collapse of the oven, and if possible, of the house, and the change from fence to children should be done during a very brief blackout. By way of wire pulling set pieces fall apart; the girls and boys crawl behind the fence which is simply pulled backstage.

Leoncavallo: *I Pagliacci*

In small theatres, Canio usually enters the stage on foot. Whenever feasible a little cart, drawn by a donkey, ought to bring him onstage. A super leads the animal to a pre-arranged spot and watches that it does not become nervous. After Canio has descended, the donkey and cart leave at once. The only difficulty is to erect a stage on the stage. Traditionally a big platform à la *commedia dell'arte* (but with a main curtain) is built at an angle near the left wings; this has the disadvantage that, in a wide auditorium with a comparatively small proscenium opening, people sitting on the same side cannot witness the entire action. Furthermore, the choristers, placed at the opposite side of the platform, have not enough contact with the incidents. A dramatically more effective answer is to build the platform on a stage wagon that in act one stands at the traditional spot but is pushed to the center during the intermezzo. This requires the choristers to sing a few passages with their backs to the conductor. However, an assistant, standing in the wing, can take care of these cues. When Canio, infuriated, kills his rival and his wife, he should use a trick dagger. (See *Carmen*.)

Mascagni: *Cavalleria Rusticana*

Traditionally, Turridu sings his serenade behind the closed main curtain, yet in recent productions a special setting has been arranged for this. The setting of the opera can stand ready; all that is necessary is to mount a Sicilian house, or part of it, center stage. For the serenade the curtain does not open completely, but just far enough to show the house. The harpist who accompanies Turridu may sit in the orchestra or directly in the wing close to the singer who indicates the guitar playing. A suggestion for Alfio: to practice the use of the horse whip he carries on stage. The whipping is first heard backstage; if the singer can do it on stage too, he adds a realistic flavor to the characterization.

Massenet: *Manon*

Some people, among them the leading lady, arrive by mail coach in act one. If the stage is deep and wide there is no difficulty; but it is not easy to find an authentic mail coach of the 18th century. A resourceful designer can add to an ordinary coach some painted cardboards that will give the impression of the historical piece. The technical director must have the wing wide enough for horses and coach. Should it be impractical to bring the coach on stage for lack of space, it will be expedient to assume its arrival in a wing left or right. The choristers on stage turn toward the wing carrying the audience along in their make-believe.

Mozart: *The Marriage of Figaro*

The setting of act one needs two doors to clarify the action; one leading to a corridor, the other to the apartments of the Count and Countess. Since Susanna and Figaro prepare this room to live in after their marriage, the arrangement of the furniture and properties has an atmosphere of improvisation The easy-chair in which Cherubino hides must have a high back! In act two it does not matter whether the main door is upstage, or left or right, but it is essential that the door to the Countess' room is rather downstage; moreover, it should open toward the stage, as this facilitates Susanna's entrance in the finale. The window from which Cherubino jumps into the garden can be in an alcove upstage or in a sidewall.

As mentioned previously, act three is sometimes performed in two settings. Thus the first more intimate scenes gain a more suitable surrounding. Before the "trial" or after it, a quick shift, just the opening of drapes, takes place to show the big hall of the castle. During the wedding ceremony the Count must have a downstage position and not be covered by the Countess so that the spectators can watch how he opens Susanna's letter and pricks his finger on a needle.

198

The last setting must give all characters the opportunity to dart quickly in and out and to hide behind a bush or tree. Furthermore, two small garden houses left and right are needed for the action; nothing superfluous should be added; certainly not a water fountain, which in one production disturbed Mozart's wonderful music with its annoying noise.

Mozart: *Don Giovanni*

The duel in the opening scene must be fought in strict accord with the music, especially the hitting of the Commendatore. Toward the end of act one Don Giovanni draws his sword against Don Ottavio; the director should elucidate the dramatic action, but not to the detriment of the ensemble's singing.

The monument in the cemetery scene raises the question whether to present the Commendatore on foot or on horseback. Both views have advocates among directors and designers. To begin with, it is a matter of fitting the statue into the composition and design as a whole and then of having a proscenium opening sufficiently high. If it is, the Commendatore on horseback is very impressive. Next, it must be decided whether the bass himself should be the "monument" or whether he should sing backstage or hide in the pedestal. In the latter case, part of the pedestal must be transparent to permit unimpaired singing. When Leporello reads the inscription the letters may be illuminated by a special spot. At the end of the opera Don Giovanni sinks into hell. The Commendatore appears of course on foot, but he must give the impression of a ghost, not a human being. Here the application of a follow spot is of great help to intensify the dramatic impact. The last ensemble should not be sung in Don Giovanni's room, but in a kind of neutral setting; a traveller may mask the preceding setting and the action is arranged in front of it.

Mozart: *The Magic Flute*

Some requirements of the librettist, Schikaneder, regarding animals may be disregarded. But a series of other problems must be properly solved and staged if the fairy tale character of this opera is to be maintained. For instance, the large snake must pursue Tamino in the opening scene. The monster pulled by a wire can emerge from behind a platform or a "rock" where it disappears after being hit by the three Ladies. Of course the throwing of the spears must be practiced. A little later, there is thunder and the background opens, revealing the Queen of Night on a high platform: the stage can be darkened, the backdrop lifted, and a special spotlight thrown on the Queen; or (and this is easier, primarily on a cramped stage) a wagon with a high platform can be pushed from the wing onto the stage during the blackout. Instead of a painted backdrop, pictures projected on a scrim are now sometimes preferred.

An extremely intricate problem is the water and fire trial. If the stage is wide, two caves should be built left and right. A few feet behind their openings

199

a scrim forms the background on which water and fire respectively are projected from the rear. Tamino and Tamina are seen walking between the opening and the scrim. Transparent flats can take the place of the scrims; they are painted in such a manner that they give the impression of water and fire; careful lighting from the rear adds much to the effect.

On several occasions Papageno plays his flute, the old Pan type; its playing presents no particular difficulty, but indeed it must be accurately tuned. Certain firms have it in stock, and instrument makers can manufacture one easily. The chimes (Glockenspiel) handed to Papageno by the Genii, are played in the orchestra while the singer pretends to play the melody in accord with the score. Wise planning must precede the staging of this wonderful opera so that the technical apparatus can function with utmost precision and speed; specifically the scene changes must not last longer than some seconds.

Nicolai: *The Merry Wives of Windsor*

As this romantic opera requires several scene changes, simple settings which afford extremely short intermissions should be devised. Falstaff needs a very large laundry basket in which he hides, and four men should be selected to carry the heavy load. Later on, Falstaff has to change quickly into the dress of an old woman, a business which must be well-timed. The most difficult scene is the forest of the last act in which every effort must be made to integrate the movements of chorus and ballet. Too often these two groups are separated definitively which is detrimental to the overall action.

Offenbach: *The Tales of Hoffmann*

Electrician and property mistress have to collaborate in the preparation of various effects, like the glowing punch bowl, the magic mirror, and the phials. In act three the Mother's portrait comes to life. It may be best to paint it on a transparent canvas and, on the given cue, throw a little light on the alto singer from behind the flat. If a real painting is used it has to be attached in a double frame from the back of the flat; a crew member removes the second frame and the singer becomes visible.

The playing of the harp in act one and of the harpsichord (spinet) in act three are merely indicated by the singers. Whereas the keyboard instrument can be set at such an angle that the audience cannot check the accurateness of Hoffmann's playing, Spalanzani's fingering the harp can be witnessed by everyone; hence he must study and memorize his music.

Two more items call for attention. At the end of act two a duel is fought with epées. The action leading to Schlemihl's death can take place in semi-darkness rather upstage. Somewhat later a gondola passes by in the rear behind a platform. If there is sufficient space behind the acting area, a few gondolas may be seen in the beginning of this act landing choristers. These little boats should run on rubber wheels, with ball bearings well-greased.

Puccini: *La Bohème*

The execution of the complicated stage business and, above all, the manipulation of numerous properties, takes a great deal of accurate practicing. To use an artist's brush, or to make fire is not very hard in itself, but singers must realize that many spectators are watching such minor incidents and are displeased if they are improperly executed. The comic duel in the last act must be thoroughly rehearsed; pokers or other tools are picked up by the singers; although the motions in this duel can be exaggerated to a certain degree, they must harmonize with the music. The setting of act three shows a winter scene. Snow falling occasionally will enhance the atmosphere. It is a simple trick; bags with little holes are filled with white flameproof confetti. Crew members standing on a catwalk or up in the flies shake the bags upon prearranged cues. Instead of several bags a single large one can be rigged with pulleys and ropes. A stage hand pulls a rope which moves a pulley up and down. In some theatres a cart with a peasant drawn by a horse or mule crosses from the upstage to a wing downstage; the effect, though good on a big stage, is not essential.

Puccini: *Tosca*

If the stage is deep, a large part of the church can be mounted for act one. This allows the deployment of many extras and choristers in the final scene. However, an intimate setting, a side chapel, has its advantages too: it brings the emotionally explosive action into sharp contrast to the solemn mood of the procession, seen upstage between pillars and perhaps trellis work.

The second act of the opera approaches the style of a drawing room drama; accordingly all stage business should be executed with natural ease. It begins with eating and drinking on the part of Scarpia; later on a passport is written, and at the end Tosca kills Scarpia with a knife and arranges candles and a cross around the dead man. As the events in this act are rather melodramatic, the characters must be careful not to fall into "ham-acting".

In the last act the tenor sings about stars; these can be produced either by projection or by means of small bulbs suspended by wires on a batten. During the execution, Cavaradossi must be visible to the entire audience; the group of soldiers can be posted opposite him if the stage is wide, or in the wing if it is not. In the latter case, however, the commanding officer should stand on the stage raising and lowering his sword for the execution Everybody is supposed to enter the stage from "downstairs"; this means through a trapdoor. But no great harm is done if singers and extras come through a door in a flat on the right or left side. The suicide of Tosca must be carefully arranged; upstage is a platform behind which the singer disappears. The height of the platform depends on the line of sight from the balcony; nobody must see Tosca after her jump. Of course, a mattress must be placed backstage for the singer's fall.

Rossini: *The Barber of Seville*

Singers of this opera have to handle many properties and execute movements and gestures with good agility. Almaviva must practice with his sword which he draws to menace Bartolo and Basilio; in the second act the shaving of Bartolo has to be rehearsed thoroughly. To be sure, a dull shaving knife must be taken by Figaro; preferably real soap is not to be used, but instead whipped cream. The only artistic-technical problem is the thunderstorm. Director and designer must decide whether it is to happen realistically, or in a stylized rather comic manner.

Thomas: *Mignon*

There is a brief duel in act two which is fortunately fought during a dialogue; its style is of the 18th century. The only other action to be watched is Lothario's playing on the lyre. At the end of act two a fire breaks out in a building, part of which should be seen. Smoke can be blown on stage from the wings but care must be taken that it does not irritate the throats of singers; a slightly yellowish glow (a strip backstage) enhances the effect of this conflagration.

Tchaikovsky: *Eugene Onegin*

Tatjana cannot start early enough to practice writing her letter while singing. The quill she has to use complicates her task, since she must not forget, as a few singers have done, to put it into an inkwell once in a while. Staging the duel in act two in a winter landscape intensifies the tragic mood of this scene. Onegin and Lenski can stand opposite each other at the wings left and right, or Lenski can take a position center downstage with his opponent far upstage; thus when Lenski falls, Onegin becomes visible which is a strong effect. By the way, the stage manager should keep a pistol ready in case of misfire on stage!

Verdi: *Rigoletto*

The violent thunderstorm that accompanies a great part of the action of the last act must be meticulously prepared. At the end of the thunderstorm, Gilda enters the little house through the side door; at the very moment when Sparafucile kills her the room should be darkened. Maddalena holds a candle (electrically managed); it is presumably extinguished by the wind. Darkness should prevail inside until the end of the opera, as against the other half of the setting, the exterior, which is to be brightened up a little.

Verdi: *Il Trovatore*

Manrico and Luna begin a duel at the end of the second scene; the best way is to have the two gentlemen rush with drawn swords upstage, or toward a wing where they are hardly visible. The great finale of act two brings two inimical groups on stage facing each other ready to fight. It is advisable not to have them draw their swords too early; by no means should the spears be lowered until the last moment, so that there are only a few measures left for the actual fighting before the curtain closes. At the beginning of act two in the gypsy camp, it is customary to have an open fire with a cauldron suspended on a tripod. Traditionally a few choristers do some hammering on swords or other weapons, a business which must be executed in the rhythm of the particular passage. Off-stage a fire may be seen at the end of the opera; in order to avoid turning the action into melodrama, only a dim glow should be created.

Verdi: *The Masked Ball*

In the second scene Ulrica sits by an open fireplace. It is more effective to place her on a low platform behind a cauldron with a fire underneath. Steam may arise from the cauldron. In the next act gallows must be erected upstage. Amelia during her aria imagines that she sees a ghost. With a little smoke and a spotlight or a striplight located behind the gallows, a good effect can be achieved. The stagefloor covered with "snow" (a whitish groundcloth) will add an eerie mood to this scene.

Verdi: *Aida*

This grand opera contains many difficulties, but none that is unsurmountable. The intriguing task of arranging a beautiful picture and, at the same time, animated action for the famous finale of act two requires close cooperation of conductor, director and designer. Fundamentally the question is an artistic one which may be resolved in various ways, depending on the size of the stage and the number of participants. The atmosphere of act three can be intensified by a veiled moon, created by means of projection. In the same act Amneris and the High Priest arrive by boat. If the upstage area has a large trap door or elevator, the boat can be omitted and the singers can walk from below up to the stage level. A trapdoor downstage is almost imperative for an effective staging of the opening scene of act four, when the Priests cross the stage from a high platform and disappear through the opening in the floor. Their straight exit through the wing somehow spoils the dramatic situation. In the next scene a double stage is needed; the tomb itself can be quite narrow; the high platform above it, however, must have enough space for a large stone and for Amneris to move around it. The chorus sings backstage.

Verdi: *Otello*

Lightning, thunder, wind, clouds, perhaps rain and stars belong to a series of phenomena illustrated in the music. More than one projector is needed: one for clouds, one for rain, and one for flashes. Later one of these can be used for stars. Before the "fire chorus" begins, extras or choristers bring pieces of firewood on stage and also a lamp or torch. The men arranging and starting the fire are covered by others. Smoke adds to the effectiveness of this scene.

Somewhat later, Cassio and Montano fight a short duel; a prerequisite for both singers is to be well-versed in the handling of their swords and in timing their fencing with the music.

Wagner: *The Flying Dutchman*

A close scrutiny of Wagner's operas and music dramas shows that the problems they pose are not too complicated for an ingenious technical director. Productions of these works are feasible, if other requirements, such as for the singers, can be met.

In *The Flying Dutchman* foremost consideration is to be given the ships in acts one and three. When the curtain opens for act one Daland's boat is already anchored, but sailors are still fastening sails and ropes. The boat should be a small one-master, as distinguished from the bigger one of the Dutchman which may have two masts. Both are mounted on stage wagons to facilitate their shifting. If a stage is wide and deep, the two ships may be fifteen and twenty feet long. If it is not, then the designer has to make believe that a part of each boat is hidden by rocks (flats). Daland's boat should be anchored parallel to the footlights; the Dutchman's can arrive almost from the rear, provided there is enough space upstage. The necessary wind is generated by a powerful fan that blows air against the sails at the beginning and the end of act one, if such a realistic effect is desired. In the opening scene the upstage area can be hidden by gauze upon which clouds and rain are projected. Any flashes the director inserts must be so directed that they do not hit the gauze. Lightning and a terrible crash accompany the arrival of the Dutchman's ship. During a blackout the gauze is raised and the ship moved against a platform.

In the first scene of act two women are spinning, a business which must be well practiced. The Dutchman's sudden entrance should be presented as described by Wagner himself. Nevertheless, the director is at liberty to arrange the door as he pleases so long as both Senta and the spectators are able to see the Dutchman in person and his painting simultaneously—that is the painting must be placed above the door or close to the door frame. For the last setting Daland's boat may be omitted; some designers like to show part of his house. The Dutchman's ship fills a good part of the stage; it must be so placed that within a few seconds, it can be pulled behind a high platform or a flat. When the Dutchman's crew sings, the men can either appear on deck or be seen below deck in a ghostlike manner through transparent walls. Toward the end of this act a series of effects must be executed in close order. Upon the departure of the Dutchman's boat, Senta jumps into the "ocean": she stands for her last words on a rather high platform behind which a mattress is prepared for her. Wagner's directive that his hero and heroine be seen rising toward heaven has been disregarded for a long time in favor of a projected aurora borealis or of another lighting effect.

Wagner: *Tannhaeuser*

An efficient fly system must be available for the quick scene shifting in act one. The grotto of Venus disappears and a forest near the Wartburg becomes visible. Counting from the last syllable of Tannhaeuser's "Maria", eleven or at the most twelve bars of music allow for this change. The second scene with its set of platforms must be ready. Arches and perhaps a backdrop of the first setting will mask some ramps, platforms and trees. The director may wish to see some action (ballet) on the platforms; for this occasion crafty lighting changes their appearance. The couch on which Venus is resting is on a dolly to facilitate its removal speedily and quietly. All stage hands must understand that every split second counts and that they must therefore be on the alert for the shifting cue. Since the change occurs during a blackout, great care must be taken to prevent accidents. At the end of act one a few huntsmen and their attendants enter. The stage director may ponder whether horses and hounds will enhance or obstruct the effectiveness of this scene.

There are singers who do not play their harp accurately in the *Saengerfest* of act two. This playing must be practiced together with music and words; presented in a slovenly fashion this marvellous scene can make the whole action ludicrous. In the last act the appearance of the evening star contributes to the mood. (See *Tosca*). Before Venus is heard, a gauze veil may be lowered in front of the platform on which she then stands. A spotlight illuminates the goddess and her maidens. On the cue "Elizabeth" there is a blackout upstage, Venus leaves the platform, the gauze is raised, and the pilgrims enter.

Wagner: *Lohengrin*

The swan, apparently pulling a small boat, captures the attention of every audience. Fortunately Wagner requires the boat to arrive rather upstage. Swan and boat alike should run on rollers and, if possible, on rails, making it easier to pull the contraption straight across the stage. The appearance of the swan and the boat has been dispensed with since the twenties. The arrival of Lohengrin is prepared in the modern version by a change in lighting; the hero himself comes on stage through a trapdoor or simply enters from behind a tree or high platform. In most productions the choristers face the wing from which the swan emerges almost until the very moment of Lohengrin's arrival. In the last act the swan arrives as in the first, but now Lohengrin, kneeling in front of it, prays for the return of Elsa's brother. The swan changes to the Duke of Brabant. The procedure is this: the swan may be pulled offstage if nearby platforms or bushes are sufficiently high; or a stage hand, hiding behind the platforms, turns the swan over, and the young Duke, hidden behind a platform, appears quickly as though coming from the embankment. A dove floats down, hanging on a wire connected with a batten or manipulated by a stagehand standing on a catwalk. The dove seems to pull the boat; another wire, handled from backstage, will create this impression. All these directives of Wagner have recently been disregarded and a light effect substituted—only the appearance of the Duke on cue remains.

Wagner: *The Mastersingers*

For all its complicated settings and many properties this opera is not particularly difficult from a technical point of view. Most problems can be solved by carefully scanning Wagner's libretto and music. Beckmesser and Sachs have to practice playing on the guitar and using chalk and hammer respectively, since these actions must be synchronized with the music. During the intermission between act one and two, the stage must be dampened; the apprentices should only indicate sweeping the street, to prevent throat irritation on the part of the singers. At the end of this act, Beckmesser is beaten up and neighbors join in the free-for-all fight. No real sticks or cudgels should be given to soloists and choristers but long thin bags filled with cotton or some other soft material. The moon may appear shortly before the closing of the curtain; suspended on wires it can be raised above a house in the background; together with light and shadow effects downstage a charming romantic mood develops.

Wagner: *The Valkyrie*

Even on a stage with limited space this opera can be produced if the lighting equipment is adequate. The first act, the interior of Hunding's hut, is the easiest. Lightning is to be seen behind the door; a border or spotlight achieves the desired impression. An open fire is burning on the hearth. A baby spot from the wing or the catwalk can simulate the glow of the fire which is supposed to illuminate the sword sticking in the tree. In act two, Fricka can enter on foot instead of in a chariot drawn by a couple of rams. (This has not been tried often, for dummies look ludicrous unless well-concealed by a low flat and besides it is impossible to turn the chariot on a rather small platform.) At any rate, Fricka should appear on a higher level than Wotan's. At the end of this act several scenic effects are prescribed. The lights on the upstage area are dimmed and rising smoke, simulating mist, and perhaps a descending gauze will screen the platform on which Hunding and Siegmund meet later on. One spotlight is needed for the two men, another for Wotan, and possibly a third for Bruenhilde, each of them covering a rather narrow area. Hunding and Siegmund should stand lower than Wotan and Bruenhilde. Flashes may be added, but they must not light up the gauze or any character.

No wholly unobjectionable solution has been worked out as yet for the ride of the Valkyries and the magic fire in act three. Small dummy horses with dolls fastened on them have been pulled across the rear of the stage; special films have been shot and projected on the background; in other productions practically everything has been left to the imagination of the spectators with only a beam of a spotlight thrown across the upstage area. None of these experiments was wholly satisfactory. The horse and doll affair looked too mechanical, the film

206

did not blend very well into the clouds of the backdrop, and the spotlight gave merely the impression of flashes. The beam of light thrown across the upstage area is probably the best procedure if properly rehearsed and exactly timed to the music. The last scene is still more trying. The magic fire begins when Wotan hits a rock with his spear conjuring Loge, the god of fire. A spark or flash may be seen. The effect is increased by a flash jumping across the stage; this can be done with a wire or string dipped into a chemical fluid. But the technical director must ascertain beforehand that no city ordinance forbids the use of open fire on the stage. At any rate, smoke, generated by steam, rises behind a platform upstage. A slightly yellow or amber glow will support this effect. Flames if so desired can be painted on cutout paper or gauze; fastened on borders and placed behind a platform they will rise by means of powerful fans. Smoke and flames can be projected too; depending on the size of the backdrop or cyclorama, two projectors possibly are needed.

Wagner: *Siegfried*

According to Wagner's libretto a variety of animals appears in Siegfried. The hero comes on stage pulling and pushing a bear with which he frightens Mime. An extra, smaller than the tenor, is dressed in a bear's skin for this purpose. The bird in act two can be featured or eliminated; a dummy may be fastened by a ring to a wire strung across the stage behind the first teaser. Stage hands can pull the bird to one or the other side by using more wires. In the last scene the horse Grane is mentioned; it is best to assume the animal standing in the wing. The only real worry is Fafner, the dragon. The size of this beast depends on the particular stage but it should be big enough to look frightful, not comical. Despite Wagner's request to show the dragon as a whole, from head to tail, it is sufficient to display its big head, shoulder and two paws. Let us presume that the entrance to Fafner's cave is on a platform from which a ramp leads into the interior toward the wing or upstage. A capable property man can mold the dragon's head of papier-mache; it is supported by a wooden construction. The "glooming eyes" can be produced by installing bulbs inside and pasting colored cellophane paper outside. From its big movable mouth steam should spout and thus a pipe with a rubber tube at its end must be inserted. The body, as far as it is seen, is made of canvas with some lumber pieces across the shoulder. The movements are directed by a stagehand or two on cues given by the stage manager or a musical assistant. A further suggestion is to keep the area near the cave almost dark in order to screen the action somewhat and also to emphasize the mood.

In act one as the story progresses Siegfried manipulates a number of tools. These must be arranged in close proximity and near the footlights, since the tenor has to sing long and strenuous passages while executing the complicated action. The anvil presents a special problem, for it must fall apart when hit by Siegfried's sword. In preparing this anvil, the carpenter constructs two halves, hooked together with any slit or crack covered by tape. A wire, connected with

207

hook or hooks, permits a stage hand in the wing to jerk one part away so that it tumbles over. To have the hammering of the sword appear more realistically, wires may be placed on top of the anvil, not touching each other, but so arranged that when Siegfried's hammer comes in contact with them, sparks will fly. In the trough for the cooling of the sword a steampipe is to be installed. The sword that Siegfried breaks into pieces must be prepared of course. All of these properties and others like the bellows and dragon, may be rented, perhaps from a professional company.

In act three Erda can come through a trapdoor, or from the wing, or appear from behind a dark cloth at the entrance of the cave, her face within the beam of a spotlight. In any event, Erda should stand higher than Wotan. The latter's spear must be prepared by the property man for Siegfried to break it. The fire at the end of this scene should only be indicated by a slight glow upstage. The atmosphere of the next sequence is similar to the one at the end of *The Valkyrie;* the glow fades until bright daylight fills the stage.

Wagner: *Parsifal*

With the exception of the moving diorama (*Wandeldekoration*) of act one and act three, this opera can be generally staged as Wagner envisioned it; however, a very good fly system and sufficient space are essential. In the opening scene a dying swan falls on stage. The bird should not be thrown but should slowly glide down on a wire and disappear in a wing. In the last act a dove descends from the cupola of the Temple; if this effect seems desirable, a stage hand can lower it with a wire, or a batten can be used. A wire tightly strung between two points must be provided for the throwing of the spear in act two; the spear itself is suspended by two rings about two or three feet apart. When Klingsor enters throwing the spear, it rolls down the wire. Twice in this music drama the holy grail lights up; a spotlight from above renders the illusion more impressive. The quick changes of scenery in act two presuppose meticulous planning and rehearsing. In the score ten measures are granted for the first shifting and twelve for the second toward the end of the act.

There remain the troublesome scene changes in act one and three. Professional opera houses have a special machinery for the *Wandeldekoration:* the characters simply mark time while the forest passes across the stage. To install this device would be financially prohibitive. The slide projector offers an effective solution. On the cue for the change, a gauze is dropped as near to the curtain line as possible and, behind it, dark heavy drapes. The stage hands can then shift from the setting of the forest to the Temple without disturbing the audience with noise. Meanwhile clouds may be projected from a booth in the balcony; a second projector can show pictures of a forest, the entrance of the Temple and a hallway; these pictures fade in and out until the gauze and the drapes rise and the interior of the Temple is visible. The transition in the last act can be performed in the same manner.

ADDRESSES

Rental Agencies

Alfred J. Mapleson. 129 West 29th Street, New York, New York 10001
Theodore Presser Company. Bryn Mawr, Pennsylvania 19010
Tams-Witmark. 757 Third Avenue, New York, New York 10017
May Valentine. 20 North Wacker Drive, Chicago, Illinois 60606

Publishers (some also serving as agent of foreign firms)

Associate Music Publishers, Inc. 1 West 47th Street, New York, New York 10036
Boosey and Hawkes. 30 West 57th Street, New York, New York 10019
Edwin F. Kalmus. P.O. Box 47 Huntington Station, L.I., New York 11748
Oxford University Press, Inc. 417 Fifth Avenue, New York, New York 10016
C.F. Peters Corporation. 373 Fourth Avenue, New York, New York 10016
G. Ricordi and Co. 16 West 61st Street, New York, New York 10023
G. Schirmer. 609 West Fifth Avenue, New York, New York 10017
(opera groups are advised to be on the mailing list of
all agencies and publishers)

Associations and Councils

American Educational Theatre Association. Suite 500, 1701 Pennsylvania Avenue, Washington, D.C. 20006
American National Theatre and Academy. 245 West 52nd Street, New York, New York 10019
Central Opera Association. Metropolitan Opera House, Lincoln Center, New York, New York 10023
National Opera Association. c.o. Martha Dick McClung, 2519 Lanark Road, Birmingham, Alabama 35223
National Council on the Arts and Government. 22 West 54th Street, New York, New York 10019
New York State Council on the Arts. 250 West 57th Street, New York, New York 10019

Services and Material

Simon's Directory (3rd edition, 1966). Package Publicity Service. 1564 Broadway, New York, New York 10036
(Although originally devised for play production this directory is valuable for opera groups because of its many addresses of firms offering theatrical material and services.)

BIBLIOGRAPHY

Anderson, John. *The American Theatre and Motion Pictures*. New York: Dial Press. 1938.

Anderson, W.R. *Music as a Career*. New York: Oxford University Press. 1939.

Apel, Willy (edit). *Harvard Dictionary of Music*. Cambridge: Harvard University Press. 1947.

Appia, Adolphe. *The Work of Living Art*. Coral Gables: University of Miami Press. 1960.

Music and the Art of the Theatre. Coral Gables: University of Miami Press. 1962.

Bamberger, Carl (edit). *The Conductor's Art*. New York: McGraw-Hill Corp. 1965.

Bekker, Paul. *The Changing Opera*. New York: W.W. Norton. 1935.

Benn, Frederick Chr. *Mozart on the Stage*. London: Ernest Benn Ltd., 1946.

Biancolli, Louis. *The Opera Reader*. New York: McGraw-Hill Corp. 1953.

Bonavia, Feruccio. *Verdi*. London: Dobson. 1947.

Briggs, T.H. *Opera and its Enjoyment*. New York: Columbia University Teacher's College. 1960.

Brockway, Wallace, and Weinstock, Herbert. *The Opera*. New York: Simon and Shuster. 1941.

Burris-Meyer, H., and Cole, E.C. *Scenery for the Theatre*. Boston: Little, Brown and Co, 1947.

Theatres and Auditoriums. New York: Reinhold Publishing Co. 1949.

Capell, Richard. *Opera, Its Nature and History*. London: Ernest Benn Ltd. 1930.

Opera. London: Ernest Benn Ltd. 1948.

Chaliapin, Feodor. *Pages from My Life*. New York: Harpers, 1927.

Man and Mask. New York: A.A. Knopf. 1932.

Cone, John F. *Oscar Hammerstein's Manhattan Opera*. Norman: University of Oklahoma Press. 1965.

Cox-Ife, William. *The Elements of Conducting*. New York: John Day. 1965.

Dace, Wallace. "A Survey of Opera in Modern Translation." *Educational Theatre Journal*. Vol. VIII, no. 3, 1956.

Dennrenther, Edward. *Wagner and the Reform of Opera*. London: Angener. 1940.

Dent, Edward J. *Opera*. London: Penguin Book. 1940.

A Theatre for Everybody. London: Boardman and Co. 1945.

Mozart's Operas. New York: Oxford University Press. 1947.

Eaton, Quaintance. *Opera Production, a Handbook*. Minneapolis: University of Minnesota Press. 1961.

Engel, Lehman. *Planning and Producing the Musical Show*. New York: Crown Publishers. 1957.

Fischel, Oscar. *Das Moderne Buehnenbild*. Berlin: E. Wasmuth. 1923.

Flagstad, Kirsten, and Biancolli, Louis. *The Flagstad Manuscript*. New York: S.P. Putnam's Sons. 1952.

Fuerst, Walter R., and Hume, Sam J. *Twentieth Century Stage Decoration*. New York: A.A. Knopf. 1929.

Garden, Mary, and Biancolli, Louis. *Mary Garden's Story*. New York: Simon and Shuster. 1951.

Gatti-Casazza, G. *Memoirs of the Opera*. New York: Scribner's Sons. 1941.

Goldbeck, Frederick. *The Perfect Conductor*. New York: Pellegrini. 1951.

Goldowsky, Boris. *Accents on Opera*. New York: Farrar, Strauss and Young. 1953.

Graf, Herbert. *Opera and its Future in America*. New York: W.W. Norton. 1940.

Opera for the People. Minneapolis: University of Minnesota Press. 1951.

Producing Opera for America. New York: Atlantis Books. 1964.

Grout, Donald J. *A Short History of Opera*. New York: Columbia University Press. 1947.

Hainaux, René. *Stage Design Throughout the World Since 1935*. New York: Theatre Arts Books. 1956.

Stage Design Throughout the World Since 1950. New York: Theatre Arts Books. 1963.

Heylbut, Rose, and Gerber, Aime. *Backstage at the Opera*. New York: Crowell. 1937.

Hoover, Kathleen. *Makers of Opera*. New York: Bittner and Co. 1948.

Huber, Louis H. *Producing Opera in the College*. New York: Columbia University Teacher's College. 1956.

Istel, Edgar. *The Art of Writing Opera Librettos*. New York: G. Schirmer. 1932.

Jones, Robert E. *The Dramatic Imagination*. New York: Duell, Sloan and Pearce. 1941.

Kerman, Joseph. *Opera and Drama*. New York: A.A. Knopf. 1957.

Kolodin, Irving. *The Metropolitan Opera*. New York: Oxford University Press. 1940.

The Story of the Metropolitan Opera. New York: A.A. Knopf. 1953.

Lawrence, Robert. *The World of Opera*. New York: Thomas Nelson and Sons. 1956.

Lehmann, Lilli. *How to Sing*. New York: The Macmillan Co. 1924.

Lehmann, Lotte. *My Many Lives*. New York: Boosey and Hawkes. 1948.

Loewenberg, Alfred. *Annals of Opera*. Cambridge, England: W. Heffer. 1955.

Marek, George R. *A Front Seat at the Opera*. New York: Allen, Town and Heath. 1948.

Opera as Theatre. New York: Harpers. 1962.

McCall, Adeline. *Adventure with the Opera.* Chapel Hill, N.C.: University of North Carolina Press. 1944.

Nemirovitch-Danchenko, Vladimir. *My Life in the Russian Theatre.* Boston: Little, Brown and Co. 1936.

Newman, Ernest. *The Life of Richard Wagner.* New York: A.A. Knopf. 1933.
Wagner as Man and Artist. London: J.M. Dent. 1914.

Oenslager, Donald. *Scenery Then and Now.* New York: W.W. Norton. 1936.

Peltz, Mary E. *Your Metropolitan Opera.* New York: Metropolitan Opera Guild. 1944.

Peyser, E.R. *How Opera Grew.* New York: Putnan Publishers. 1956.

Rosenthal, Harold D., and Warrack, J.H. *Concise Oxford Dictionary of Opera.* New York: Oxford University Press. 1964.

Schubarth, Ottmar. *Das Buehnenbild.* Munich: G.D.W. Callway. 1955.

Shea, George E. *Acting in Opera.* New York: G. Schirmer. 1937.

Siegmeister, E. *Music and Society.* New York: Critics Group Press. 1938.

Simonson, Lee. *The Stage is Set.* New York: Dover Publications. 1946.
Part of a Lifetime. New York: Duell, Sloan and Pearce. 1943.

Smith, Cecil M. *Musical Comedy in America.* New York: Theatre Arts Books. 1950.
Worlds of Music. Philadelphia: J.B. Lippincott Co. 1953.

Sonneck, Oscar G. *Early Opera in America.* New York: Ben. Blom. 1964.

Stanislavsky, Constantin. *My Life in Art.* New York: Theatre Arts Books. 1948.
Building a Character. New York: Theatre Arts Books. 1949.

Strauss, Richard. *Letters of Richard Strauss and Hugo von Hofmannsthal.* New York: A.A. Knopf. 1927.

Taubman, Howard. *Music on my Beat.* New York: Simon and Schuster. 1937.
Opera Front and Back. New York: C. Scribner's Son. 1938.

Thompson, Oscar. *The American Singer.* New York: Dial Press. 1937.

Toy, Francis. *Giuseppe Verdi.* New York: A.A. Knopf. 1931.

Turfery, Corsar, and Palmer, King. *The Musical Production.* London: Sir Isaac Pitman and Sons. 1953.

Wagner, Ludwig. *Der Szeniker Ludwig Sievert.* Berlin: Verlag Buehnenvolksbund. 1926.

Walter, Bruno. *Gustav Mahler.* New York: Greystone Press. 1941.
Theme and Variations. New York: A.A. Knopf. 1946.
Of Music and Music Making. New York: W.W. Norton. 1961.

Weingartner, Felix. *On Conducting.* Scarsdale, N.Y.: Ed. F. Calmus. 1946.

Wido, Charles M. *The Technique of the Modern Orchestra.* London: J. Williams. 1946.

PERIODICALS

Musical America, New York
Musical Journal, New York
Musical Quarterly, New York
Opera, London
Opera News, New York
Opernwelt, **Velber-Hanover**

Penguin Music Magazine, London
Revue Théâtrale, Paris.
Show, New York
Theatre Arts, New York
Theatre Today, London
World Theatre, Paris

INDEX

(Page numbers in italics indicate illustrations.)

216

217

218

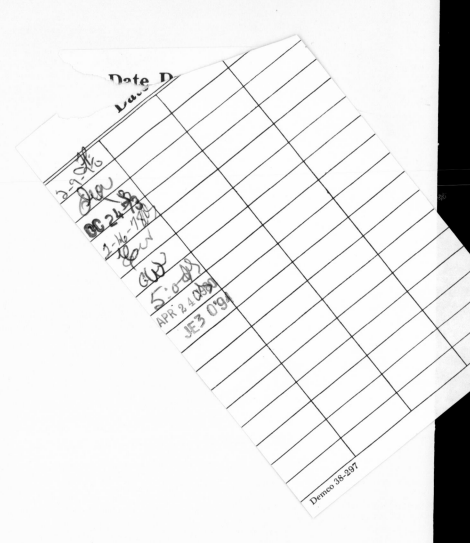

Date D...

OC 24 75
1-16-79

APR 24
JE 3 0'94

Demco 38-297